THE RENAISSANCE SOCIETY OF AMERICA

RENAISSANCE TEXT SERIES, II

DE FRUCTU QUI EX DOCTRINA PERCIPITUR

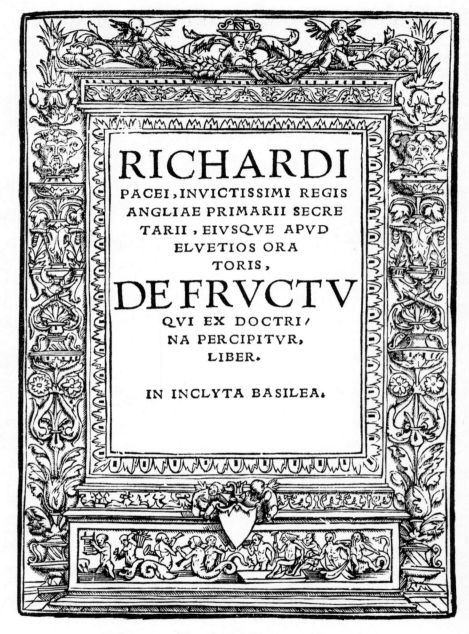

RICHARDI

PACEI, INVICTISSIMI REGIS
ANGLIAE PRIMARII SECRE
TARII, EIVSQVE APVD
ELVETIOS ORA
TORIS,

DE FRVCTV

QVI EX DOCTRI/
NA PERCIPITVR,
LIBER.

IN INCLYTA BASILEA.

Title page of Pace's *De Fructu*, Froben, 1517

DE FRUCTU QUI EX DOCTRINA PERCIPITUR

(The Benefit of a Liberal Education)

BY

RICHARD PACE

Edited and translated by
FRANK MANLEY
and
RICHARD S. SYLVESTER

Published for
THE RENAISSANCE SOCIETY OF AMERICA
by
FREDERICK UNGAR PUBLISHING CO.
NEW YORK

ACKNOWLEDGMENTS

We should like to express our thanks, first of all, to the Renaissance Society of America, and particularly to Professor George B. Parks, Chairman of its publication board, who has strongly encouraged our work on Pace since its inception some years ago. Mr. John Deason Ogden of Ithaca, New York, has most generously allowed us to make free use of his unpublished Yale Ph.D. dissertation, "Richard Pace's *De Fructu Qui Ex Doctrina Percipitur*" (1951), and we gratefully acknowledge the help which his study has given us. Professor Craig Thompson of Haverford College read our manuscript in its final form and we are very grateful to him for many revisions and corrections. In more than one sense, this book is the product of a collaboration in which several scholars have pooled their talents and resources—their own particular benefits of a liberal education—in order to restore to the present a lost fragment of our cultural heritage.

Our thanks are also extended to Mrs. Virginia Fortino, who typed the manuscript in its various stages and who has served us efficiently and well on this and on previous projects. In the tracking down of Pace's allusions and in the checking of his Greek quotations, Mrs. Linda F. Kaufman has given us the full benefit of her classical knowledge. The English Department of Yale University and the Research Fund of Emory University assisted financially with the typing.

Finally, the editors wish to thank one another and to shake hands here at the beginning of the work—which is for them the ending—and to regard it not as a true ending, but as a bond between them forged by their friendship in their years together at Yale and a pledge of its continuance. Last but not least, we thank our wives, who had in different ways much to endure while this book was in process—and in particular Joy. For her there is no consolation. But it is to Patrice that this book is dedicated.

F. M.

R. S. S.

Atlanta and New Haven, March, 1966

TABLE OF CONTENTS

INTRODUCTION

The main facts concerning the life of Richard Pace can be briefly summarized.[1] Born about 1483, probably in Hampshire,[2] Pace served as a page in the household of Thomas Langton, Bishop of Winchester, during the 1490's. Much impressed with the young Pace's musical ability, Langton gave him an annual stipend and sent him, about 1499, to study at the University of Padua.[3] If he had not already met them in England, then it was certainly at Padua that Pace became close friends with Cuthbert Tunstal and William Latimer, both of whom were students there at that time.[4]

Bishop Langton died in January 1501; his will left Pace, described as a student at Bologna, the sum of £10 per year for seven years. This pension enabled Pace to support himself while he was continuing his education in Bologna, Ferrara, and Venice. By the fall of 1508, Pace was well known to Erasmus, who had been in Italy since September 1506. The two met at Ferrara in December 1508, and Erasmus entrusted several of his manuscripts to Pace for safe-keeping.[5] In a letter to Mountjoy, he spoke highly of Pace as "a young man so well equipped with knowledge of the two literatures, as to be able by his

---

[1] The *Dictionary of National Biography* account of Pace has been superseded by Jervis Wegg's *Richard Pace, A Tudor Diplomat* (London, 1932). Wegg's monograph is the only biography, but it can be supplemented by items from Erasmus' correspondence (*Erasmi Epistolae*, ed. P. S. Allen *et al.*, 11 vols., Oxford, 1906-58) and from the *Letters and Papers of Henry VIII* (ed. J. S. Brewer, J. Gairdner, and R. Brodie. Revised edition by Brodie, London, 1920). It is also probable that a good deal of Pace's correspondence still reposes in diplomatic archives.

[2] Wegg, pp. 3-4.

[3] For the date, see Charles Sturge, *Cuthbert Tunstal* (London, 1938), p. 9, n. 7. Pace thanks Langton profusely in the *De Fructu* itself, below, p. 39.

[4] See below, p. 125.

[5] These included the *Antibarbari*, which was later lost. See Allen, *Eras. Ep.*, 1, 121, and below, p. 141, n. 2.

genius alone to bring honor to England, and of such purity and modesty of character as to be worthy of your favor." [6]

But Pace's literary activities were soon to be interrupted. In 1509, he entered the service of Christopher Bainbridge, Archbishop of York, and Henry VIII's newly appointed agent at Rome. Bainbridge was Langton's nephew, and this fact may have figured in Pace's appointment. In any event, he was to serve Bainbridge faithfully until the latter's death in 1514. About September 1513, the long sequence of Pace's diplomatic letters to Henry VIII and Wolsey begins. At the same time, he starts to be mentioned frequently in Erasmus' correspondence. English policy, and that of Bainbridge, was strongly anti-French during these years and, throughout his diplomatic career, Pace was to adhere closely to this position. He seems to have plunged whole-heartedly into his work, perhaps with a view to rapid promotion. On December 21, 1513, Erasmus wrote to his friend Ammonius that "Pace seems to me to forget his scholarship, and to assume a style more agreeable to Midas than the Muses." [7]

At some time in the spring of 1514, if not before,[8] Pace was back in England, where he probably met Thomas More for the first time. On May 20, he became Archdeacon of Dorset and by June 12, he was in Zurich to negotiate for Swiss aid against the French. A treaty was signed at Berne on July 31, 1514, but by then Pace had received news of Bainbridge's death in Rome (about July 13), and he hastened there to act as the cardinal's executor.[9] When an autopsy indicated that Bainbridge had been poisoned, Pace vehemently conducted an investigation, which implicated Silvester de Giglis, Bishop of Worcester, and Wolsey's agent in Rome. But Wolsey's star was rising, and Pace could do little without his protection. By September 25, he was writing cordially to the new Archbishop of York; just before Christmas a papal consistory absolved de Giglis. Pace reached Paris by March 29, 1515, and in April was back in England, serving as secretary to Wolsey.

In October 1515, Pace was again abroad and, from then until 1525, his life was one long series of missions to the continent. His negotiations with the Swiss and the Emperor Maximilian dragged on

---

[6] Allen, ibid., *1*, 445.

[7] Allen, ibid., *1*, 543.

[8] For a discussion of the date, see Wegg, pp. 45-46.

[9] For Bainbridge's death and Pace's role in the investigation of it, see D. S. Chambers, *Cardinal Bainbridge In The Court Of Rome 1509 to 1514* (Oxford, 1965), pp. 131-40.

through 1517, most of which Pace spent at Constance, where the *De Fructu* was written. He had become principal secretary to the king in 1516, but his health was not of the best and several serious attacks of fever hit him before his return to London about Christmas, 1517. Several contemporaries noted [1] that Pace was not perhaps perfectly suited for the life of an ambassador. He was subject to fits of depression or elation, given to violent enthusiasms, and there was some doubt about his discretion. One might conjecture that, on occasion, Pace's moral probity did not stand him in good stead. Like many another courtier, he was constantly forced to shift with the tide of royal affairs, now flattering, now abusing. Instructions and money did not always reach him in time for a scheme to be carried out effectively and he was not the sort of man to float serenely through the sea of troubles in which he was involved. Even if we do not credit the rumor [2] that Wolsey deliberately kept Pace on diplomatic business in order to prevent his rise in the king's favor, it remains true that Pace was constantly discovering how difficult it could be for a devoted humanist to maintain his ideals amidst the pragmatic environment of court life and royal service. [3]

For a time at least, Pace breathed a bit easier in England, where he remained until May 1519. He was granted a coat of arms on February 12, 1518, and spent most of his time attending on the king as the court moved from place to place in an effort to escape the plague. On October 3, Pace delivered an oration before the papal legate, Campeggio, and the French, Spanish and Venetian ambassadors, who had assembled in London to sign a treaty of universal peace and to proclaim war against the Turk. [4] Bouts of fever continued to bother him, but on May 14, 1519, he was at Calais, ready to leave for the meeting of the Frankfort Diet which would elect a successor to the Emperor Maximilian, who had died the previous January. Pace was to work for Henry's election, but if this proved impossible, he was to support that of Charles, Prince of Spain, against the candidature of Francis I. Charles was elected on June 28 and Pace returned

---

[1] See Wegg, pp. 99 f.

[2] Ibid., pp. 269 f.

[3] The best dramatization of this problem occurs in Book I of Thomas More's *Utopia*. See the discussion by J. H. Hexter in vol. 4 of the *Complete Works of St. Thomas More* (New Haven, 1965), pp. lxxxi-xcii. Wyatt's satire, "To Mine Own John Poins," also describes the difficulties of life in the Tudor court.

[4] *Oratio in pace nuperrime composita*, R. Pynson, London, 1518 (STC 19081a).

to England at the end of July. A series of lucrative benefices came Pace's way in 1519, and these were crowned by his appointment, on October 25, to succeed John Colet as Dean of St. Paul's. In April 1520, he was named lecturer in Greek at Cambridge, but he does not seem to have taken up the post.

By the spring of 1520, Pace was abroad again, this time with the court at the Field of the Cloth of Gold, the sumptuous meeting of Henry and Francis I between Guines and Ardres. The court returned in July, and the round of royal business began again for Pace. In May 1521, he was present at the burning of Luther's works before Paul's Cross, later translating into Latin the sermon which Bishop Fisher delivered. He remained in England while Wolsey was at Calais in the summer of that year, zealously forwarding his patron's interests. On December 2, Leo X died and Pace was dispatched at once on what was to become his last mission. He set out for Rome, to try to make Wolsey Pope.

Pace's health, as his letters indicate, had not been improving. He was accustomed to speak of his "troublesome passion," and in November 1521 he had written to Wolsey that he lacked both sleep and appetite.[5] These statements may indicate the gradual onset of the madness that was later to seize him; certainly the pressure of diplomatic work during the next four years might well have broken a much stronger man. Pace did not reach Florence until January 12, 1522; already, on the 9th at Rome, Adrian VI had been elected. Continuing on to Rome late in January, Pace awaited instructions from England and busied himself by translating Plutarch. At the end of June 1522, Pace was instructed to proceed to Venice in order to wean the Venetians away from the French. He did not leave Rome until August 4, nine days before Adrian finally reached it. The Venetian negotiations dragged on for over a year, but a treaty was eventually signed on July 29, 1523. Pace left on a brief Swiss mission, but finding them bound to Francis I, returned to Italy.

In September, he was again at Rome. Adrian had died and the Wolsey campaign was on once more. Pace and his colleague, John Clerk,[6] could do nothing, however, to prevent the election of Clement VII on November 17. Henry then recalled Pace from Rome, ordering him to Lombardy to take part in negotiations with the Duke of Bourbon, Francis' rebellious vassal. This Pace did and then started for home, only to be ordered back to Bourbon by a dispatch which

---

[5] Wegg, pp. 159 and 175.

[6] Pace mentions Clerk in the *De Fructu*. See below, p. 35, n. 3.

reached him at Malines in May 1524. He remained with Bourbon's army when the latter invaded France that summer, retreating again to Italy with him after the failure of the siege of Marseilles in September. Once more Pace was ordered to persuade Venice against Francis I, and he scurried back and forth from Brescia to Mantua to Venice throughout the fall and winter. Fortunately, he was able to spend some time at Padua with his friends Reginald Pole and Thomas Lupset.[7] On February 24, Francis I was defeated and taken prisoner by the imperial forces at Pavia. Pace was at Venice, sick and unwell. The Signory sent physicians to him.[8]

In March, Pace wrote to Wolsey, asking to be recalled, but he did not begin his return voyage until October, and it was November 17 before he reached London, a broken man, whose brain had been affected by his illness. For the last ten years of his life we hear of him only occasionally. Coadjutors were appointed for his deaneries in 1526. The next year he was retired to Sion monastery at Isleworth, but he was living in London again in the autumn. Later Pace was placed in the custody of the Abbot of Beaulieu in Hampshire; but, after Wolsey's fall in October 1529, he returned to court on a few occasions. It had become quite clear, however, that his madness was incurable, and he lived in retirement from 1530 until his death on June 28, 1536. He was buried at St. Dunstan's, Stepney, where his epitaph, now no longer extant, spoke of his eloquence and affability, his sharp wit, and the good services which he had rendered to many.

Although Pace published several other volumes during his lifetime,[9] his modest claim to literary fame rests upon his *De Fructu* of 1517, reprinted here for the first time since its original publication. We know, as a matter of fact, a good deal about the composition, printing, and reception of Pace's book, partly because he himself discourses at some length about his circumstances and intentions as he writes, and

---

[7] See F. Gasquet, *Cardinal Pole and His Early Friends* (London, 1927).

[8] Wegg, p. 260.

[9] In addition to the *Oratio* of 1518 and the translation of Fisher's sermon noted above, these include his translations of Plutarch (Venice, January, 1522-23, with a revised edition in the same year) and his work on the text of the Old Testament, which seems to have engaged him at Venice in 1525 and later during his retirement. D. S. Chambers (*Cardinal Bainbridge In The Court Of Rome*, p. 119, n. 5) calls attention to an earlier (1515, Rome) edition of *Opuscula Plutarchi . . . Richardo Paceo Anglico interprete.* STC 19082 [London, 1530?], *Praefatio in Ecclesiasticen recognitum ad Hebraicam veritatem*, a copy of which is in the Bodleian Library, seems to be the only published evidence of Pace's later biblical studies. See also Wegg, pp. 273-74.

partly too because of the series of comments which his contemporaries, particularly Erasmus, made once the volume had appeared from Froben's press in October 1517. Pace evidently wrote out his book very quickly during the latter part of August and early September 1517 while he was waiting at Constance for new instructions from the king. In his preface "To All Professors of Knowledge" (p. 11), he says that the work was composed in one month. Paulus Bombasius (Paolo Bombasio, d. 1527), who had been Pace's teacher at Bologna and who introduces the *De Fructu* to the reader, was in Switzerland in September; he met Pace at Constance and read most of the book then, suggesting a few revisions and additions. Bombasius went on to Zurich and there received the finished volume, which he immediately dispatched to Froben's press at Basel.[1] Other internal evidence confirms this account, for at one place in his book (p. 93) Pace speaks of Andreas Ammonius, Latin Secretary to Henry VIII, as still alive. Ammonius died on August 17, 1517 and we might expect that, by October 1, Pace would have received news of his death.[2]

The *De Fructu* begins, after *three* prefatory letters from Pace,[3] as a traditional *laus*, an oration designed to praise the various branches of learning and to indicate the benefits which each confers on humanity. Pace thus considers Theology, Law, and Philosophy in that order, but when he turns to Music (p. 39), he ceases to speak in the first person and lets the Art herself usurp the stage. From this point until the very last section (pp. 111-141), where Pace again appears directly as the speaker, the Arts of Music, Astronomy, Astrology, Geometry, Arithmetic, Rhetoric, Grammar, and Dialectic almost literally 'sport their stuff.' They praise themselves and wrangle with each other in witty repartee. Nor is this all—at times (e.g., pp. 69-73, 93) they even tell stories about Pace himself, who, towards the end of Grammar's speech (p. 111) merges rather gracelessly into the figure of the personified Art.[4]

Equally disconcerting, at least on first reading, is Pace's seeming

---

[1] Bombasius' prefatory letter is dated September 29, from Zurich.

[2] Erasmus had heard the sad news concerning Ammonius on August 28 (Allen, 3, 637).

[3] "To All Professors of Knowledge" (pp. 11-13), "To Good Students" (pp. 15-19), and "To John Colet" (pp. 21-25).

[4] Grammar begins her address on p. 101 ("Then Grammar directed her speech to the boys:"). It runs on to p. 111 without a break, sounding more and more like Pace himself, who finally interrupts, apparently in his own person, with "When I had said all that, etc." For a possible explanation of the situation here, see below, p. 109, n. 1.

indifference with regard to his audience. Although the three introductory letters envisage three different classes of readers, it soon becomes apparent that it is really only the boys of Colet's school who should be listening to the various speeches of the Arts. In the last section, first Colet, then the boys again, and finally Henry VIII and Wolsey are appealed to, the latter in terms of perhaps the most fulsome eloquence ever bestowed on the all-powerful cardinal. At the same time, the reader is constantly disconcerted by shifts in tone as the discourse proceeds. Windily oratorical on occasion, as in the *Laus Musicae* section (pp. 39 f.), Pace often drops into the most vulgar sort of anecdote, as with his story of the man (p. 55) who "dreamed he was walking along naked and squeezed out a turd so big and long that it dragged along behind him like a tail." Learned quotations from the classics [5] jostle uncomfortably with a racy idiom of the streets; maxims from Plato or Plutarch are illustrated by stories of Erasmus' poverty or the little horse belonging to Doctor Aquila. A topsy-turvy book indeed, and where, through it all, is our learned humanist and royal secretary, Richard Pace?

Such, certainly, was the reaction of Erasmus himself when he first received a copy of the *De Fructu* at Antwerp on February 22, 1518.[6] In the previous December, Erasmus had told Beatus Rhenanus that Pace had boasted that Rhenanus had praised the work and, as we have seen, he had a very high opinion of Pace's intelligence. But the *De Fructu* embarrassed Erasmus in every possible way. First of all it offended him personally with its allusions to his previous poverty. "You have made me absolutely notorious," he wrote Pace in March 1518, "with the ill report of my poverty, although I seem to myself almost a Midas." [7] Moreover, Pace had stirred up the scholastic theologians again with his defense of Erasmus against them and, Lord knows, Erasmus had his hands full with them already. Although the Germans read the *De Fructu* avidly, they were irate over Pace's description of them as tippling illiterates. Pace had been too personal in

---

[5] For the most part, Pace rattles these off from memory. Thus he is often inexact and at times he will blend several sources together in one quotation. See, for example, p. 23, n. 3; p. 59, n. 9; p. 75. n. 3, etc.

[6] Allen, 3, 218-19. A succinct account of contemporary opinions on Pace's book is given by Edward Surtz, S.J., "Richard Pace's Sketch of Thomas More," *JEGP*, 57 (1958), 36-50, which is drawn upon in the following paragraphs.

[7] Surtz, p. 38; Allen, 3, 242. Erasmus' chagrin on this point was only temporary and should not be over-emphasized. He went on, lightheartedly, in the same letter, to ask Pace to dispel the libel of poverty by appealing to patrons on Erasmus' behalf!

his anecdotes; friends were friends and their names should not have
been bandied about as if they were fictitious characters. Erasmus asks
More to advise Pace that, in the future, he should not abuse literature
again in this fashion. His book is neither serious nor humorous, it lacks
unity and coherence, like the dreams of a sick man in Horace's *Art of
Poetry*.[8] To Rhenanus, Erasmus speaks of his regret and shame: the
book is most lifeless and it will certainly disappoint the expectations
of Pace's learned friends. Even Bombasius comes in for a lashing, for
he should have known better when he recommended the publication
of the work.[9]

Pace, as far as we know, never made any direct attempt to defend
his little book. He seems, instead, to have taken Erasmus's advice [1]
that he devote himself to translating from the Greek. The modern
reader may well find, however, that the *De Fructu* arouses interest
today for precisely those reasons which led Erasmus to reject it so
indignantly. For the student of Renaissance social history, Pace's chat-
tiness brings to life the day-to-day affairs of the humanist milieu as do
few other literary works from the period. We value the character
sketches that he gives of his contemporaries, especially the description
of Thomas More (pp. 103-107), which agrees in so many details with
Erasmus' portrait in his famous letter to Ulrich von Hutten of 1519.[2]
The *De Fructu* is, after all, a very "in" book. At times it even seems
that Pace is deliberately trying to convince his readers that he knows
all the gossip circulating among the group of humanists whom he
portrays. Certainly he has read all the latest books, as his casual
allusions to the *Utopia* and Erasmus' *Novum Instrumentum* (both just
published in 1516) show, and he is soaked in all the great classical
commonplaces which humanistic scholarship was now reviving and
revivifying. Pace has all the quick answers, all of the new jargon, on
the tip of his tongue, and woe be to those pretenders to knowledge
who, like the Scotist theologian (pp. 117-21), have never heard of the
Adagia,[3] or are unfamiliar with the latest scholarly opinion (Linacre's

---

[8] *De Arte Poetica*, ll. 6-9.

[9] Allen, 3, 254-55. Erasmus had a high opinion of Bombasius as a textual
critic. See below, p. 13, n. 8.

[1] As given to More to be passed on to Pace. See Allen, 3, 218-19.

[2] Allen, 4, 12-23. The parallels are noted by Surtz, pp. 41-49.

[3] This whole scene recalls the anecdote of the Friar in Cardinal Morton's
household in Book I of the *Utopia*. The Friar, like Pace's Scotist, also misquotes
Scripture in an effort to defend himself.

and Beroaldus') on the proper way to make *theriaca,* "the most famous
and healing of all medicines" (pp. 63-65).

Of course none of this dazzling display of knowledge on Pace's part
makes for any real profundity. The *De Fructu,* at this level, is hardly
more than a *tour de force,* parading its superficial wisdom in a highly
ostentatious manner. Erasmus, one can see, must have felt as if the
Epistolae Obscurorum Virorum had been turned back on their humanist authors with a vengeance. That famous satire, the first install-
ment of which had appeared in late 1515, purported to be the letters
of a group of semi-literate monks who exchanged the most trivial
gossip with each other in the most barbarous Latin imaginable.[4] But if
it was one thing for the humanists to make fools of their opponents in
such an ironical fashion, it was quite another for one of the bright
young men in their own circle to retail racy anecdotes about themselves—even if he did it in a fine classical style! The dignity, the
gravitas, of the new learning had been compromisd by Pace's performance—the last thing one would expect from a diplomat.

It is also possible that Erasmus resented the *De Fructu* on more
purely literary, albeit still personal, grounds. There was, after all, a
right way to do the kind of thing which Pace seemed to have attempted. Erasmus himself, in *The Praise of Folly,* had provided a
model for the satiric oration, and there could be little doubt that Pace
knew Erasmus' masterpiece and at times seemed to imitate the manner
of its heroine. Like the *De Fructu,* the *Praise of Folly* was written on
a sudden inspiration. Conceived while Erasmus crossed the Alps on his
return from Italy in 1509, it was composed during six weeks of leisure
at More's house in London the same year. In his dedication to More,
Erasmus outlined, with consummate irony, the logic that underlay his
satiric technique:

> For what an injustice it is, when we allow to each way of life its own
> recreations, that none should be permitted to studies! Especially when
> literary trifles may lead to serious matter, and fooleries may be so
> handled that a reader who is not altogether a fathead may garner more
> of profit from them than from the bristling and pompous arguments of
> some whom we know. As, for instance, one fellow praises rhetoric or
> philosophy in a pieced-up oration, another paints the glories of some
> prince, another exhorts to the end of making war against the Turks,
> another foretells the future; and still another works up a new set of
> little essays relating to—a lock of goat's wool. Nothing is more puerile,

---

[4] See the edition and translation of F. G. Stokes (London, 1925).

certainly, than to treat serious matters triflingly; but nothing is more
graceful than to handle light subjects in such a way that you seem to
have been anything but trifling. The judgment of others upon me will
be what it will be. Yet unless self-love deceives me badly, I have
praised folly in a way not wholly foolish.[5]

If the *Folly* turned foolishness into wisdom, subtly modulating its
central theme with the greatest artistry, then how appalling to meet
with a work like the *De Fructu*, which, while ostensibly praising learning, succeeded only in transforming wisdom into foolishness. "Nothing
is more puerile, certainly, than to treat serious matters triflingly." Pace
should have been forewarned; his "Praise of Wisdom" was, most as-
suredly, a far cry from the kind of thing which Martin Dorp, himself
troubled by the satire in *The Praise of Folly*, had suggested that Erasmus might set his pen to.[6]

In the face of such strictures, what can be said for Pace and his
book? Beyond the liveliness of its anecdotes, which parallel to a certain extent, the 'newsiness' of Pace's official correspondence, is the *De
Fructu* merely a slightly spectacular literary failure? Comparison with
Erasmus' masterpiece would suggest so, but a closer look at the *De
Fructu* itself may allow us to sympathize a bit more fully with its
author and the dilemma which he faced when he attempted to set
forth 'the benefits of a liberal education.'

In a sense, Pace gives himself away on the very first page of his
address to "All Professors of Knowledge." Staying at Constance, he
was "confused and unsettled" in his mind over what to do with himself (p. 11). The instability suggested by this sentence is reflected even
more strikingly a few lines later when he tells us that he "began to
consider (*cogitare coepi apud me*) that nothing is more suitable for
an educated man than to devote all his leisure time to learning."
Surely, we may note, the true humanist did not have to *begin* to consider. He would have thought such a conclusion obvious and would
automatically have turned to intellectual pursuits. It was with this
kind of casualness that More had penned the second book of *Utopia*,
while he waited in Flanders for new instructions from the king and
the emperor's commissioners.

---

[5] Desiderius Erasmus, *The Praise of Folly*, trans. H. H. Hudson (Princeton,
1941), p. 3.

[6] Dorp's letter (c. September 1514) was published by Thierry Martens in
October 1515 and could thus have been seen by Pace. See Allen, 2, 13: "Sed
spero pro meo captu omnia facillime consequeris, si contra Moriam composueris
Sapientiae laudem eamque aedideris."

But what was a reflex action for a More or an Erasmus quickly becomes a deliberately set and ardently pursued task for Richard Pace. We soon learn that his topic, "the benefit of a liberal education," makes him thoroughly uneasy. Hence his triple set of prefaces, each reaching out for a different sort of audience,[7] and hence too his remark (p. 11) that the subject seemed "*both* beautiful *and* useful" to him. Even though Pace is employing the conventional Horatian formula of *dulce et utile,* it is clear that he wants things both ways at once: knowledge should be its own end, the leisurely pursuit of educated men, but at the same time it should be useful, leading perhaps to advancement or promotion for just such manipulators of it as Pace will soon show himself to be. On the one hand, the title which he chose for his book—*De Fructu Qui Ex Doctrina Percipitur*—suggests the pragmatic motive which will lead him to compromise his ideals. The "fruit" or the reward that can be extracted from knowledge is not merely the moral wisdom so dear to Erasmus; it also entails a shrewdness in practical affairs that any quick young man might, either unconsciously or unscrupulously, or both, *use* for his personal advantage. But at the same time the "fruit" is the work itself. If one is educated, Pace says in effect, this (the *De Fructu*) is the sort of thing he can do with his leisure hours. It is the living proof of the benefit of a liberal education.

As Pace's prefaces continue, he worries more and more over the difficulty in which he has involved himself. Since he serves the "invincible King as the servant of the wise Cardinal of York" (p. 13), he is "free by nature, but not by choice." As a public servant, he must find that "to serve one's country exceeds all freedom"—but how can such abject servility, which startles the reader at the conclusion of the *De Fructu,* where Pace calls Wolsey his "God" (*quasi alter Deus*), how can such a position be reconciled with his attempt to disprove, in his address "To All Good Students" (pp. 15 f.), that "the more learned you are the less wise you become"?

In fact, Pace never reconciles the two positions. The very form of his book, so distressingly incoherent to Erasmus, mirrors perfectly his artful attempts to dodge a decision on the central problem that disturbs him so much. Although he certainly writes for the boys of St. Paul's School, he is nevertheless trying to impress the great with a display of sparkling virtuosity. He has many good things to say about the educational process, about what classical authors should be read

---

[7] See above, p. xiv, n. 3.

and how, about the need for studying Greek along with Latin, and about the value of imitating good men. In these passages, most of which come after the Arts have spoken their pieces (pp. 113-141), Pace shines as one of the first Englishmen to articulate clearly the new humanistic theories of education. Colet had spoken in much the same terms in his *Accidence* for the St. Paul's boys,[8] and Ascham was later to cite at length the passage from the younger Pliny to which Pace refers in his discussion of suitable classroom exercises.[9]

At this level, the *De Fructu* can well be viewed as an educational treatise and linked with other early Tudor admonitions to schoolboys. Thomas More, it will be recalled, had written two poems in praise of knowledge for John Holt's *Lac Puerorum* (c. 1497),[1] and Erasmus himself composed five verse pieces for Colet's school.[2] To the same tradition belong the Tudor *vulgaria* by Stanbridge, Whittington, and Horman, with their many lively passages of contemporary anecdotes that were set for the schoolboys to translate.[3] Colloquialism of this kind is not unrelated to Pace's own witty stories, and he may perhaps have felt that their inclusion in the *De Fructu* would enhance its appeal for young students. In this way learning could be brought out of the classroom and applied to daily life, just as Pace himself, in his own book, makes use of knowledge in the "hypocaust" of an inn.

Yet, when all due tribute has been paid to Pace's educational zeal, it is hardly conceivable that John Colet would have seriously considered the possibility of placing the *De Fructu* in the hands of the boys at St. Paul's. Even if the good Dean might have been willing to allow Pace's occasionally off-color wit to pass ("A whore is like a *sphaera*

---

[8] See J. H. Lupton, *A Life of John Colet* (London, 1909), pp. 290-92.

[9] Below, pp. 137-39. See also Roger Ascham, *English Works*, ed. W. A. Wright (Cambridge, 1904), pp. 244-45. On the humanists' misinterpretation of the Pliny passage, see William E. Miller, "Double Translation in English Humanistic Education," *Studies in the Renaissance, 10* (1963), 163-74.

[1] See *The Latin Epigrams of Thomas More*, ed. L. Bradner and C. A. Lynch (Chicago, 1953), pp. 117-18.

[2] See J. H. Rieger, "Erasmus, Colet, and the Schoolboy Jesus," *Studies in the Renaissance, 9* (1962), 187-94. Pace too includes a poem on the virtues of learning (below, p. 139).

[3] The *vulgaria* of Stanbridge and Whittington have been edited for the Early English Text Society by Beatrice White (Original Series 187, London, 1932) and that of Horman by M. James for the Roxburghe Club (London, 1926). See also the fine set of passages in William Nelson, *A Fifteenth Century School Book* (Oxford, 1956).

and *harpastum* because she doesn't stay in one spot, but rolls around all over," p. 55), he would probably have seen, as Erasmus did, that most of the book devastatingly undermines the eulogy of learning which it is apparently promoting.[4] Take, for example, the now well-known story that Pace relates to Colet (pp. 23-25) about the drunken nobleman who insists that aristocrats should know how "to blow the horn properly, hunt like experts, and carry a hawk gracefully." Studies can be left to country boys. Many a historian has treated this anecdote as indicative of the opposition which the humanists faced from the semi-literate, old-school gentry and have connected it with Ascham's later denunciation of the poorly-educated nobility. But, as Pace tells the story, such interpretations will hardly do. The nobleman, even in his cups, can quote Greek, and he has read Erasmus; he is, in fact, turning a typical humanist complaint (that their labors were not sufficiently rewarded) against themselves. And when Pace, preening his feathers, relates how he silenced the fox-hunter, he betrays his supposedly pure devotion to learning by meeting his opponent on the latter's own terms. Knowledge *is* useful—without it, how could a courtier speak to a visiting royal ambassador?

There would be little point in attempting to decide whether or not the irony implicit in this episode was consciously Pace's. If he did not quite realize what he was in fact doing, it remains true that the pattern suggested by the story persists through much of his book. Whenever Pace, or one of the personified Arts, begins to wax portentously idealistic, laughter suddenly begins to echo from the wings of the stage. Frequently it is a quickly tossed in joke ("Pliny said of them: 'only doctors can kill a man and get away with it.'") or a digressive, but amusing, personal anecdote (Pace's account of his friendship with John Clerk, p. 35) that interrupts the staid scene. The author seems unable to distinguish between the system, the whole structure of learning being praised, and the man himself, the daily life of Richard Pace who, whatever his allegiance to lofty wisdom, is continually reminding us of the way in which all too incongruous reality forces men—even good humanists—to compromise their ideals. One could even argue that Pace was no abstract thinker like many of the humanists, but the sort of person who could conceive of things only in

---

[4] One wonders, at times, if Pace himself really believed in the new learning. Perhaps he felt that studies (which, in the *De Fructu,* he describes as too harsh) were unreal and deadening, and perhaps he wrote his book to remedy this defect. If this was the case, then it implies an entire educational theory that Pace was not consciously aware of or able, apparently, to articulate for himself.

terms of the personal and concrete—thus, perhaps the form of the book, the alternating colloquialism and formality, anecdote and address, and thus too Pace's ill-concealed dissatisfaction with the educational system of his day. Greece and Rome may indeed have mattered once, and they may still provide both information and models; but, in the *De Fructu,* the pedagogic benefits which they afford often appear unreal and unrelated to the contemporary scene.

The gusto with which Pace indulges in his digressions and asides is matched by an analogous movement in the speeches of the Arts themselves. As the *De Fructu* opens, Pace himself praises Theology rather perfunctorily. For two pages (27-29) he is straightforward enough, but as soon as he begins to discuss law and lawyers we find him not praising, but condemning the faculty and its practitioners in the sharpest satirical terms. Philosophy follows next, together with Medicine, both of them very nearly treated as personifications. Then, with Music (pp. 39 f.), Pace drops out of sight and the Art praises herself to the skies, damning all other claimants to the highest wisdom. But the joke here, as with the orations of the Arts which follow, is that Music, without knowing it, taints her own dignity with irrelevant little witticisms (Pythagoras marching a young man in and out of a whorehouse to the sound of the lyre, p. 43) or satiric anecdotes like that of Brother Egidius (pp. 43-45).

"So Music, in praise of herself," Pace concludes, but now the bickering among the Arts becomes more intense as Astrology and Astronomy appear. Again the slanted anecdotes crop up, and again the argument becomes more laughable than serious. Geometry intervenes (p. 57), to hold the stage for the entire center of the book (pp. 57-77). Judiciously, and appropriately, she balances and measures all things, including the other Arts, many of them still to speak; but her arbitration consists of little more than scathing attacks on her sisters, or on those men who are devoted to them. The marginal glosses highlight the tone of this central section: "Disagreement of theologians" (p. 61), "Discord of lawyers" (p. 63), "Disagreement of astrologers" (p. 67), and so on until the palace of wisdom is turned into a marketplace of wrangling hucksters.

Any individual point which Pace scores amidst all this quarrelsomeness does indeed have its satiric effect. But the whole is not merely the sum of its parts, and even Pace's final effort to reestablish control over his book in the relatively friendly conversation between Rhetoric and Grammar (pp. 93-101) scarcely lessens our sense of a rapidly disintegrating learned cosmos. Rhetoric and Grammar get the

last words because, of course, they loomed largest in the humanistic system of education,[5] but their casual banter is delightful in itself rather than indicative of what verbal eloquence can contribute to real learning. Like all the other arts, Rhetoric and Grammar are pompous asses, more concerned with their own prestige than with the value of the humane disciplines which they are supposed to represent.

It almost seems, in fact, that once Pace starts to speak again *in propria persona* (p. 113), addressing Colet and the boys directly, he is trying to apologize for most of what has preceded. Yet even here, where, as has been seen, he comes closest to enunciating some sober educational ideals, he still is torn between the abstract validity of the precepts which he offers and the considerably less intellectual usefulness of the ambitiousness which he encourages. Poverty is the scholar's bane, and the long anecdote which Pace relates about Erasmus (pp. 117 f.) will hardly convince a student that the life of a truly learned man is free from care. The world wins in the end, triumphing over both wisdom and Pace himself; flattery may be bad for princes but "people set a value on utility in human affairs" (p. 125) and Pace, at Constance in 1517, was in no position to avoid the route which could and did (at least temporarily) lead him to preferment, honor, and wealth.

Was the strain, through the next eight years, too much for Pace? Given our poor knowledge of his medical record, it would be foolish to read into the whirlygig rhetoric of the *De Fructu* some indications of his future madness. Yet the relevance of his book to the general predicament of the court humanist in the Renaissance cannot be ignored. Pace was to discover, if he had not already discerned (particularly in the Bainbridge affair) that an ambassador is indeed an honest man sent to lie abroad for the good of his country. Wotton's knowing maxim [6] would not be out of place in the *De Fructu*, however much Pace's own sensibility and temperament were unsuited to the harsh world of Tudor politics. In the last analysis, Pace himself, for all his wit and enthusiasm, emerges as a distinctly sad figure. Greater things had been expected of him, both as a humanist and a diplomat. No one blamed him for his failure, and even Erasmus could,

---

[5] Dialectic, the darling of the Middle Ages, tries to speak at pp. 111-113, but she is kicked off the stage as a mere fortune teller.

[6] For the story, see Izaak Walton's *Life of Wotton*, originally written for the *Reliquiae Wottonianae* of 1651, and included in all editions of the *Lives* from 1670 on.

at the worst, see his faults as merely puerile. If he never really grew up, his childishness never detracted from his lovability. In his letter to Colet (p. 25), Pace anticipated that some might notice a childish element in the *De Fructu;* but, at this distance, his folly seems rather to reach the childlike plateau which Erasmus' speaker attained at the end of the *Encomium Moriae.* "Nulli unquam nocuit," said his epitaph, he never harmed anyone. When wisdom offers better fruits, then folly will be ready to claim them.

TEXT, TRANSLATION, AND COMMENTARY

The Latin text of the *De Fructu* has been taken directly from the Yale Library copy of the first and only previous edition, that published by John Froben, Basel, 1517. The abbreviations in the Froben text have been silently expanded, but spelling, capitalization, and punctuation, with a few rare exceptions, have been retained. We have, where necessary, corrected misprints in the original, recording our emendations in footnotes to the text. The marginalia in the 1517 edition have been cut into the present texts, both in the Latin and in the English translation. In the original, the marginalia are sometimes followed by a full stop, sometimes not. We have omitted the full stop throughout. Pace's Greek quotations posed a problem. On the few occasions where they differed from the readings of modern editors, we have recorded this fact in notes to the Latin text. While retaining Greek characters in the Latin, we have transliterated the quotations in our English translation. It is our hope that this procedure will enable the modern reader, forced to make do with small Latin and less Greek, to recapture something of the humanistic flavor which the Greek quotations contributed to the original edition.

In the English translation itself, we have striven first of all for accuracy, but we have not hesitated to introduce modern sentence structure and idiom (even, on occasion, slang) where the force of Pace's Latin seemed to demand such measures. A merely literal translation of the *De Fructu*, we believe, would do scant justice to the extraordinary liveliness of the original in which highly colloquial dialogue continually interrupts a respectable Ciceronian eloquence.

Our commentary, embodied in the notes to the English translation, endeavors to locate and verify Pace's quotations from the classics and from contemporary writers. When citing Latin and Greek authors in short-title form we have used the abbreviations listed in the *Oxford Classical Dictionary* (Oxford, 1949); wherever possible, we have taken classical quotations from the Loeb editions. Biblical quotations, unless otherwise noted, are from the Revised Standard Version. References to Erasmus' letters are abbreviated as "Allen" (P. S. Allen, ed., *Erasmi Epistolae*, 12 vols., Oxford, 1906-1958). For citations from the *Adagia*,

a work to which Pace, directly or indirectly, constantly alludes, we have used the system employed by Margaret Mann Phillips in her *The 'Adages' of Erasmus* (Cambridge, 1964). Thus *"Adagia,* I.II.lvii" refers to the first thousand, second hundred, number 57, and enables the reader to locate the adage in any of the collected editions as well as in the *Opera Omnia* (Leyden, 1703-1706). The titles of other authorities or sources are given in full as they occur.

CAMPEIUS: My Lord of York was not one Doctor Pace
    In this man's place before him?
WOLSEY: Yes, he was.
CAMPEIUS: Was he not held a learned man?
WOLSEY: Yes, surely.
CAMPEIUS: Believe me, there's an ill opinion spread then,
    Even of yourself, lord cardinal.
WOLSEY: How! of me?
CAMPEIUS: They would not stick to say you envied him,
    And fearing he would rise, he was so virtuous,
    Kept him a foreign man still; which so griev'd him,
    That he ran mad and died.

WILLIAM SHAKESPEARE
Henry VIII

RICHARDI PACEI,
INVICTISSIMI REGIS ANGLIAE
PRIMARII SECRETARII,
EIVSQVE APVD ELVETIOS ORATORIS,

DE FRVCTV QVI EX
DOCTRINA PERCIPITVR, LIBER.

IN INCLYTA BASILEA.

THE BENEFIT OF A LIBERAL EDUCATION

BY
RICHARD PACE, FIRST SECRETARY
TO THE INVINCIBLE KING OF
ENGLAND AND HIS AMBASSADOR TO
SWITZERLAND

PRINTED IN FABULOUS BASEL

PAVLVS BOMBASIVS BONONIENSIS
AD LECTOREM.

QVID MIHI DEBEAS CANDIDE LECtor, tunc plane intelliges, cum opusculum hoc uel ipsis Musis dignum perlegeris, meo potissimum suasu & impulsu editum. quomodo autem res processerit, uolo tibi commemorare. Proximis diebus cum ex Turrego Eluetiorum pago, Constantiam profectus essem, nec antiquius quicquam habuissem quam RICHARDVM PACEVM, summa mihi necessitudine coniunctum conuenire, forte fortuna hominem reperi literis inuolutum, qui simulac me respexit inopino gaudio quasi attonitus, est ne inquit, hic BOMBASIVS meus? Ipsissimus inquam ego. Sed (obsecro) nunquid ego te regis tui negocijs occupatum interpellaui? Regis mei inquit ille, negociorum plane Alcedonia nunc mihi sunt, ac ne nihil prorsus agam, totus in nugis nostris uersor, nec opportunius quicquam te esse potuit, in his praesertim locis, ubi nulla neque librorum copia, neque doctorum facultas adest, ac propterea te rogo ut operam mihi reddas, & sicut olim te Bononiae profitentem saepius audiui, ita me nunc inuicem Constantiae ociantem audire non graueris, libero, (ut consueuisti) iudicio tuo utens. Et cum dicto disiectas hincinde chartas in unum colligens, haud ita pridem inquit sub incude libellum habeo, cui titulum esse volui, Quis fructus ex disciplinis percipiatur. cuius summam cum diligenter enarrasset, loca plurima, ac fere omnia, quae iam perfecta erant, mihi perlegit. quae uero adhuc perficienda restabant, ita lucide exposuit, ut paulominus quam illa iam elaborata, oculis atque animo subiecta uiderentur. Postea me interrogauit ecquid crederem opus dignum fore, non quod aederetur, (nam id plane se facturum negabat),[1] sed quod studiosi quidam in Britannia iuuenes, citra temporis iacturam legere possent. Ego cum miram quandam, multiplicemque operis eruditionem annotassem, stilo supra quam dici possit, elegantem, salibus urbanam, praeceptis grauem, ipsaque

---

[1] negabat,) *1517*

4

PAULUS BOMBASIUS OF BOLOGNA [1]
TO THE READER

Dear reader, you'll understand clearly what you owe me after you've read this little book, which is worthy of the Muses and was published primarily at my insistence. I want to tell you how it happened. Recently, when I set out for Constance from Zurich, Switzerland, I wanted nothing more than to meet Richard Pace, whom I'm very close to, and, as luck would have it, I found him. He was writing something. As soon as he saw me, he was almost struck dumb, he was so happy, and said, "Is that really you, Bombasius?"

"In the flesh," I said, "but tell me, have I interrupted any official business?"

He said, "The King's affairs [2] are in the doldrums as far as I'm concerned, and in order to keep myself busy, I've taken to writing some nonsense of my own. I couldn't be happier to see anyone, especially in this place, where there're no learned men and no libraries. So I wonder if you would mind doing me a favor? I used to listen to you when you were lecturing at Bologna, and now you ought to be willing to take turns and listen to me when I'm taking my ease at Constance. Just remember to be as critical as you used to." And with that, he gathered up the papers scattered about and said, "I've had a little book in the works for a short while. I want to call it 'The Benefit of a Liberal Education.'" And after carefully describing the main idea, he read many parts of it to me, almost everything he had written. And he described the rest of it so clearly that it seemed almost as real to me as what he had already finished. As soon as he was through, he asked me if I thought it was worth, not publishing—for he flatly denied he would ever do that—but being read by a few students in Britain without wasting their time.

Since I had noted the wonderful and complex erudition of the book, the inexpressible style—elegant, sophisticated in wit, weighted with moral precepts, pleasing because of its very variety—which would

uarietate iucundam, nec studiosis tantum iuuenibus, sed uiris etiam quamlibet doctissimis admodum utilem futuram, per Musas inquam te rogo mi Pacee, ne tantum ac tam multiplex bonum cuiquam inuideas, sed publice omnibus (uel meo periculo) edas. Opus, inquit ille, absolutum paulo mox quam Turregum redieris, ad te mittam. Quod ubi diligentius examinaueris, tuum erit, uel Basileam mittere, ut illic imprimatur, uel ad me (quod fortasse tutius erit) remittere, ut supprimatur. Quod amice promiserat, fideliter praestitit. paucis siquidem interiectis diebus, librum extrema iam manu diligenter expolitum ad me mittens, ministro suo qui eum afferebat, praecise [2] mandat, ut quod ego iuberem, sine cunctatione faceret. Toto libro acrius perpenso & curiosius examinato, cum primo gustui omnia felicissime responderent, ministrum ipsum iubeo recta Basileam ire & curare ut quam primum liber imprimatur, quod ne temere fecisse, ac re missius alieno (ut aiunt) corio lusisse uidear, ex hoc ipso libro ingenij ac iudicij mei aestimationem fieri ualde cupio. nec recuso, quin me literarum omnium penitus ignarum iudicent, qui hanc editionem summopere non probabunt. Sed iam Vale humanissime lector. auresque tuas uerbositate mea defessas, suauissimo Pacei eloquio refoue. Ex Turrego, tertio Calendas Octobris.

M. D. XVII.

---

[2] paercise *1517*

obviously be useful not only to students, but also to well-educated men, I said, "By God, Pace, don't begrudge so great and rich a benefit to anyone, but publish it by all means, even if I have to assume the risk myself."

He said, "I'll send you the book when it's finished, probably by the time you get back to Zurich. Then, after you've looked it over carefully, it'll be up to you. Either send it to Basel and have it printed or (and this would probably be safer) send it back to me, and I'll shelve it."

He faithfully carried out what he had promised, for after a few days he sent me the book carefully polished, with all the finishing touches, and he expressly commanded the servant who brought it to do whatever I ordered without delay. After weighing the entire work more carefully and critically, I found that it agreed completely with my first impression. I therefore ordered the servant to go directly to Basel and see to it that the book was printed as soon as possible.

If anyone thinks I've acted rashly in this and, as they say, played free with another man's purse, I ask only that he form an opinion of my intelligence and critical abilities from the work itself. And as for those who don't think highly of the book, they can believe I'm totally ignorant of all literary matters.

But now farewell, gentle reader, and refresh yourself, after the din of my verbosity, with the sweet eloquence of Pace.

From Zurich
29 September 1517

PAVLI BOMBASII BONONIENSIS
IN LAVDEM ANGLIAE EPIGRAMMA.

Sceuo Marte potens & mercibus Anglia diues
    Quid tibi cum Musis improba? Momus ait.
Paceum pluresque ostentans Anglia doctos,
    Immo inquit mecum quid (rogo) Mome tibi?
Si me auro uincentem omnes, belloque superbam,
    Eloquio haud superat Graecia nec Latium.

EPIGRAM OF PAULUS BOMBASIUS OF BOLOGNA
IN PRAISE OF ENGLAND

"Since you're rich in trade and strong in war,
    What does a hussy like you care about art?"
Said Momus.[3] And England replied,
    Pointing to Pace and many other learned men,
"The question is, why are you criticizing me, Momus?
    Though I am richer than everyone else and proud in war,
Neither Greece nor Rome is superior to me in eloquence."

RICHARDVS PACEVS OMNIBVS OMNIVM SCIENTIARVM PROFESSORIBVS, S. P. D.[3]

LIBRVM, o doctissimi uiri, non adeo breuem, unius spatio mensis scriptum mirabimini. Mirabimini & illud, tam praecipitanter fuisse aeditum, & quod utroque est mirabilius, eo in loco compositum, ubi nec doctorum commercium, nec ulli fuerunt libri, hoc est, Constantiae in publico hypocausto, ubi nihil minus, quam de literis agitur. Tria aeditionis infelicissimae futurae indicia audistis. Res iam postulat, ut nostras quoque rationes intelligatis, quae nos ad hoc opus, cum scribendum, tum aedendum impulerunt. Commorabar Constantiae perplexus, & pendens animi, abeundum ne cito, an diu manendum esset. Qua animi fluctuatione effectum est, ut nescirem in qua potissimum re, me exercere deberem. Sed quum tempus in longum protraheretur, postpositis omnibus istiusmodi abeundi, & permanendi curis, cogitare coepi apud me, nihil magis homini studioso conuenire, quam ut omne ocium suum in literis consumeret. Hic illico se offert incredibile illud incommodum inopiae librorum, & doctorum. Suadet tamen ratio, aliquid etiam sine doctis, & libris tentandum esse, & experiendum quantum per se ualeret ingenium. Decernitur aliquid omnino scribendum esse. Deest materia. inuenitur haec, de fructu, qui ex doctrina percipitur. Arrisit haec ut pulchra, & utilis. Datur principium rei. redeunt in memoriam uetera, & multis ante annis lecta, affluunt & noua, adeo ut nihil unquam uerius dictum fuisse iudicarem, quam ἀρχήν ἥμυσι [4] τοῦ παντὸς,   id est, dimidium facti, qui bene coepit, habet. Pergo ulterius, & peruenio ad illum locum, ubi tracto nullum laborem detrectandum esse, qui ad doctrinam consequendam adiuuet. Interea dum circa hoc uersarer, longe praeter spem & expectationem meam, appulit ad ciuitatem casu quodam felicissimo, Paulus Bombasius, uir utriusque linguae doctissimus, & meus olim Bononiae praeceptor. Hunc cum uiderem, subijt mentem illud Aristophanicum, ἀγαθῶν σωρὸς ἐις τὴν ὀικίαν ἐπισπέπαικεν, [5] id est, cumulus omnium simul bonorum in domum meam incidit. Hunc rogo, ut meas audiat nugas, & de erroribus moneat. Is ut est in his rebus

Paulus Bombasius Bononiensis

---

[3] S P D. *1517*

[4] The correct Greek form is ἥμισυ.

[5] The reading here is an impossible formation. Modern editors of Aristophanes print either ἐπεισπέπαικεν or ἐπεσπέπαικεν.

RICHARD PACE TO ALL PROFESSORS OF KNOWLEDGE: GREETINGS

Learned gentlemen, you'll wonder at a book, and not a very short one, written in the space of one month. You'll also wonder at the fact that it was published so quickly and, more remarkable, that it was written in a place where there were neither learned men nor books, that is to say, in the public room of an inn [4] at Constance, where literature ordinarily is of little concern. That makes three reasons why the book should be unsuccessful. But you should also know why I wrote the book in the first place and afterwards published it.

I was staying at Constance, confused and unsettled in my mind whether I should leave at once or remain longer. Because of my uncertainty I did not know what to do with myself. But as time dragged on and I forgot about whether I should go or stay, I began to consider that nothing is more suitable for an educated man than to devote all his leisure time to learning. Then all at once I remembered my incredibly unfortunate lack of books and learned men. Yet my reason persuaded me that something could still be done and that I should try to find out what my mind was worth by itself. I decided therefore that I had to write something. Material was lacking and from that lack this was found: the benefit of a liberal education. The subject pleased me, for it was both beautiful and useful. And once I began, many old things read years before poured into my mind as well as things of more recent date, so that I thought nothing truer had ever been said than *archên hêmisy tou pantos.* That is to say, well begun is half done.[5] In fact I'll go further and say that no work should be avoided which helps in the pursuit of learning.

Meanwhile, as I was turning this over in my mind, Paulus Bombasius, a man versed in both Greek and Latin and my teacher once at Bologna, arrived at Constance by some happy coincidence far beyond my hope and expectation. As soon as I saw him, I remembered the line from Aristophanes,[6] *agathôn sôros eis tên oikian epeispepaiken,* that is, a heap of good things befall my house at once. I asked him to listen to the nonsense I had written and to correct the mistakes. And since he is a very kind person in things like this, he

Paulus Bombasius of Bologna

humanissimus omnia ad uerbum perlegit, immo tam seria, quam iocos nostros, & facetias approbauit. Monet illum quem dixi de labore locum, ampliandum esse, quia res ita postularet, & plus eo quem audierat, salis aspergendum. In utroque, consilio eius obtemperaui. Tum uero non ad adulationem, sed ex iudicio (quod in eo maximum est) ut aiebat, locutus, hortatus est ad aedendum. Non putaui doctissimo uiro hoc negandum, ne eius iudicio diffidere uiderer. Et haec est una, & quidem praecipua tam praecipitatae aeditionis causa. Aliae uero sunt hae. Liber sum, natura quidem, sed non uoluntate. Addixi enim me inuictissimo meo Regi, sapientissimo famulor Cardinali Eboracensi. patriae etiam seruire omnem superat libertatem. Itaque quum ex alieno pendeam arbitrio, nec hic sit manendum, sed abeundum, nescio quo, aut quạ, & longum simul & periculosum iter conficiendum, malui, si ita contingeret, ut homo potius quam pecus mori, id est, aliqua mei posteris memoria relicta, etiam si talis esset quae a multis emendaretur. Nam ut omnia quae scripsi, parum erudita sint, certe institutum omnibus probatum sit oportet. Primo, quod tempus non contriui, deinde quod iuuenes ad doctrinam, omnium uirtutum reginam, diligentissime sum hortatus, postremo fructus ex doctrina collectos, in scopum mihi proposui, quem si non attigi (quod nescio an fecerim) poterunt alij sua in eundem destinare iacula, & a quo ego uincar, ei libentissime palmam dabo. Vestrum igitur erit, o Musarum omnium cultores, & disciplinarum studiosi, nostris fauere coeptis, nec nostram aspernari humanitatem, qui uestra omnium nomina, ut olim clarissima fuerunt, ita his quoque temporibus maxime illustrare studuimus. Quod si quis fortasse tantum iocorum rei tam seriae admixtum esse cauillabitur, nescio quid huic nocebit paulisper risisse, imitanti non infacetum illum Atheniensem, qui profligato, & deleto in Sicilia (duce Nicia) Atheniensium exercitu, maxima celeritate Athenas se contulit, & omnia felicissime cecidisse nunciauit, insignemque ab hostibus reportatam esse uictoriam. Hunc deosculati, & amplexi sunt omnes, indicta est in triduum laetitia publica. Quarta uero die, allatae sunt literae Ducis, cladem longe maximam acceptam esse. Vocatur ille in Senatum, arguitur mendacij, mille mortes, principes ei minantur. Quibus auditis, quid, inquit (malum) est hoc, o ciues mei? quid obfuit uobis, triduum, me autore, in summa transegisse laetitia? Sed & huic malo θεραπεία, & medela fortasse erunt illa, quae de praeceptis, exhortatione ad doctrinam, & exercitationum generibus scripsimus. Valete igitur, & omnia boni consulite.

read every word and approved not only the serious parts, but also my puns and jokes. He said that I should expand what I had said about work [7] because the material itself demanded it and that I should spice up the parts he had gone over. And I have complied with each of his suggestions. Then, speaking not in flattery, as he said, but critically (he is an outstanding critic),[8] he urged me to publish it. I didn't want to say no to such a learned man for fear of seeming to distrust his opinion. And that is one—perhaps the primary—reason for this quick publication.

The others are these. I am free by nature but not by choice. For I have bound myself to serve my invincible King as the servant of the wise Cardinal of York.[9] To serve one's country exceeds all freedom. And so, since I am dependent on the will of another and cannot remain here, but must go away—I know not where nor how—and undertake a long and dangerous journey, I preferred, if it should turn out that way, to die like a man, not a beast—that is, to leave behind me something to be remembered by even if it were imperfect. For since what I have written is not very learned, my intentions at least have to be good. People should realize, first, that I have not wasted time; second, that to the best of my ability I have persuaded the young to search for learning, the queen of all virtues; and finally, that I have set up as my goal the benefit of a liberal education. And if I have not attained it (I am not certain that I have), others can aim at the same target,[1] and if they beat me, I'll gladly give the prize to them. It's therefore up to you professors, who cultivate the arts and all fields of learning, to approve of my beginning and not scorn my attempt to do you a favor and make your names as famous in our own times as they once were in the past.

But if anyone happens to object to my mixing so many jokes with such serious matter, I don't see that it would hurt him to laugh a little, like that wry Athenian who hurried as fast as he could to Athens after the army, under Nicias,[2] was routed and wiped out in Sicily and announced that everything had turned out fine and that they had won a famous victory. Everyone hugged and kissed him, and they proclaimed a three-day holiday. But on the fourth day letters came from the general saying that they had suffered a great defeat. The Athenian was called before the Senate, accused of lying, and threatened with a thousand deaths. After he had heard the accusations, he said, "What's wrong, gentlemen? How did it hurt you to spend three days in great happiness?" But perhaps the *therapeia* and remedy for this difficulty will be the remarks I make about precepts, encouragement to learning, and kinds of training. Therefore, farewell, and take all in good part.

RICHARDVS PACEVS STVDIOSIS
IVVENIBVS, S. P. D.

VVLGATVM EST APVD NOS PROuerbium, o studiosi adolescentes, cui nec euentus ullus, nec ulla ratio (quod in plerisque omnibus fit) sed hominum ignorantia, & fatuitas originem dedisse uidetur. Est enim multis in ore, doctiores uiros non esse sapientiores. Et quoniam hoc prouerbium alienissimum est a nostro instituto, qui aggressi sumus doctrinam omnibus alijs humanis bonis praeferre, uel tentandum nobis est, ut istud prouerbium ridiculum esse demonstretur, uel permittendum, ut periclitetur doctrina, priueturque illa ui & potestate, quas nos in opusculo, quod huic subiungitur epistolae, tantopere extulimus. Quamobrem intueamur diligentius, & acutius oportet, quod genus hominum est, quos huius prouerbij autores fatentur, doctos quidem, sed non sapientes. (Nam ex hoc solo tota prouerbij huius dependet subuersio).[6] Qua in re equidem illud obseruaui, modo astutiores istos & callidiores, quibus nulla scientia notior est, quam impostura, modo imperitum uulgus illis solis huius prouerbij notam inurere, qui sacrarum rerum contemplationi apud nos totos se dedunt, & omnibus humanis uoluptatibus, & friuolis oblectamentis spretis & contemptis, soli deo inhaerent, & malunt uerbum dei populo praedicare, quam chartulis & taxillis, modo astute, modo fraudulenter, diu noctuque ludere. Hos inquam fatentur doctos, sed negant sapientes, ac si dicerent illum desipere, qui Christi praecepta sequitur, eiusque insistit uestigijs, illum uero qui eiusdem nunquam est memor, sed pertinaciter damnatas & pestilentes persequitur artes, esse sapientissimum. Ille euoluit chartas euangelicas, & Paulinas, dum tu lusorias & perniciosas. Ille studet, ut deum lucrifaciat, tu ut eundem una cum facultatibus (quod saepe accidit) amittas. Ille neglecta hac misera & momentanea uita, totis laborat uiribus, ut assequatur sempiternam, & in coetum caelestis societatis ascitus ea perfruatur, Tu omnes neruos intendis, ut exiguo temporis momento, in huius uitae ergastulo te contineas, non ut bene & beate, sed ad libidinem instar beluarum uiuas, & omni animi curae, omni sacrae Theologiae, omnibus denique diuinis religionis nostrae praeceptis, unam

Contra prouerbium Anglicum, quo dicitur doctiores non esse sapientiores

---

[6] subuersio) *1517*

RICHARD PACE TO GOOD STUDENTS:
GREETINGS

Students, there's a proverb in English
that seems to have originated from the
ignorance and foolishness of man and
not from some particular thing or event,
as is usually the case. For many people

Against the English proverb
that says learned men
are not wiser

say that the more learned you are the less wise you become.[3] And
since this proverb is the opposite of what I hope to prove—that learning is superior to all other human goods—I either have to show that
the proverb is absurd or else endanger learning and let it be stripped
of the strength and power I've praised so much in the little book that
follows. Therefore we ought to consider more carefully and precisely
what kind of men the authors of the proverb say are learned, perhaps,
but not wise. (For on that alone the refutation of the entire proverb
depends.) Along this line, I've noted that the ignorant masses sometimes apply this proverb to big-time operators and con men, who know
nothing so well as they know how to cheat, and sometimes only to
those of us who dedicate themselves entirely to the contemplation of
sacred things, who cling to God alone, scorning all human lusts and
empty pleasures, and who would rather preach the word of God to the
people than play cards and dice day and night, sometimes with skill,
sometimes by cheating. These are the ones, I say, who're supposed to
be learned but not wise. It's the same as if they said a man is foolish
if he follows the commandments of Christ and walks in his footsteps,
but wise—most wise—if he never thinks of Him, but constantly pur-
sues a damned and unhealthy way of life. My man opens the books
of the Evangelists and St. Paul, whereas you open destructive novels
and romances. He takes pains to find God, whereas you take pains to
lose Him, along with your own wits, as often happens. He neglects
this miserable, momentary life and works with all his might to attain
eternity and enjoy it as part of the company of saints in heaven. You
strain every muscle in the workhouse of this life to remain here for a
brief moment of time, not in order to live properly and blessedly, but
to live for lust like a beast. You place one sect of the Epicureans before
all care for the soul, all sacred theology, and all divine precepts of our

anteponis Epicureorum sectam, solo uoluptatis nomine titillatus. Quam ut assequaris, nullum dolum postponendum, nullam fraudem omittendam, nullam rapinam negligendam censes. Et in hoc uno, quo maxime sapere tu te existimas, maxime insanis. Neque enim tibi notum est, quid sit uel Epicurus, uel eius uoluptas, adeo ut ego, si daretur optio, mallem esse Diogenes, quantumuis Cynicus, quam tui similis Christianus, nisi mores hos peruersos emendare uelis, & a recta doctrina sapientiam separare desieris. Nam non nomen (mihi crede) Christianum facit, sed res, id est, doctrinam Christi noscere, & imitari, sicut ille doctus facit, quem tu negas sapientem. Porro Diogenes sua usus familiari linguae libertate, quicquid male uidebat factum, id taxabat, reprehendebat, damnabat. & e diuerso, quicquid bene, id approbabat, laudabat, imitandum ducebat. Vnde ipsius, & omnium Cynicorum selectae exierunt sententiae, quas κυρίας δόξας uocabant. At tu contra facis, blandiris semper, assentaris, adularis. quod maxime uituperandum est, id maximis in caelum laudibus tollis. quod pessimum & uitiosissimum, id solum omni studio sectandum proponis. Seminauit Diogenes ut Ethnicus, in genere humano praecepta bona, & documenta clara. quae licet duriora uisa sint, tamen nemo non illa suspiciebat, ceu ex ipso uirtutis fonte emanantia, praesertim quum de contemptu rerum humanarum ageretur. Sed quid seminas tu? Profecto odia, simultates, inimicitias, discordias, bella, plura denique mala, quam in Iliade continentur. Diogenes denique nemini nocuit, tu omnibus. At inquis, non omnes sic fecerunt Cynici. Fateor, Sed qui Diogenem non sunt imitati, hi peruerterunt sectam Cynicam, sicut tu peruertis sanctam Christi religionem, dum a sanctissima doctrina sapientiam stulte separare conaris. Nunquid haec tua magna est, & laudabilis sapientia? & illius de quo superius dixi, boni & innocentis uiri doctrina ex Christo profecta, stultitiae nomen reportare debet? Absit. Mutabis igitur prouerbium si sapies, & neminem sapientem iudicabis, nisi idem doctus sit. Circunspice teipsum, & consydera, quantum aberras a recto. Saepissime enim ad hunc audiendum, quum populo concionatur, eumque Christi praeceptis erudit, accedis, ut sapere docearis, (neque enim id negas),[7] negas tamen ridicule sapientem esse, a quo tuipse cupis sapientior fieri. Sed dixerit hic quispiam, Nonne sunt quidam ex his quos tu doctissimos, cum nominas, tum iudicas, qui nobiscum sentiunt, & dicunt se malle prudentiam sine literis, quam literas citra prudentiam? Sunt, fateor. Telum torsisti ualidum quidem, sed quod facile tamen retorquebitur. Nam & hos ipsos qui haec dicunt, si rem bene notabis, nihil unquam famae, nominis,

---

[7] negas,) *1517*

faith. You are titillated by the mere mention of sensual enjoyment. And in order to pursue it, you think that one should postpone no deceit, omit no fraud, neglect no theft. And in that one thing the smarter you think you are, the crazier you are. You certainly don't know anything about Epicurus or his concept of pleasure, and therefore if given a choice, I would rather be Diogenes, even though he was a cynic, than a Christian like you, unless you're willing to change your evil ways and stop separating wisdom from true learning. For believe me, the word alone does not make a Christian, but the deed, that is, to know the teaching of Christ and to imitate it, like the learned man to whom you deny wisdom. Besides, Diogenes censured, reprehended, condemned with his customary freedom of speech whatever he saw done badly, and on the other hand he approved, praised, held up for imitation whatever was done well. That was the origin of his choice sayings and those of all the Cynics,[4] which they called *kyrias doksas*. But you do the opposite. You flatter, agree, and fawn. You praise to the sky whatever should be cursed the most. You set up whatever is worst and most corrupt as the only thing worth pursuing enthusiastically. Though he was a pagan Diogenes sowed good rules and clear examples in the human race. They seemed hard, but everyone looked up to them as if they had flowed from the spring of virtue itself, especially since they had to do with contempt for human affairs. But what do you sow? Nothing but hatred, sham, enmity, discord, war—more evils, in short, than in *The Iliad*.[5] In other words, Diogenes hurt no one; you hurt everyone.

But you say not all the Cynics were like that. True. But those who did not imitate Diogenes corrupted the sect of Cynics, just as you corrupt Christ's holy religion when you stupidly try to separate wisdom from holy learning. Is this your great, praiseworthy wisdom? And that good, innocent man I mentioned earlier, should his learning, which originated in Christ, be called stupidity? God forbid. Therefore, if you're smart, you'll change your proverb and call no one wise unless he's also learned. Consider yourself and see how far you're wrong. For when that good man preaches to the people and teaches them the commandments of Christ, you often draw near him to learn wisdom. You don't deny it. And yet you foolishly deny that he is wise, even though he's the one you want to use to increase your own wisdom.

But someone will say, "Don't some of those who you really believe are learned agree with us in preferring common sense without learning to learning without common sense?" I must admit that there are some who do. You hit hard, but I'll return the punch easily.[6] For if you look at the matter closely, you'll find that no one who says things

aut gloriae, nisi ex solis literis & doctrina consecutos esse inuenies.
Praeterea ut dem tibi istum tuum prudentem aliquid esse sine literis,
uideamus quid hoc aliquid est, & conferatur cum doctrina. Iste tuus
bene dispensat familiam, acute stipulatur contractum, non inepte
loquitur, non male consulit, umbram sequitur honesti, ut dicam omnia,
ad uulgi opinionem non improbe uiuit. Sed si ab his uel paululum eum
retrahes, ad illa quae maxime hominis sunt, hoc est, ad cognitionem
rerum naturalium, uel quod altius est, ipsius dei, ad cuius imaginem
est factus, haeret, caecutit, nihil penitus est. Contra doctus, quae
maxime decent, in his maxime ualet. Et illa alia etiam si eis animum
applicat, callet. Si non applicat, illarum rerum est imperitior, non quia
non possit assequi, sed quia non uult, & contemnit illa. ut sequatur
meliora. At inquis, prudens meus non curat quae supra nos sunt. Haec
opinio non minus damnanda est, quam ipsum adagium. Nam si deum
qui supra te est, nihil ad te pertinere iudicas, peruertis omnia, non est
amplius tecum disputandum. Mutandum est igitur, o iuuenes, doctrinae
sacris iniciandi, inane istud prouerbium (ut iam dixi) & uel sapientia
nihil aliud intelligenda est, quam doctrina, uel saltem doctrina, praecipua sapientiae pars habenda. Valete.

like that has ever attained any fame, renown, or glory except through books. But granted your man of common sense has something or other in his favor without book learning, let's see what it is and compare it with real learning. He manages his house well, runs his business shrewdly, speaks well, gives good advice, walks in the shadow of honesty, and, to sum it up, leads a proper life according to the opinion of most people. But if you turn him away from this, even a little, and direct him towards what concerns man particularly—the consideration of nature or, what is higher, of God Himself, in whose image he is made—he's stuck, confused; he's absolutely nothing. A learned man, on the other hand, is best at the things that really matter. As for the rest, if he applies his mind to them, he understands them. If he doesn't apply himself, he doesn't understand them, not because he's unable to, but because he doesn't want to. He ignores them in order to pay attention to better things. "But," you'll say, "my man of common sense doesn't care for what's above us." [7] That's about as bad as the proverb itself. For God is above you, and if you think He doesn't matter to you, you've overturned everything, and there's no sense arguing with you.

Therefore, O students, novices in the holy mysteries of learning, that insane proverb must be changed, as I've said. Either wisdom is identical with learning, or learning is at least an important part of wisdom.

Farewell.

RICHARDVS PACEVS IOANNI COLETO THEOLOGO
ERVDITISSIMO ATQVE OPTIMO VIRO
S. P. D.

NVLLAE (mi Colete) occupationes quantumuis magnae, efficere possunt, ut meorum isthic amicorum, doctorum praesertim, quorum in
numero tu excellis, non saepissime recorder, eorumque iucundissimam
consuetudinem uehementer desyderem. Quemadmodum igitur alijs quibusdam amicis meis nuper literarum aliquid a me efflagitantibus libenter scripsi, ita tibi quoque mea sponte in praesentia feci. Et ne aegre
feras, me in scribendo tibi quam alijs fuisse tardiorem, tarditatem
scribendi ipso muneris precio compensare uolui. Quod tametsi nec
argenteum, nec aureum sit, (est enim literarium) tibi tamen non ingra-
tum fore puto, immo certe scio. Quippe qui magno studio laborasse
uideris, ut omnes literarum studiosos, tui amantissimos reddas, tibique
deuincias. Siquidem hinc & non aliunde, sentiunt omnes celeberrimum
illud ludi literarij tui, quem Londini erexisti, & pulcherrime sustentas,
monimentum prodijsse. Et (quod ipsi scholae non est postponendum,
ne dicam praeferendum) curasti, ut honestissimus simul & peritissimus
uir, pueros, adolescentesque erudiat, Isocratem imitatus, qui sapienter
(ut omnia) nemini pueros ad erudiendum tradendos censuit, nisi in
quo doctrinam satis magnam, par quoque honestas uitae sequeretur, ut
non doctrinam solum, sed etiam bonos mores, quum ad imitationem
praeceptorum totos se dederent, imbiberent. Quorum utrunque nunc
te autore, facillime possunt assequi. Habent enim praeceptorem, cuius
uita, moresque sunt probatissimi. Tanta praeterea eruditio, ut extrusa
pene omni barbarie, (in qua nostri olim adolescentes solebant fere
aetatem consumere, & longissimo tempore, ut nihil boni discerent,
laborare) politiorem latinitatem, atque ipsam Romanam linguam, in
Britanniam nostram introduxisse uideatur. Quae quum ita sint, cum
alios omnes, tum praecipue doctos, & doctrinae studiosos, his coeptis
fauere, id est, in commune prodesse, uehementer conuenit. Sed quia
ita natura comparatum est, ut qui maxima uellent, minima possint. illi
qui benignissimis animis suis re ipsa satisfacere nequeunt, uerbis suum
implere officium coguntur, id quod mihi cum alijs (puto) multis contigit. Nam cum libentissime laudatissimum opus a te inceptum, pro-

RICHARD PACE TO JOHN COLET,[8] THE MOST LEARNED OF
THEOLOGIANS AND THE BEST OF MEN:
GREETINGS.

No matter how great my business, dear Colet, I often remember my
friends at home and long for the pleasure of their company, especially
the learned ones like you. And just as I was happy to write recently
to some of my friends who begged me for letters, so I am happy to
write to you now of my own free will. And so you won't feel bad that
I'm writing to you after the others, I want to make up for it by the
richness of the gift. Although it's not gold or silver (for it is literary),
I think—in fact I know—that it will please you. For you seem like a
person who has worked with great energy to make everyone interested
in learning love you and feel attached to you. For everyone knows
that through your energy and labor you alone were responsible for
the famous monument, your grammar school,[9] which you founded in
London and handsomely maintain. And (not to put it after the school
when it should come first), you've chosen a virtuous and at the same
time a skilful man [1] to teach the boys and young men. In this you've
imitated Isocrates,[2] who wisely thought (as usual) that boys should
be educated only by someone whose virtuous way of life went hand
in hand with a sufficient amount of learning. That way, when they
give themselves over to the imitation of their teachers, they'll absorb
not only a certain amount of learning, but also good character. And
now, because of what you've done, they can easily do both. For they
have a teacher whose life and character are impeccable. Besides that,
his learning is so great that he has driven out almost all the barbarism
our boys once spent their youth on, working long to learn nothing, and
as a result he seems to have introduced into our Britain a more polished use of Latin, in fact, the Roman tongue itself. That being so,
everyone is obliged to help along his work and advance the common
good, especially the learned and students of learning. But it's a trick
of nature that those who want to do the most can do the least. Therefore, anyone who's not able to carry out his good intentions by
actually doing something is forced to do it by words alone. This has
happened to me and I think to many others. For although I would
honestly like to further the important work you've begun (if I could,

mouere in maius, atque (si facultatum angustia non obesset),[8] augere
uellem, cogit necessitas uerbis efficere, quod re ipsa praestare mallem.
Accipe igitur meum libellum tuo dedicatum nomini, cui titulus est, de
fructu qui ex doctrina percipitur. In quo si res tam bene a me tractare-
tur, quam pueris & iuuenibus titulus conuenit, haud scio an in primis
illis esset legendus. Solent enim omnes homines illis libentius uacare
rebus, quarum fructus percipiendus, manifeste ante oculos proponitur.
Sed si meum exiguum me fefellit ingenium, tibi, alijsque relinquam, ut
Vergilium imitati, aurum colligatis ex stercore, & ex persona quadam
uiuam effingatis imaginem. Ego uero hoc solo contentus ero, quod tibi
atque illis pulcherrimum, in quo uos exerceretis, (quippe in utilitatem
omnium studiosorum adolescentum) argumentum praebuerim. Restat ut
iam tibi explicem, quid me moueat ad libellum hoc titulo conscriben-
dum & publicandum. Quum duobus annis plus minus iam praeteritis,
ex Romana urbe in patriam redijssem, interfui cuidam conuiuio multis
incognitus. Vbi quum satis fuisset potatum, unus, nescio quis, ex
conuiuis, non imprudens, ut ex uerbis uultuque conijcere licuit, coepit
mentionem facere de liberis suis bene instituendis. Et primum omnium,
bonum praeceptorem illis sibi quaerendum, & scholam omnino frequentandam censuit. Aderat forte unus ex his, quos nos generosos
uocamus, & qui semper cornu aliquod a tergo pendens gestant, acsi
etiam inter prandendum uenarentur. Is audita literarum laude, percitus
repentina ira, furibundus prorupit in haec uerba. Quid nugaris, inquit,
amice? abeant in malam rem istae stultae literae, omnes docti sunt
mendici, etiam Erasmus ille doctissimus (ut audio) pauper est, & in
quadam sua epistola uocat τὴν κατάρατον πενίαν uxorem suam, id est,
execrandam paupertatem, & uehementer conqueritur se non posse illam
humeris suis usque in βαθυκήτεα πόντον, id est, profundum mare excutere. (Corpus dei iuro) uolo filius meus pendeat potius, quam literis
studeat. Decet enim generosorum filios, apte inflare cornu, perite
uenari, accipitrem pulchre gestare & educare. Studia uero literarum,
rusticorum filijs sunt relinquenda. Hic ego cohibere me non potui,
quin aliquid homini loquacissimo, in defensionem bonarum literarum
responderem. Non uideris, inquam, mihi bone uir recte sentire. nam
si ueniret ad regem aliquis uir exterus, quales sunt principum oratores,
& ei dandum esset responsum, filius tuus sic ut tu uis, institutus, inflaret
duntaxat cornu, & rusticorum filij docti, ad respondendum uocarentur,
ac filio tuo uenatori uel aucupi longe anteponerentur, & sua erudita usi
libertate, tibi in faciem dicerent, Nos malumus docti esse, & per doc-

---

[8] obesset,) *1517*

with my meager talents), I'm forced to do with words what I would rather do with deeds.

Therefore accept the dedication of my little book entitled, "The Benefit of a Liberal Education." If the content is as good as the title, I almost think students should read it first, before anything else. For people are usually willing to take pains with something they can clearly see will benefit them. But if my meager talent has deceived me, I leave it to you and to others to imitate Vergil [3] and gather gold from dung and make a living face from a mask. In fact, I'll be content with this thought alone, that I've furnished you and them with an excellent subject for exercise (which is certainly useful for all studious young men). It now remains for me to explain to you why I wrote and published a book with this title.

About two years ago,[4] more or less, when I returned to my country from the city of Rome, I was at a banquet where I was unknown to most of the guests. After we had drunk a sufficient amount, one of them (I don't know who, but, as you could tell from his speech and appearance, he was no fool) began to talk about the proper education for his children. He thought first of all that he should find them a good teacher and that they should by all means attend school and not have a tutor.[5] Now there happened to be a certain person there, a nobleman, or so we call them, who always carry horns hanging down their backs as though they were going to hunt while they ate. When he heard us praise learning, he became wild, overwhelmed with an uncontrollable rage, and burst out, "What's all this stuff, buddy? To hell with your stupid studies. Scholars are a bunch of beggars. Even Erasmus is a pauper, and I hear he's the smartest of them all. In one of his letters [6] he calls *tên kataraton penian,* that is, goddamn poverty, his wife and complains bitterly that he's not able to get her off his back and throw her in the ocean, *bathykêtea ponton.* God damn it, I'd rather see my son hanged than be a student. Sons of the nobility ought to blow the horn properly, hunt like experts, and train and carry a hawk gracefully. Studies, by God, ought to be left to country boys."

At that point I wasn't able to keep myself from making some reply to the loudmouth in defense of learning. I said, "I don't think you're right, my good man. For if some foreigner came to the king, a royal ambassador, for example, and he had to be given an answer, your son, brought up as you suggest, would only blow on his horn, and the learned country boys would be called on to answer him. They would obviously be preferred to your son, the hunter or hawker, and using the freedom that learning gives, they would say to your face,

trinam non imprudentes, quam stulta gloriari nobilitate. Tum ille hinc-inde circunspiciens, Quis est iste, inquit, qui haec loquitur? hominem non cognosco. Et quum diceretur in aurem ei quisnam essem, nescio quid submissa uoce sibimet susurrans, & stulto usus auditore, illico arripuit uini poculum. Et quum nihil haberet respondendum, coepit bibere, & in alia sermonem transferre. Et sic me liberauit, non Apollo, ut Horatium a garrulo, sed Bacchus a uesani hominis disputatione, quam diutius longe duraturam uehementer timebam. Ad ultimum, illud unice rogem necesse est, ut siquid in hoc meo opusculo minus erudi-tum, quam eruditis tuis auribus conuenit, reperies, non omnia meae imperitiae & ignorantiae, sed aliquid huic quoque attribuas incom-modo, quod hic nunc sum, ubi nec docti uiri sunt, nec libri, quos aliunde mihi aduehendos curassem, si ita fuisset consultum. Sed hic non tam permaneo, quam pendeo, ut ubi sum hodie, nesciam an sim futurus cras. Atque tu probe nosti hominem literis deditum, si desint libri, similem esse militis, cui desunt arma. Quare si qui erunt, qui aliquid puerilius in hoc libello notabunt, quam longum deceat studium, sciant illi opusculum pueris esse scriptum. Vale. Ex Constantia.

'We would rather be learned, and thanks to learning no fools, than to be proud of our stupid nobility.'"

Then, glancing about him on all sides, he said, "Who's this, talking to me like that? I don't know the man." And when someone whispered in his ear who I was, he mumbled something to himself—I don't know what—and finding a fool to listen to him, he snatched up a cup of wine. Since he had no answer to give, he started to drink, and the conversation passed on to other things. And so I was saved not by Apollo, who saved Horace [7] from a blowhard, but by Bacchus, who saved me from an argument with a madman, which I was afraid would go on a lot longer.

Last of all I ask only this, that if you find anything in this little book that sounds less learned to you than it should, don't attribute it entirely to my inexperience and ignorance, but allow something for this difficulty, that here where I am now there are neither learned men nor books, which I would have had sent here if I had thought of it. But I don't exactly remain here—I hang here, so that I don't know tomorrow whether I'll be where I am today. And as you well know, a man devoted to learning who lacks books is like a soldier without weapons. And so if anyone notices anything in this little book more childish than there should be after long years of study, I want him to know that it was written for children.

Farewell.

FROM CONSTANCE

RICHARDI PACEI, SERENISSIMI BRITANNIARVM REGIS SECRETARII, DE FRVCTU QVI EX DOCTRINA PERCIPITVR, LIBER.

OMNES HOMINUM in uniuersum actiones, tribus praecipue rebus inniti uidentur, iusto, honesto, & utili. De illa autem utilitate loquor, quam ab honestate Stoici non separant, nec Christiani commode separare possunt, nisi uolunt illam laudare utilitatem, quam fraus, dolus, auaritia, & aliae innumerabiles malae artes comparant. Itaque si ostendero nihil horum, nisi doctrina adiutrice, homines uere assequi posse, tam late patebit doctrinae campus, ut nemo non in eo (ut opinor) libentissime uelit expatiari. Principio igitur illud notandum esse iudico, quomodo Catonem, omnium uirtutum radicem esse amaram, fructus uero iucundos dixisse constat, ita Isocratem eandem de sola doctrina protulisse sententiam, nimirum quod tanquam uir prudentissimus, omnes ad unam uirtutes a doctrina originem trahere, eamque ueluti omnium matrem existimaret. Quod ut manifestius clariusque fiat, singulas scientias ad humanam uitam instituendam pertinentes, & eidem utiles, percurramus necesse est. Igitur si omnem humanam uitam accurate & penitus introspicias, nihil laudabiliter, nihil bene, nihil recte fieri absque doctrina, liquido patebit. Atqui ut a maioribus incipiamus, & ordine quodam perueniamus ad minora, quid prodesset Theologus populo, ad quem concionatur, & praecepta praedicat diuina, nisi illam calleret doctrinam, quam Christus ipse de caelo descendens, generi reliquit humano, ut per eam omnes a communi calumniatore, id est, diabolo capti, redimerentur, & aeterna condemnati morte, in aeternam uitam liberarentur. Praeterea quum duae duntaxat res sint, quibus deus humanum genus conseruauit, harum altera est eius doctrina, alter est sanguis Christi effusus. Hae autem hoc inter se distant (si modo aliqua distantia sit) quod sanguis Christi semel & cito effusus est, doctrina uero in omne aeuum durat, & duratura est. Et sicut uis & beneficium effusi sanguinis nunquam delebitur, ita doctrinae huius salutiferae effectus sempiternus est. Quo fit, ut his duabus plane admirandis rebus, non tam ulla dif-

THE BOOK OF RICHARD PACE, SECRETARY TO HIS SERENE HIGHNESS, THE KING OF BRITAIN

THE BENEFIT OF A LIBERAL EDUCATION

All the actions of men in general seem to be based on three things in particular: justice, honor, and utility. I speak of the utility which the Stoics regard as part of honor and which Christians cannot easily distinguish from it, unless they want to praise the utility of fraud, deceit, greed, and innumerable other evil arts. And if I show that man cannot truly attain any of these three things without the assistance of learning, the fields of learning will stretch so wide that everyone, I believe, will want to wander in them freely. First of all, therefore, I think we should note that Cato [8] said that the root of all virtue is bitter, but the fruit is sweet. Similarly, Isocrates extended the same idea to learning itself, probably because he was a sensible man and thought that all virtues originate in learning as if it were the mother of them all. To make this clearer it is necessary to survey the various fields of learning that are useful to human existence and that have to do with its organization.

If, therefore, you look deeply and carefully into all human existence, you'll clearly see that nothing can be done laudably, correctly or properly without learning. But to begin with the greater and arrive by degrees at the lesser, how can a theologian benefit the people to whom he preaches the word of God unless he understands the teaching which Christ Himself, who descended from heaven, left to mankind? Through it all those captured by our common deceiver, the devil, may be redeemed, and although they are condemned to eternal death, they may be freed into life everlasting.

Moreover, there are only two things through which God saved mankind. One is his teaching, the other is the blood poured out by Christ. If there is any difference at all between them, they differ in this: Christ's blood was poured out quickly and only once, but His teaching endures and lasts for all ages. And just as the virtue and benefit of the blood which He shed will never be destroyed, so also the effect of His life-giving teaching is eternal. And so there seems to be a sacred correspondence between these two completely wonderful

ferentia, quam quaedam sancta paritas inesse uideatur, & doctrina caelestis, & diuina res habenda sit. Vnde & sacrarum literarum sanctissimi professores, Christum ipsum magistrum appellant, ut diuus Augustinus, quum inquit, Non in Petrum, sed in Petri magistrum, id est, Christum credimus. Sed nec Christus ipse hoc nomen dedignatur. siquidem in diuinis euangelijs ubique legimus, Dixit Iesus discipulis suis, qui ad magistrum semper referuntur. Iam uero ipsius Theologiae uocabulum, quid aliud significat quam doctrinam, qua rerum diuinarum ratio redditur? Quae scientia ut reliquis excellentior, sic ab ipso deo profecta esse uidetur. Quo modo Poetae finxerunt deam sapientiae natam esse ex capite Iouis, significantes sapientiam rem supremam, non nisi ex supremi dei altissima & excelsissima parte ortam fuisse. Atque hinc est, quod omnia quae haec scientia complectitur, & tradit, pure sunt diuina, & ob id aliqua captum humani excedunt ingenij. Hinc etiam est, quod uniuersa ex deo & sanctis eius Prophetis (qui diuino inspirati numine, sunt locuti) ad nos effluxit. Hos autem quid aliud dixerimus, quam diuinos doctores & magistros, illiusque doctrinae prouulgatores, qua omnia religiose, sancteque uiuendi instituta continentur? Quocirca quum doctrina, (& praesertim haec, de qua nunc uerba facio),[9] tam excellens res sit, ut omnem laudem longe superet, in ea uerbis nunc extollenda tempus terere nolo. Sed qui tam incomparabili dono dei assidue incumbet & assequetur, hunc plane felicem iudicabo.[1] Nam ut sapientiam prisci praecipuam felicitatis partem esse tradiderunt, ita mea quidem sententia, doctrina sapientiae praecipua pars est habenda. nimirum quum rectam, cum ad aliam omnem, si qua est, tum ad diuinam sapientiam uiam monstret. Quae sola, si ei inhaereatur, ad uitam ducit caelestem & sempiternam. Ergo nolite o pueri,

Fructus Theologiae, uita aeterna

iuuenesque senesque (ut Poeta ait) fructum huius doctrinae negligenter colligere. Nam si ita feceritis, non in carne [2] (quod aiunt) & quauis uili re est periculum, sed ipsa salus animae in manifestum uocatur discrimen. Et non haec illa est, quam Dauid intellexit, alloquens deum, Declaratio sermonum tuorum intellectum dat paruulis. Sane illud minime pratermittendum est, ut caute agatur in legendis huius doctrinae autoribus, id est, ut deligantur optimi, ut diuus Paulus, Hieronymus, Augustinus, Gregorius, Ambrosius, & siqui sunt alij horum similes. Nam in Scoto, & eius sectatoribus, plus est, ut uidetur, & etiam peritissimi Theologi sentiunt, loquacis subtilitatis, quam uerae & salutaris doctrinae. Porro

---

[9] facio,) *1517*   [1] iudicacabo. *1517*   [2] Care *1517*

things, not a difference. And that correspondence should be considered as both heavenly teaching and something divine. For that reason the saintly doctors of Holy Writ call Christ Himself their teacher, such as St. Augustine,[9] for example, when he says, "We do not believe in Peter, but in Peter's teacher," that is, in Christ. Christ Himself did not scorn the term, for we read everywhere in the holy Gospels, "Jesus spoke to His pupils," and they always referred to Him as their teacher. In fact the very term *theology*, what else does it mean but that branch of learning by which divine things are made accessible to man? Thus this science, more excellent than the rest, seems to have proceeded from God Himself. Therefore the poets imagined that the goddess of wisdom was born from the head of Jupiter, indicating that wisdom was something most high, derived from the highest and most lofty part of the ruler of the gods. And so it is that everything this science embraces and transmits is divine in its purity and therefore exceeds in some measure the grasp of the human mind. And so also this universal knowledge flowed forth to us from God and His holy prophets, who were filled with the divine presence. What shall we call these men if not divine teachers and masters and lecturers of the learning that contains all the fundamental principles for a holy and religious life?

Therefore, since learning (and especially the kind I now speak of) is such an excellent thing that it far surpasses all praise, I don't want to waste more time praising it. But whoever applies himself constantly to this incomparable gift of God and attains it will be, in my opinion, truly happy. For just as the ancients taught that wisdom is the most important part of happiness, I think that learning is the most important part of wisdom. And no wonder, for it shows the direct route not only to all other wisdom, if there is such, but also to divine wisdom, which is the only thing that leads to eternal life in heaven, if one sticks to it. Therefore, all you boys, young men, and old men (as the poet says),[1] don't forget to derive the benefit from this branch of learning. For if you do, the danger is not

The benefit of theology, eternal life

to the flesh, as they say, or any worthless thing, but to the salvation of the soul. Isn't this the same thing David [2] understood, when he spoke to God: "the disclosure of your words gives understanding to children"? It's obvious that you should read carefully the authors who contain this learning, such as (to mention only the best), St. Paul, Jerome, Augustine, Gregory, Ambrose, and any others like them. For it seems (and the most learned theologians agree) that in Scotus and his followers there is more fine-spun subtlety than true and wholesome learning.

Doctrina legum

iurisconsulti (nam horum scientiam sacrae Theologiae adnectam, tum quia inter leges aliquae sacrae & diuinae sunt, tum quia in hac sicut in illa, doctores non nascuntur hodie, sed creantur) adeo nihil faciunt absque doctrina, ut in euoluendis legum uoluminibus nunquam non uersentur, & ut ipsorum uerbis utar, ad perpetuam chartarum reuolutionem condemnentur, (Sunt enim commentaria plura quam leges) nempe ut aliquid addiscant, uel aliquam stropham explicent. Sic enim aduocati & causidici, tam reum quam actorem defendere discunt, quibus si desit doctrina (& aliquando si superfluat) saltem unus perit, & saepissime uterque. Nam indocti aduocati & causidici, non student ut lites cito dirimantur, sed ut quam diutissime prorogentur. Quod quum accidit, non minus actum est de illo, secundum quem sententia est lata, quam de altero, qui in iudicio succubuit. nam ut hunc amissa perdidit lis, ita illum consumpta res depauperauit. At docti (quorum numerus est longe minor) contra faciunt. Nam hi ad honestatem & iustitiam respicientes, non tam lucro augendo, quam iuri summa (ut decet) aequitate respondendo, & beneuolentiae omnium hominum comparandae student, ac consyderant, Legem (secundum Graecorum sententiam) δῶρον μὲν εἶναι θεοῦ, δόγμα δὲ ἀνθρώπων, id est, donum quidem esse dei, sed dogma hominum. Item illud, nihil aliud esse legem, quam ἐπανόρθωμα κακῶν ὧν αἱ τύχαι ποιοῦσιν, id est, fortuitorum malorum correctionem. Nam progenitores nostri, ut Aphthonius scribit, quum fortunae uarietatem, & humanarum mentium mutationem notassent, fortunae inconstantiam & inaequalitatem, legum aequitate corrigere uolentes, leges inuenerunt, effeceruntque ut per eas una esset omnibus mens & sententia. Sed non ab re fuerit ipsius Aphthonij de progenitoribus suis loquentis, uerba subijcere, quorum sensum iam explicauimus. ἐπειδὴ γὰρ ἄλλοτε ἄλλαι τοῖς ἀνθρώποισ᾽ τύχαι προσπίπτουσιν, καὶ μεταποιοῦσι τὰς τῶν ἀνθρώπων γνώμας, ἐπανορθούμενοι τὸ τῆς τύχης ἀνώμαλον τῇ τῶν νόμων ἰσότητι, νόμους ἐξεῦρον, μίαν πᾶσιν ἐξ αὐτῶν, ἐργαζόμενοι γνώμην. Ad haec, quot sunt iuris scientiae antiqui & recentiores doctores, quibus quotidie discendi causa student, notius est omnibus, quam ut a me nunc dici sit necesse. Igitur uel hinc liquet, iurisconsultum nihil esse aut posse absque doctrina, quae sola eum iurisconsultum facit, iuuenibusque hunc fructum colligendum offert, ut (quod pulcherrimum est) possint cum priuatim amicis, tum in com-

Next the lawyers, for I connect their
field of learning with sacred theology,   *The field of law*
partly because some of their laws are
sacred and divine and partly because in this field as in others learned
men are made nowadays, not born. Lawyers do so little without the
aid of learning that they're always busy opening up law books, and—
to speak their language—they're sentenced to life imprisonment turning the pages, for there are more commentaries than laws. Obviously,
their purpose is to learn something new or to untangle some trick or
other. So lawyers and casuists learn to defend not only the defendant,
but also the plaintiff, and if they're not very learned (and sometimes
if they are), at least one side loses and most often both. For incompe-
tent lawyers are not eager to settle a case quickly, but stretch it out as
long as they can. When that happens, both sides are done for, the one
who wins and the one who loses. For the loss of the case ruins one,
and the loss of his money ruins the other. But competent lawyers (and
there are far fewer of them) do otherwise. Since they're concerned
with honor and justice, they want to give a legal opinion with the
greatest possible fairness (as they should) and secure equal rights for
all men rather then increase their own wealth. They regard the law, to
quote the Greek phrase,[3] as *dôron men einai theou, dogma de an-*
thrôpôn, that is, as a gift of God, but a decree of man. So too law is
nothing but *epanorthôma kakôn hôn hai tychai poiousin*, that is, an
amendment of accidental misfortunes. For as Aphthonius writes, when
our forefathers observed the vicissitudes of fortune and the changeableness of man's mind, they wanted to rectify the inconstancy and
inequality of fortune by the moderation of law. They invented laws,
therefore, and brought it about that through those laws there was one
mind and one opinion for all men. But it will not be out of place to add
the words of Aphthonius [4] himself, which I have just now paraphrased:
epeidê gar allote allai tois anthrôpois' tychai prospiptousin, kai meta-
poiousi tas tôn anthrôpôn gnomas, epanorthoumenoi tô tês tychês anô-
malon têi tôn nomôn isotêti, nomous ekseuron, mian pasin eks hautôn,
ergazomenoi gnômên. Moreover, it's too well known for me to mention
how many doctors of law, ancient and modern, lawyers study each day
in order to be learned.

It is obvious, therefore, that a lawyer is nothing and can do nothing
without learning, which is the only thing that makes him a lawyer. The
law offers this benefit to young people: that they can be of assistance to their friends in private as well as to everyone else in general,
which is a fine thing and is quite rightly the cause of the greatest
good will among men. They finally attain the goal when they become

Fructus ex studio legum est,
prodesse omnibus, &
beneuolentiam simul cum
utilitate comparare

mune omnibus prodesse, unde maxima honestissime comparatur hominum beneuolentia. quod tum demum assequuntur, quum maior iustitiae reddendae, quam turpis lucri accumulandi ratio habetur. Nam ut illa hanc scientiam maxime illustrat & ornat, ita hoc maxime obscurat & deturpat. Istud uero tunc est uituperosius, quum a pauperibus (quorum sors etiam iurisconsultis est miseranda) fraudulenti laboris, nimis magna exigatur merces. Vnde factum est, ut nulla maior horum sit aut frequentior conquestio, quam aduersus legum strophas & intricamenta, a malis aduocatis & causidicis studiose exquisita, ut omnem iuris aequitatem peruertant. Nam quod expeditum est, tricis inuoluunt, dum in testamento, uel codicillis, uel alio quouis instrumento apertissime scripto, duplicant uel triplicant intellectum, & nodum plane in scirpo quaerunt. cui rei iam nunc finis imponi potest, non procrastinant modo, sed in aeuum prorogant. Quae quum ita sint, qui huic doctrinae recte, & ut decet, studere uolunt, & eam exercere, haec praecepta sequantur oportet, ut iustitiam & aequitatem ante oculos semper proponant, fraudem uero, dolum, & auaritiam longe abijciant, & potentiori ad gratiam non faueant, ut pauperem subuertant, ne illi in uituperium leguleiorum dicto sint obnoxij, Leges consimiles esse aranearum telis. quae muscas quidem irretiunt, grandiora uero animalia prendere non possunt. A nimia praeterea seueritate, ip-

De legum seueritate

sius Christi exemplo abstineant, & tum praesertim, quum de uita hominum agitur. Est enim ipsius dei uox, Neminem occidas. Denique seueritas clementiae prorsus est inimica, quam Christus quum in mundo esset, in omnibus suis actionibus prae se tulit. Item Draconis Atheniensis leges, ut nimis seuerae, male audierunt, quum dicerentur non atramento, sed sanguine scriptae. quo eleganter allusit Angelus Politianus in Disticho. Actaei inuentum dicuntur iura Draconis, Fama nimis uera est, nil nisi uirus habent. Est & illud in omnibus legibus, siue hae diuinae sint, siue ciuiles, siue municipales, in primis spectandum, bonas leges a sapientibus collatas esse cum ipsa natura. Nam quomodo natura omnia recte disposuit, ita leges omnia recte administrare & regere debent. Vnde extat illa Graecis antiquissima sententia, πᾶς ὁ τῶν ἀνθρώπων βίος φύσει καὶ νόμοις διοικεῖται, id est, omnem humanam uitam, natura & leges dispensant, & administrant. Sed de scientia iuris satis de professoribus aliquid addam, de quibus quum loquor, non Accursium, & alios huius non dissimiles imitandos dico, sed Vlpianum, Paulum,

more concerned about rendering justice
than they are about piling up filthy
money. For just as the former intention
graces and adorns the study of law, so
the latter disgraces and defiles it. But it's
even more shameful when they squeeze

*The benefit of law is
to be helpful to
everyone and to join
kindness with utility*

a large fee for phony work from the very poor—whose sad lot even a
lawyer should pity. And that's why you hear of no greater or more frequent complaints than those raised against the tricks and intricacies
of the law, which rotten lawyers eagerly search out to corrupt all justice. Whatever is clear, they involve in perplexity. They double or
triple the meaning in a will or codicil or any other plainly written
instrument of the law and obviously look for a knot in a bulrush.[5] They
not only put off something that could be settled at once, they drag it
out for ages.

Since that's the case, those who want to study law and practice it
properly (as they should) ought to follow these rules. They must
always keep before their eyes justice and equality. They must get rid
of all fraud, guile, and greed, and they must not favor the more powerful party to ruin the poor. If they do, they'll be guilty of the saying
that damns pettifoggers: laws are like spider webs: [6] they catch flies,
but they can't bag bigger game. Moreover, they should follow the
example of Christ and refrain from exces-
sive severity, especially when it's a ques-   *The severity of law*
tion of human life. For God's own words
are: Thou shalt not kill. In short, severity is the direct opposite of
mercy, which Christ showed in all His actions when He was on earth.
Similarly, the laws of Draco the Athenian [7] had the reputation of being
too severe. They were said to have been written in blood, not ink.
Angelus Politianus [8] alludes to this gracefully in the distich:

> Laws are said to have been invented by an Athenian dragon.[9]
> Too true. There's nothing in them but poison.

And it should be particularly noted that wise men have made all good
laws—whether divine, civil, or municipal—agree with nature itself.
For just as nature set everything in order, so law ought to govern and
control all things. That's the origin of the ancient Greek saying,[1] *pas
ho tôn anthrôpôn bios physei kai nomois dioikeitai,* that is, nature and
law direct and regulate all human life.

But enough about the science of law. I shall add something about
the professors. When I speak of them, I don't mean Accursius and

Gallum, Scaeuolam, & alios huius sectae multos, in quibus reperio singularem sapientiam una cum eleganti doctrina coniunctam. Nam Accursij interpretamentis & glossematibus, tum demum ego credere soleo, quum ait, dic nescio. non possum tamen simplicitatem hominis non uehementer laudare, qui ingenue fatetur se nihil scire. Hic non possum tacere fidelissimum meum amicum Ioannem Clerke, qui (ut grauem [3] claritatem omittam) hac scientia non semetipsum modo, sed patriam quoque suam illustrat. Nam

Amicitia Ioannis Clerke
& Pacei

quum is & ego olim in Italia operam daremus literis, tam arctam, tamque fidelem & constantem iniuimus amicitiam, ut nullum unquam par amicorum ex his, quae apud omnes scriptores sunt celebratissima, in religiose obseruando illo Pythagorico prouerbio, Amicorum omnia communia, nos superaret. Siquidem non interponebantur inter nos preces, ut quicquid esset, ex aequo diuideretur, sed alter alteri sua sponte omnia, si qua premeret inopia, afferebat ut uteretur pro suo, & maluit ipse egere, quam deesset amico. quod tunc liquido patebat, quum ad calculum (quod non coactum, sed spontaneum erat, ut amicitiae uerae conuenit) deueniretur. Est enim persaepe inter nos uisum, ut quum ego perparum, ipse nihil haberet. & e contrario, quum ipse pusillum, ego ne obolum quidem. & tunc uenit in mentem illud Horatianum, Tribusque diebus nil erat in loculis. Et istud uere erat Pythagorae satisfacere, sicut & in futurum quoque facturi sumus, & acturi communi diuidundo. Nec facultates solum inter nos communes erant, sed etiam studia. Prouocasti enim me (ut audio) mi Ioannes, ad perlegenda tecum omnia digestorum uolumina, currentem, ut aiunt, incitas. & si quum simul erimus, te lentiorem uidero, pungam, mihi crede, nam nec mihi meus deest aculeus. Iam de iure canonico, quod idem diuinum appellatur, cum sacra Theologia, unde originem habet, coniungendum asseuero. Et qui huius doctrinae studium non probat, idem potest ipsum quoque deum stulte improbare. Est enim haec scientia comes Theologiae, & ob id pari ueneratione prosequenda. Sequitur philosophia (male tamen libenter sequitur, quia praecedere uoluit) cuius tam celebre, tamque insigne nomen fuit semper atque apud omnes gentes (sicut adhuc quoque floret) ut nullus fere antiquorum ei serio studuerit, quem omnes homines in caelum laudibus non extulerint, non doctrina solum illorum, sed etiam morum & uitae probitate incitati. Nam ex huius officina prodijt Pythagoras, Socrates, Plato, Aristoteles, Zeno, Xenocrates, Cleanthes, & alij innumeri, nunquam satis laudati uiri. Sed quid causam praebuit tam communi laudi atque eorum gloriae? Profecto nihil praeter doctrinam,

---

[3] grauis *1517*

others like him, but rather Ulpianus, Paulus, Gallus, Scaevola,[2] and others of that school, in whom I find singular wisdom combined with choice learning. For I believe Accursius' commentaries and glosses only when he says, "Let's say I don't know," though I can't help but praise the simplicity of a man who frankly admits he knows nothing.

At this point I can't fail to mention my faithful friend John Clerk.[3] Not to mention his great distinction, his knowledge of law graces not only himself, but also his country. For when he and I were once students together in Italy, we started a friendship so close, so loyal and constant that none

Friendship of John Clerk and Pace

of the friends celebrated in literature ever surpassed us in observing the Pythagorean proverb, friends share everything.[4] We never asked each other to share whatever we had, but each of us of his own free will offered everything to the other to use as his own if he needed it. Each of us preferred to lack something himself rather than have his friend do without. This was most obvious when it came to paying the check; it was not forced, but spontaneous, as befits true friendship. For, when I had little, he had nothing, and, on the other hand, when he had next to nothing, I did not have an obolus.[5] And then that line from Horace [6] came to mind: "after three days there was nothing in the bank." That was really satisfying Pythagoras. And we're also going to do it in the future by sharing things in common. We not only shared our money, but also our studies. For I admit, dear John, that you stimulated me to read through all the volumes of the Digests with you. You spurred a willing horse,[7] as they say. And when we're together again, if I see that you're slower, believe me, I may prick you, for I have not lost my sting.

Now, as for canon law, which is called divine, I claim that it should be considered a part of sacred theology since it takes its origin there. Anyone who doesn't approve of studying this is stupid enough not to approve of God Himself. For this science is the companion of theology and for that reason should be pursued with equal respect.

Philosophy follows next, but it follows unwillingly since it wants to go first. It has always been so well known and so famous among all people (just as it is today) that almost any of the ancients who studied it seriously was praised to the skies not only for his learning, but also for the goodness of his morals and his way of life. From its workshop came Pythagoras, Socrates, Plato, Aristotle, Zeno, Xenocrates,[8] Cleanthes,[9] and innumerable other men who have never been praised enough. But what's the reason for such universal praise and glory? Actually, nothing at all but learning. Through it they left to posterity

qua praediti, excellentissima ingenij sui monimenta posteris reliquerunt (quorum excellens pars adhuc extat & est inter manus hominum.) Nam uel in contemplatione rerum tam caelestium & humanarum semper sunt uersati, uel assidue laborarunt in his quae ad formandos bonos mores spectant. Quae duae res effecerunt, ut haec doctrina priscis perfectissima haberetur, tanquam nihil non complexa. Vnde Cicero philosophiam omnium uirtutum matrem, & omnium uitiorum expultricem appellat, & omnem autoritatem philosophiae in comparanda beata uita consistere scribit. Ad hanc itaque non modo omni studio, sed omnibus quoque uotis expetendam, non tam mea inuitare iuuenes oratio, quam ratio ipsa excitare debet. Est enim haec non ex his rebus, quae alieno tantum laudantur ore, sed αὐτὴ αὐτὴν αὐλεῖ (quod prouerbio dici solet) id est, seipsam laudat & praedicat. Fructus igitur huius doctrinae est uberrimus, tametsi paucis uerbis explicetur. siquidem

Fructus philosophiae, morum honestas, & uitae probitas

honesta appetere, turpia auersari, fugere uitia, uirtutes sequi, usquequaque docet. Huius comites multae sunt, ut mathematicae scientiae omnes, sed omnium prima & princeps est doctrina medica, inter pulcherrimas & utilissimas illius partes numerata. Nec immerito, nam periti medici, quamplurimos & grauissimos, in quos solemus morbos incidere, curant. a quibus si non liberaremur, ipsa uita (nemini non suauissima) omnibus esset tedio. & nisi adesset, inquit ille, ualitudo, omnes in poenam uiueremus. Et quum omnes homines in hoc consentiunt, ut sanitatem omnibus humanis bonis praeferant, immo illa, si haec non adsit, uilipendant, & pro nihilo ducant, plurimum

Fructus artis Medicae, conseruatio sanitatis

haud dubie debemus rei medicae, eiusque professoribus, quorum arte & diligentia ipsa sanitas nobis conseruatur. Vnde sapienter (ut omnia) Pythagoras, trium magnarum quae solebat optare rerum, primam fecit sanitatem. Nam optabat ille ὑγιαίνειν, καιὸν [4] εἶναι καὶ πλουτεῖν, id est, sanitatem, pulchritudinem, & diuitias. Fructum igitur huius doctrinae tanto alijs anteposuerim, quanto aliarum quidam doctrinarum fructum quodammodo uidemus magis, quam sentimus, hunc uero & uidemus, & sentimus. Hinc est quod apud omnes celebratissimi sunt duo illi huius doctrinae principes, Hippocrates & Galenus. quorum prior doctrinae tam studiosus fuit, ut doluerit artem esse longam, uitam uero breuem. Sed illud o iuuenes, huic scientiae operam daturi, diligenter obseruate, ut graecam linguam cum latina coniungatis. nam sicut aliae scientiae, in quibus aliquid latini scriptum reliquerunt, e graecis fontibus emanarunt, ita haec potissimum, adeo

---

[4] An error for καλόν.

the finest monuments of their intellect (the best part of which still survives and remains in the hands of men). For they were always engaged in the contemplation of human and divine things, or else they worked constantly on whatever led to the formation of good habits. And because of those two things philosophy was considered to be the most perfect branch of learning in ancient times, as if there were nothing it did not encompass. Cicero [1] therefore calls philosophy the mother of all virtues and the destroyer of all vice, and he writes that the entire use of philosophy consists in making a happy life. Reason itself, not my reasons, ought to persuade young people to search for this not only with all their strength, but also with all their heart and soul. For this is not one of those things that needs to be praised by someone else, but *autê autên aulei* as the proverb says,[2] it praises and commends itself. The benefit therefore of this branch of learning is extremely rich, though it can be expressed in a few words: it teaches us on every occasion to seek out honor, avoid disgrace, flee from evil, and pursue virtue.

The benefit of philosophy, good morals, and an upright life

Philosophy has many companions, such as all the branches of mathematics, but first and foremost is the science of medicine, which is the most beautiful and useful of all. And with good reason, for skilful doctors cure the many serious diseases we are subject to. If we were not free of them, life itself, which is sweet, would be loathsome to us. If we were not healthy, it's said, we would all live in suffering. All men agree that they would rather have health than any other human good, and in fact if they're not healthy, they think everything is worthless and consider it nothing. We obviously owe much therefore to medicine and doctors, through whose skill and care our health itself is preserved. Pythagoras therefore

Benefit of the art of medicine, preservation of life

wisely (as always) placed health first on the list of the three great things he desired.[3] For he wanted *hygiainein, kalon einai kai ploutein,* that is, health, beauty, and riches. I would therefore place the benefit of this field of learning before all others. For we see the benefit of certain other fields more than we feel it, but this one we both see and feel.

Among all the leaders in this field Hippocrates and Galen are the most famous. The former was so eager for learning that he lamented that art was long, life short.[4] But O you young men who intend to be doctors, be sure that you study Greek as well as Latin. For all the sciences in which the Romans wrote something flowed from the fountains of Greece, and this one especially. So you'll hardly be able to under-

ut in ea uix aliquid possitis assequi, linguae graecae ignari. Quam si contempseritis, in illorum medicorum numerum referemini, qui impune homines occidere solent. De quibus Plinius, Soli medico hominem occidere, summa est impunitas. Exigit iam suum musica quoque doctrina locum, a me praesertim, quem puerum inter pueros illustrauit.

Thomas Langton

Nam Thomas Langton Vyntoniensis episcopus, decessor huius qui nunc uiuit, cui eram a manu minister, quum notasset me longe supra aetatem (ut ipse nimis fortasse amans mei iudicabat, & dictitabat) in musicis proficere, Huius inquit, pueri ingenium ad maiora natum est. & paucos post dies in Italiam ad Patauinum gymnasium, quod tunc florentissimum erat, ad bonas literas discendas me misit, annuasque impensas benigne suppeditauit, ut omnibus literatis mirifice fauebat, & aetate sua alterum Mecoenatem agebat, probe memor (ut frequenter dictitabat) sese doctrinae causa ad episcopalem dignitatem prouectum. Adeptus enim fuerat per summam laudem, utriusque iuris (ut nunc loquuntur) insignia. Item humaniores literas tanti aestimabat, ut domestica schola pueros & iuuenes illis erudiendos curarit. Et summopere oblectabatur audire scholasticos dictata interdiu a praeceptore, sibi noctu reddere. In quo certamine qui praeclare se gesserat, is aliqua re personae suae accommodata, donatus abibat, & humanissimis uerbis laudatus. Habebat enim semper in ore ille optimus Praesul, uirtutem laudatam crescere. Et siquis ei uidebatur hebetioris ingenij, uoluntatem tamen non deesse, huic naturae culpam non imputauit, sed suauiter hortabatur, ut diligentia contenderet cum natura, proponens aliorum quorundam exempla, qui ita fecerant. Quod siquem notasset, non per ingenium, sed peruersam suam negligentiam, alieniorem a literis, hunc sapientissimis uerbis obiurgabat, demonstrabatque argumentis, nihil unquam ei feliciter euenturum, quem tantae uirtutis, quanta est doctrina, contemptorem esse non puderet. Idem in munere episcopali ita se gessit, ut apud tres reges ingenij, doctrinae & experientiae causa, in maxima fuerit autoritate. Libuit in hoc paulo extra propositum uagari, ut excellentissimi uiri memoria, per me (de quo optime meritus fuit) posteris commendaretur. Exigit, in-

De Musica

quam, musica suum a nobis locum, & incipit contendere, & primas inter omnes scientias sibi uendicare, affirmans intrepide caelum ipsum ruiturum, nisi una pars ipsius, id est, harmonia quaedam, musica caelestem illam fabricam contineret. nec pateretur admirandam illam aptitudinem dissolui, quam ideo ab hominibus non audiri, quod sensum aurium humanarum longe superat, quod etiam in

stand anything about it if you don't know Greek. If you disregard it, you'll be one of those doctors who literally get away with murder. Pliny said of them: "only doctors can kill a man and get away with it." [5]

Now Music demands her place. She has a claim on me particularly since she singled me out when I was still a boy among boys. For when I was a page in his household, Thomas Langton,[6] the Bishop of Winchester, the predecessor of the one now living, noted that I was talented in music *Thomas Langton* far beyond my years (or so he thought, perhaps because he loved me too much) and said, "The boy's bright; he was born for greater things." A few days later, he sent me to Italy to study liberal arts at the University of Padua, which was then in its prime, and kindly paid the expenses himself since he encouraged all learning and acted the part of another Maecenas for his age. As he often said, he would never forget that it was through learning that he was promoted to the rank of bishop. Through his great merit he achieved distinction in both the laws, as they say nowadays.[7] He thought so much of the liberal arts that he had them taught to boys in his own household school, and he especially liked to hear the students recite for him at night what they had learned from their teacher during the day. Whoever did well in the examination was given a gift suited to him personally and was praised with great kindness. For that great and good bishop always said that virtue praised increases.[8] If anyone seemed to him slower than the rest, but willing, he didn't blame his lack of native ability, but urged him to make up for it by working harder, mentioning examples of others who had done so. But if he saw anyone who didn't know his lessons because of his own wilful negligence, he corrected him with words of wisdom and proved to him that nothing would ever turn out well for a person who wasn't ashamed of despising such a great virtue as learning. He was such a good bishop that he remained in a position of great authority under three kings [9] through his ability, learning, and experience. I've enjoyed digressing a little here to commend to posterity the memory of this distinguished man, a tribute he most richly deserved.

As I was saying, Music demands her place and begins to argue and claim first place for herself, confidently stating that the sky itself would fall in *Music* ruin if one part of it that has to do with music—that is, a certain harmony—did not hold it together. This wonderful concord cannot be destroyed, and men cannot hear it because it exceeds the range of the human ear, which is also said to be true in

humanis rebus accidere dicitur, ut in Nili cataractis. Vnde Theologos illos antiquos, non aliam ob causam mystice nouem intellexisse musas, nisi propter octo sphaerarum caelestium musicos concentus, & unam maximam concinnentiam, quae constat ex omnibus, harmoniam (ut dictum est) nomine. Hanc uero in causa esse, ut ipsum etiam caelum canat. Porro continuus, inquit musica, motus ille animae, quae (ut Flaccus ait) diuinae est particula aurae, non nisi harmonicus est & musicus. Quod si ego illa sum, quae rebus diuinis perpetuitatem largior, cur non & ego diuina habenda sum? Iam uero nonne hymni, qui in deum ubique gentium canuntur, mei sunt? Tum quis me fidelius clarissimorum uirorum gesta, aeterna donat memoria? Nonne Homerus, Vergilius, & reliqui omnes nobiles Poetae alumni fuerunt mei? Viuit ne per me Vlysses? perijsset ne omnino Aeneae memoria, nisi cecinisset Vergilius, Arma uirumque Cano? Hinc est quod apud priscos, quum omnis uirtus floridior esset quam nunc, habiti sunt indoctiores, qui citharam pulsare & canere nescierunt, & lyram pro more in omnibus conuiuijs circunlatam recusarunt. quae nota celebratissimo illi Themistocli inusta fuisse narratur, ut contra, laudatum ferunt Epaminondam, quod ad citharam canere esset eruditus. Extant in me Platonis quoque & Aristotelis praeconia, quorum alter musicam, omni ciuili uiro necessariam, alter uero inter disciplinas maxime liberales, collocandam censet, ideo quod ego non minus sum sine noxa delectabilis, quam philosophia salubris. Ego enim illa sum, quae curas abigo, clementiam suadeo, ad leniendos affectus plurimum ualeo, moerentibus moerorem adimo, hilares hilariores efficio. Eadem denique uarijs, moribus accommodata, animos auditorum quocunque uolo, sensim traho. Porro non solum animorum perturbationibus, sed etiam corporis morbis mea medetur modulatio, quippe quum ad febrem & uulnera cantiones soleant adhiberi. Quapropter laudatus fuit olim Xenocrates, qui musicis modulis, lymphaticos etiam & insanos liberabat. Item Asclepiades, qui tubarum cantu surdissimis medebatur. sicut & Theophrastus, qui animi affectiones tibijs moderandas censuit. Quinetiam memoriae posteritatis commendatum est, Thaletem Cretensem citharae suauitate, cum alios morbos, tum pestilentiam fugauisse, & cantus tibicinum mederi ischiacis. Iam uero in ueteri instrumento scriptum reperitis, quemadmodum Dauide citharam perite pulsante, Saul refocillabatur a furore dementiae, quo identidem [5] corripiebatur. Sed de curandis morbis satis, ne uidear id agere, ut sororem meam artem medicam omni honore & dig-

---

[5] ideutidem *1517*

human experience, as at the cataracts of the Nile.[1] Because of the musical agreement of the eight celestial spheres and the one great harmony that rises from them, the ancient theologians symbolically perceived that there were nine muses.[2] In fact, that is the reason the sky itself sings.

"Besides," says Music, "take that eternal motion of the soul, which Flaccus [3] says is a particle of the divine breath, what is it if not harmonious and musical? And if I therefore bestow the gift of eternity on things divine, why shouldn't I be considered divine myself? And what about the hymns everyone sings to God, aren't they mine? And who is more faithful than I in bestowing immortality on the deeds of famous men? Weren't Homer, Vergil, and other great poets my nurslings? Doesn't Ulysses still live through me? Wouldn't the memory of Aeneas have been lost entirely if Vergil hadn't sung of 'Arms and the man'? And so it was that in the past, when virtue was more vigorous than it is now, the ancients considered a person uneducated if he didn't know how to sing and play the harp or if he refused the lyre when it was passed around at banquets, as was the custom. They say that Themistocles,[4] as famous as he was, had that mark against him, whereas Epaminondas, on the other hand, was praised because he knew how to accompany himself on the harp. Plato's and Aristotle's recommendations of me are still well known.[5] One thought that music was necessary for all civilized men; the other thought it was one of the more liberal of the liberal arts. And so I'm as harmless and pleasant as philosophy is useful. For I banish care, incline people towards mercy; I can soothe many moods. I take away sorrow from those who're sad, and I make happy people more happy. I'm always the same, but fitted to different natures, I softly draw wherever I want the souls of those who hear me. Besides, I cure with my melody not only disturbances of the mind, but also diseases of the body. For songs are usually prescribed for fever and wounds. Xenocrates, for example, was once praised for curing the mad and insane with the sounds of music. Similarly, Asclepius treated the deaf with the sound of trumpets, and Theophrastus thought that disorders of the mind could be soothed with flutes.[6] In fact, it's even recorded that Thales of Crete [7] cured the plague as well as other diseases with the song of the harp, and he treated sciatica with the music of the flute. You'll even find it written in the Old Testament how David [8] strummed the harp like an expert and revived Saul from the rage of madness that seized him at times. But that's enough about curing diseases. I don't want to seem to deprive my sister, the Art of Medicine, of all her honor and dignity.

nitate sua priuem. Laudandus sane est Socrates, qui Apollinis oraculo
sapientissimus iudicatus, noluit hoc nomen agnoscere, priusquam .lxxx.
aetatis natus annum, fidibus canere didicisset. Nimirum nullam ubi ego
non adsum, perfectam sapientiam existimans, huc accedit, quod non
solum homines ratione praediti, sed etiam bruta animalia, ratione
carentia, me mirifice capiuntur. Quae est enim tam fera belua, quae
quum sentit me adesse, non placatur? Cerui fistularum cantu adeo
demulcentur, ut cantus dulcedine trahantur in praedam.[6] Aues uero
fistulis allici, & capi, uulgatissimum est. Quid delphinum uobis commemorem? qui Arionem meum citharoedum, suauitate artis ipsius
captus, in mare proiectum, dorso excepit, & ex Italia Tenarum usque
peruexit. Atqui quum omnes res humanae duo duntaxat tempora,
nempe pacis & belli, sortitae sint, uolo intelligatis uires meas non infir-
miores in uno esse, quam in altero. Nam Timotheus in arte musica adeo
excelluit, ut Alexandrum Magnum modo arma corripere, modulamine
illo uirili & erecto (quod Graeci orthion nomon uocant) usus, modo
mutata harmonia, deponere compelleret. Sicut & Pythagoras adolescen-
tem sono lyrae ad lupanar impulit, & eadem ratione eundem reuocauit.
Ad haec, ego in omnibus bellis ad praelium milites excito, eisque animum & uires suppedito. Eadem, si opus erit, reuoco, & in unum colligo,
& istud est, quod apud omnes legitis, receptui canere, adeo ut nihil
sine me in bellis bene fiat. Quid enim sine me fecerunt celebratae illae
Romanae legiones, id est, sine lituis, tubis, & cornubus, quorum concentus equos pariter & milites acuebat? Quid Cretenses sine cithara,
ad cuius sonum semper dimicabant? Quid Lacedaemonij & Sybaritae
sine tibijs? Quid Amazones sine calamis? Quid Alyattes Lydorum rex,
sine fistulatoribus & fidicinis? Caeterum ut uerum dicam, bellis inuita
intersum, ideo quod minime bella sunt. Vnde Erasmus nec contra
Turcas quidem bella probat. At nec Dauid a me dissentire uidetur,
quum inquit, Dissipa gentes, qui bella uolunt. Addam duo, quae sub-
tilia quidem sunt, uera tamen. Vnum, quod periti musici longe melius
& acutius, quam illi qui musices sunt ignari, percipiunt, quia sunt apud
omnes rhythmi, & eis aptius scient uti, etiam si oratorum de illis praecepta nunquam legerent. Nam plurimum in his potest aurium iudicium,
cui musica magna est adiutrix, nempe in omnibus quae modulatione
nituntur, quod genus sunt rhythmi. Docet igitur Musica & orare bene,
& concionari. Quarum rerum non ignarus, fons ille Theologiae, frater

---

[6] praedam, *1517*

"Socrates certainly should be praised. When the oracle of Apollo judged him the wisest of all men, he didn't want to claim the title till he had learned to play the lute at the age of eighty.[9] No doubt he thought that no wisdom is perfect without me. In addition, I miraculously captivate not only men, who are gifted with reason, but also brutish animals, who lack it. Is there any wild beast that's not calmed when he feels my presence? Deer are so soothed with the song of the pan pipes that they're drawn into the trap by its sweetness and killed.[1] It's common knowledge that birds are lured and caught by the sound of the pipes. And do I need to remind you of dolphins? When my dear harper Arion [2] was thrown overboard into the sea, a dolphin who was charmed by the sweetness of his art took him on his back and carried him all the way from Italy to Taenarus. And since all human history is divided into two ages, the time of war and the time of peace, I want you to know that I'm just as powerful in one as in the other. For Timotheus [3] was such an excellent musician that he used the virile and arrogant song the Greeks call *orthion nomon* and forced Alexander the Great to grab up his weapons; and then by changing the mode, he forced him to put them down again. Similarly, Pythagoras [4] drove a young man into a whorehouse with the sound of the lyre and in the same way called him out again. Besides, in every war I call soldiers to battle and give them strength and courage. Similarly, if necessary, I recall and regroup them, and that is what it means *to sound a retreat* that you read about everywhere. So nothing can be done properly in war without me. For what did those famous Roman legions do without me—without clarions, horns, and trumpets, whose din excited both men and horses? What did the Cretans [5] do without the harp, for it always played while they fought? Or the Spartans and Sybarites [6] without flutes, or the Amazons without reed pipes, or Alyattes,[7] King of the Lydians, without pipers and lutists? But to tell the truth I'm not eager to go to war. It's not very pretty. That's why Erasmus [8] doesn't approve of it, not even against the Turks. And David [9] seems to agree with me when he says, 'scatter the peoples who delight in war.'

"Let me add two things that are subtle, but nevertheless true. First, experienced musicians understand things much better and more clearly than people who don't know music, for rhythm is natural to man, and musicians know how to use it more suitably than others, even if they've never read the rules of oratory. A good ear, which music helps considerably, is particularly useful in these things, in fact, in everything that depends on modulation, which is a kind of rhythm. Music, therefore, teaches you how to speak well and deliver an oration. Brother Egidius,[1]

Egidius, egregie in pulpitis ecclesiasticis,
De fratre Egidio nunc Cardinale   etiam contra ipsos summos Pontifices saepissime cecinit, nunc creatus Cardinalis,
ut taceat. Caeterum in eo creando, Leo Pontifex uere Maximus honori
suo maxime consuluit, non solum quia ob admirabilem scientiam dig-
nissimus fuit, qui crearetur, sed quia uiuente (ut intellexi) Iulio II,
Leo adhuc Cardinalis, motus doctrina huius excellentis uiri, apud eum
intercessit, ut tunc in sacrum collegium asciretur. Sed Iulius, ut erat
uir iustus & timens deum, quum audisset Cardinalem nulla moueri nisi
doctrinae ratione, Probe, inquit, nosco incredibilem doctrinam fratris
Egidij, filij nobis in primis chari & dilecti, & sola doctrina est in causa,
ut non possim illum illaesa conscientia in Cardinalium numerum re-
ferre, quo possit commodius uerbum dei quotidie (ut facit) populo
praedicare, quod Cardinali creato minime liceret. Est enim, ut scitis,
hoc a Cardinalium dignitate & consuetudine longe alienum, sed diuina
prouidentia factum est, ut quod Leo tunc Cardinalis procurauit, nunc
Pontifex Maximus per se facere posset. Sane utriusque Pontificis in hoc
uiro iudicium, nemo non merito probauerit. Nam Iulius, ut pius uir, &
Christiani gregis studiosissimus pastor, noluit eum creare, ut commodius erudiret populum. Leo omnino creandum censuit, ut uel unus
saltem in sacro collegio summus esset theologus, nisi siquis fortasse
alius clam me, aeque doctus, in idem dulcedine purpurei pilei captus,
irrepsit collegium. Alterum est, cuius Victruuius quoque meminit, musicam in primis esse necessariam omnibus ballistarum, catapultarum,
scorpionum, hydraulicarum machinarum artificibus, quippe efficacem
ad harum temperaturas moderandas, adeo ut haec, iuxta illius sententiam, non possint ullo modo recte effici sine musicis ratiocinationibus.
Sed si omnes, o studiosi adolescentes, uirtutes meas & ornamenta in
medium adducere uellem, dies quantumuis longa, me deficeret. Volo
igitur de industria multa silentio praeterire, ne ex ambitione magis,
quam ex ueritate loqui existimer. Haec musica in laudem suam, quae
omnia nos non possumus uerissima esse, non fateri & confirmare. Volu-
mus tamen de hac scientia nostram aperire sententiam, ideo quod illa
tempora, quibus (ut ipsa narrauit) tam insigniter musica floruit, sunt
mutata, & maxima pars huius artis negligentia hominum perijt. Nam
omnia quae musici nostri faciunt hodie, sunt fere triuialia, si cum his
quae fecerunt antiqui, comparentur, adeo ut uix unus aut alter reperia-
tur, qui quid sit harmonia (quam semper habent in ore) intelligat.

that fountain of theology, was not ignor-
ant of these things. He intoned magnifi-   *Brother Egidius, now a cardinal*
cently in the pulpit at church, often
against even the Popes themselves. He's now made a cardinal to shut
him up. Yet Leo, a very potent pontiff indeed, achieved a triumph of
his own while conferring the honor on Egidius. For Egidius was not
only the most suitable one he could choose because of his wonderful
knowledge, but also because (as I understand it) when Julius II was
living and Leo was still a cardinal, he was led by the learning of this
excellent man to ask the Pope to admit him to the sacred college. But
Julius was a just and God-fearing man, and when he heard that the
Cardinal was influenced only by Egidius' learning, he said, 'Of course
I know of Brother Egidius' incredible learning. He's a son especially
loved by us, and it's precisely because of his learning that I cannot
with a clear conscience make him a cardinal. If I did, he would hardly
be able to preach the word of God to the people suitably as he now
does.' For as you know that's far from customary with cardinals and
well beneath their dignity. But Divine Providence brought it about
that what Leo asked for when he was a cardinal he was able to do
when he became the Supreme Pontiff. Obviously everyone would agree
with both Popes about this man. For Julius was a pious man and an
extremely zealous pastor of the Christian flock, and the reason he
didn't want to make him a cardinal was so that he could teach the
people better.[2] Leo thought that he absolutely should be made a cardinal so that at least one person in the sacred college would be a great
theologian—unless, unbeknown to me, there's someone equally learned
who has been charmed by the red hat and crept into the sacred college.

"Another thing (which Vitruvius [3] also mentions) is that music is
particularly necessary for all makers of balistas, catapults, scorpions,
and hydraulic engines, particularly in judging proportion. According to
Vitruvius these things couldn't be done properly at all without the aid
of musical theory. But, students, if I wanted to bring out in the open
all my virtues and charms, one day wouldn't be enough, no matter
how long. Therefore I would rather pass over many of them in silence.
I don't want to seem vain; I just want to tell the truth."

So Music, in praise of herself. All of which we must confess is true.
Nevertheless, I want to tell you what I think about this science. For
the times in which music flourished so remarkably (as she tells it) have
changed, and most of this art has died out through man's neglect. For
everything our musicians do today is insignificant if we compare it
with what the ancients did. There're hardly one or two people today
who know what harmony is, though they're always talking about it.

Huic itaque restituendae, quum Romae essem, nactus in bibliotheca
summi Pontificis magnam librorum copiam, quos in hac scientia multi
& summi Philosophi scripserunt, magna & miranda continentes, uacare
coepi, instigatus ab honestissimo simul & doctissimo uiro Gulielmo
Latymero. Sed repentina Cardinalis Angliae defuncti morte (cuius
memoria in perpetuum mihi est colenda) impeditus, & Romam relin-
quere coactus, institutum prosequi non potui. Verum quoniam, ut dixi,
mutata sunt tempora, & perijt maxima artis huius pars, qui uolunt ei
studere, ita illis meo iudicio est agendum, ut cum musica aliquam aliam
liberalem scientiam coniungant, sicut apud antiquos multi fuerunt &
summi musici, & excellentes philosophi. Nam omnem in hac scientia
sola aetatem conterere, nihil ad rem pertinet, praesertim quum sub-
cisiuae horae huic sufficiant & ab aliud agentibus possit disci, sicut

Morus Musicus

Morvs meus didicit pulsare tibias cum
coniuge, nisi siquem natura (quod aliquando uidetur accidere) ab omnibus
alijs studijs penitus alienarit. Nam huic concedam, ut canat semper, &
psallat, & in omni genere musices se exerceat, ne si aliquid aliud inuita
Minerua conetur, operam & oleum (quod dici solet) perdat. Sed finem
postulat haec de musica oratio. Est igitur huius scientiae fructus proculdubio magnus, siquis eum penitus in-

*Fructus Musices, deum
honorare, homines celebrare,
& delectare*

tueatur. Siquidem haec (ut supra dictum) deum honorat, homines celebrat &
delectat, tristicias animi discutit, omne
genus animantum placat & demulcet.
Quae omnia si in summam contrahas, inuenies musicam prodesse quidem omnibus, nocere uero nemini. Sed his diebus non tam innocentiae
ratio, quam utilitatis habetur, unde requisiui, ut musicus cum musica
aliam coniungat scientiam. His de musica auditis, proruperunt in
medium affines eius Astrologia & Astronomia, scientiae syderales, quarum altera a ratione,[7] altera uero a lege & norma syderum uocabulum
sibi deduxit. Hae quum diu multumque inter se utra utri anteponeretur,
contendissent, tandem lex & norma cesserunt rationi, & sese ab ea
originem traxisse confessae sunt. Quippe quum nulla lex absque ratione
condatur, nedum ulla norma introducatur. Sublata itaque hac conten-

astrologia loquitur

tione, Astrologia sic est exorsa. Ego inquit (o charissimi iuuenes, doctrinae
operam daturi) maiorem curam uerae

---

[7] tatione, *1517*

When I was in Rome, I came across a great number of books in the Vatican Library that many eminent philosophers wrote on music. They had great wonders in them, and, urged on by William Latimer,[4] an honorable as well as a learned man, I began to devote my leisure time to the revival of music. But I was hindered by the sudden death of the late English Cardinal[5] (whose memory I shall always cherish) and forced to leave Rome. So I was not able to carry out what I had begun.

But since, as I've said, times have changed and most of this art has died out, I think anyone who wants to study music should join it to one of the other liberal arts, like many of the ancients who were both fine musicians and excellent philosophers. To waste all your life on this one science accomplishes nothing since your spare time is enough. Music can be learned by someone who's actually doing something else, as in the case of my friend More, who learned to play the flute with his wife[6]—unless one's nature is such that he's incapable of any other study, as *More a musician* sometimes happens. I would let someone like that sing and play all the time and keep himself busy with all sorts of music for fear that if he were to try anything else against his nature,[7] he would lose both his time and his trouble,[8] as they say. But enough about music.

No doubt there's a great benefit to be derived from this science if anyone looks at it closely. For as I've said above, it honors God, praises and pleases men, *Benefit of music, to honor God, praise and please men* drives away sadness of the soul, and soothes and calms every kind of living thing. Put it all together, and you'll find that music is helpful to everyone, harmful to no one. But these days it has to be more than simply harmless. It has to be useful, and for that reason I've required the musician to join his music to some other science.

When they heard all that about Music, her relatives, Astrology and Astronomy, the sciences of the stars, ran out to the middle of the stage. One of them gets its name from the calculation of the stars, the other from their law and order. After they argued for a long time about which one should go first, law and order finally gave way to reason and admitted that she took her origin from her—naturally enough, since no law and still less any order can be established without reason. With the argument settled in that way, Astrology began. "Dear boys," she said, "future scholars, I've always cared more for real honor than empty glory, *Astrology speaks* and I've always been especially eager for

honestatis, quam inanis gloriae semper habui, & ueritatis in primis
studiosa fui, quapropter uolo uobis citra fucum & fallaciam simpliciter,
ne decipiamini, quantum possum & ualeo, declarare. Apud maiores
igitur uestros (quibus longe notior fui, quam huius aetatis hominibus)
clara & illustris his nominibus fui. Primo quod meo freti auxilio, defec-
tus Solis uarios, Lunaeque labores, ut Poeta ait, deinde motus syderum,
postremo agrorum foecunditates & sterilitates in multos annos uere
praedixerunt, ideo quod haec sunt quae naturae ipsius necessitas (ut
Physici docent) perfectura est. Motus enim syderum non temerarij aut
fortuiti sunt, sed certo & constanti ordine fiunt. Et ut harum rerum
unum uobis, quo apertiores fiant, producam exemplum.[8] Democritus
ille astrologus, cuius & Plinius meminit, quum a quodam stulto diuite
derideretur, ob praedictionem magnae olei inopiae, in unum praefixum
annum futurae, ut scientiam suam ueram esse comprobaret, coepit
omne oleum (erat enim diues & ille) quod hincinde in tota regione
colligere poterat, emere, & conseruare in illum, quem nihil olei pro-
ducturum annum praedixerat, ut accidit. Tunc uero quum omnes ad
illum olei emendi causa confluere cogerentur, uenit & ille diues, qui
eum, ut dixi, deriserat, huic Democritus, Te inquit, contumeliae nomine in ius uocabo, sed nolo alia condemneris, quam stultitiae poena,
& doctrinam astrologicam quomodo ego eam exerceo,[9] ueram esse
fatearis. Nam ut omnem mentem meam intelligas, ego non coemi tantum olei, ut opes quibus ante iam abundaui, augerem, sed ut quod ex
doctrina praedixi, uerum esse comprobarem. Et ut istud manifestissimum fiat omnibus, minuam quod auxi, olei precium, & absque ullo
lucro quicquid habeo uendam, & partiar ex aequo in commune, ut
omnibus (quoad eius fieri poterit) satisfiat. Is itaque sectator meus,
non modo diuitem & doctum, sed etiam bonum & honestum uirum se
declarauit, quales hodie perpauci reperiuntur. Haec & his similia ea
sunt, quorum cognitionem & praesensionem ipsa mihi uendico. Est
enim in his praedicendis sua ratio, causa, atque etiam necessitas. At
qui thesauros inueniendos, aut haereditates, aut dignitates uenturas
praedicunt, (quod hodie in summo Pontificatu promittendo maxime
fit) quid sequuntur? aut in qua rerum natura inest id futurum? Vnde
Ciceronem uestrum uehementer laudo, qui de istis impostoribus optime & elegantissime scribit in primo de diuinatione libro, in haec
uerba, Non agnosco de circo Astrologos, non Isiacos, non coniectores,
non somniorum interpretes. Non enim hi aut scientia, aut arte diuini,

---

[8] exemplum, *1517*
[9] exreceo, *1517*

truth. Therefore, I want to tell you without tricks or sophistry, so you won't be fooled, precisely what I can do and what I'm worth.

"With your ancestors, then (for I was better known to them than I am to men of this age), I was famous and important for these reasons: first of all, with my help they accurately predicted the various eclipses of the sun and 'labors' of the moon (as the poet says),[9] the motion of the stars, and the sterility and fruitfulness of the fields for many years to come. The reason they could was that nature itself, the necessity involved in it (as the physicists teach), was going to bring them about anyway. For the motion of the stars is not haphazard and accidental but occurs in a regular, fixed order.

"To make it clearer, I'll give you an example. When Democritus the astrologer—the one Pliny mentions [1]—was laughed at by a certain rich man for predicting that there was going to be a great shortage of olive oil one year, he wanted to prove that his science was exact, so he began to buy up all the olive oil he could get in the entire area, for he was rich himself. And he saved it for the year when he had predicted there would be no oil. And there wasn't. Then, when everyone had to flock to him to buy oil, that rich man came too, the one I said had laughed at him. Democritus said to him, 'I ought to take you to court for slander, but I don't want you to be sentenced to any other punishment than your own stupidity. And I also want you to admit that the science of astrology the way I practice it is true. To let you in on the whole thing, I didn't buy up all this oil to make money. I had enough already. But I wanted to prove that what I had predicted was true. And in order to make that obvious to everyone, I'll cut the price of oil, which I've inflated, and I'll sell whatever I have without profit. Moreover, I'll divide it equally among all so everyone will be satisfied (as much as he can be).' In that way my disciple proved himself not only a rich and learned man, but also a good and honest one. There are very few like him today.

"I claim as my own the knowledge and presentiment of these things and things like them. For each of these predictions has its own reason, cause, and even necessity. But those who predict how to get a pile of money, or inheritances, or high positions that are just around the corner (which is done today, especially in predicting who the Popes will be) [2]—what sort of principles are they going on? Where is it in the nature of things? That's why I praise your man Cicero so much. In the first book of his *De Divinatione* [3] he writes sensibly and gracefully about those imposters in these words: 'I do not recognize the astrologers at the Circus, nor the priests of Isis, nor soothsayers, nor the interpreters of dreams. For they are not prophets through knowledge

sed superstitiosi uates, impudentesque harioli, aut inertes, aut insani, aut quibus egestas imperat, qui sibi semitam non sapiunt, alijs monstrant uiam. quibus diuitias pollicentur, ab his petunt drachmas. de his diuitijs sibi deducant drachmam, reddant caetera. Porro in Cornelio Tacito de istis loquente, non ueritatem modo & elegantiam, sed etiam breuitatem impense laudo. Nam Mathematici, inquit (sic enim isti prognostici nominantur) genus hominum, principibus infidum, credentibus fallax, a ciuitate nostra semper prohibentur, sed expelluntur nunquam. Item extat scitum contra aruspices, Catonis dictum, qui mirari se aiebat, quod non rideret aruspex, aruspicem cum uidisset. Nam eiusdem generis sunt aruspices, extispices,

Artes damnatae   augures, necromantici, pyromantici, aeromantici, hydromantici, phytonici, catoptromantici (id est, qui ex speculorum inspectione, occulta siue futura nunciant) Magi, quorum ars initio quidem non nisi ex deorum cultu & syderum obseruatione constabat, sed postea ad incantamenta & ueneficia prolapsa est. Denique illi qui in hoc stultitiae genere caeteris longe antecedunt, nutrientes spiritus malignos in ampullis, si modo aereum corpus uitro pasci potest. Quantum autem haec insania fugienda & abominanda sit, non modo sanctis praeceptis (quae omnia huiusmodi damnant) monendi homines sunt, sed etiam rerum experientia. Nam egomet in Italia uidi & cognoui, quos haec ars non modo praecipitauit, sed etiam ad extrema calamitosissime perduxit supplicia. Et miserrimi homines, quod [1] alios diligentissime docere sunt conati, hoc est, futura indubie praescire, id in semetipsis perfectissime ignorarunt. In horum numerum intrudam & Alchimystas, ceu additamentum (alium enim locum eis non reperio) quo-

In Alchimystas   rum nomen nouum & obscurum est, & scientia plusquam ridicula & stulta, & ex qua nihil fructus praeter risum, capiunt homines, quum uideant illos enixissime & diutissime laborare, ut argentum non in aurum sed in cineres transmutent. Recte igitur de uniuerso hoc hominum genere scripsit, qui illud scripsit, Istis non credo

Sententia   qui aures uerbis diuitant alienas, suas ut auro locupletent domos. Sane Alchimystis & Necromanticis debemus prouerbium hodie uulgatum, Nec Alchimystam bene uiuere, nec Necromanticum bene mori. Quamobrem ab harum artium malarum, & prorsus damnandarum studio, omnes

---

[1] qnod *1517*

or skill, but superstitious fortunetellers, shameless gut-gazers, loafers, or crazy, or driven by poverty. Those who don't know the dirt roads point out the highway to others. They wheedle drachmas [4] from those to whom they promise riches. From all that wealth they want only one drachma for themselves and let the rest go.'

"Cornelius Tacitus [5] has also spoken of them. I admire not only his truthfulness and grace, but also his brevity. For he says, 'Mathematicians (as, in fact, these fortunetellers are called) are a race of men who are traitors to their princes, deceivers of those who believe in them. They are always forbidden to live in our country, but they are never driven out.' Along the same line there's a wise saying of Cato's [6] against fortunetellers. He said he 'always marvelled that one fortuneteller didn't laugh when he saw another.' For they're all the same—diviners, soothsayers, augurs, necromancers, pyromancers, aeromancers, hydro-   *Black magic*
mancers, pythonists,[7] catoptromancers
(that is, those who tell what's hidden or in the future from looking at mirrors), magi, whose art at first consisted of nothing but worship of the gods and observation of the stars, but afterwards fell into charms and sorcery. And finally there are those who are far more gone in this stupidity than the rest and who grow malignant spirits inside bottles,[8] as if an airy body could eat glass. Men ought to be warned not only by sacred precepts (which damn everything of this sort), but also by experience itself how much this insanity should be shunned and detested. For I myself saw and knew men in Italy who were not only ruined by this art, but most disastrously led to suffer the extreme penalty. And these miserable men were completely ignorant of what they tried so hard to teach to others, that is, to see clearly into the future.

"Let me stick the alchemists in here as
a kind of supplement, since I don't know   *On alchemists*
where else to put them. The word is
recent and obscure,[9] and their science is more than ridiculous and stupid. Men get no benefit from it other than laughter when they see them working long and hard to turn silver not into gold, but ashes. Whoever wrote this,[1] therefore, wrote the right thing about this whole species of man: 'I do not trust those who
fill the heads of others with thoughts of   *A wise saying*
riches in order to fill their own houses
with gold.' No doubt we owe to alchemists and necromancers the proverb [2] that's common nowadays: no alchemist lives well; no necromancer dies well. That's why I urge everyone as strongly as I can not

quam uehementissime possum, dehortor, quippe quum nec cum astrologia quicquam habeant commune, nec alia quauis liberali & appro-
bata sapientibus uiris scientia, sed aliam quandam turpissimam reginam sortitae sint, nomine imposturam. quae cum suis mox nominatis
discipulis, nullum alium fructum praebent hominibus ipsarum studiosis, quam infamiam, paupertatem, & extremam miseriam. Neque enim
debet illud aliquem mouere, quod aliquando incidunt in ueritatem.
Nam hoc fit, ut siquis tessaris uel talis tota ludat die, possit semel
seniones uel Venerem iacere, quod nulla ratione, sed fortuitu accidit.
Et ut horum fallaciae uobis sint notiores, scitote istos in hoc uehementissime laborare, ut principum intelligant secreta, & ob id in ipsorum
aulis suos habere exploratores, illos praecipue, qui aliquam rerum mutationem expectant. Et siquid hac uia odorari uel scire poterunt, tunc
quod uerisimilius est, id coniectant futurum. Quod si uel semel, non
scientia, sed coniectura ueritatem futuram assequantur, tunc non humana ratio, sed credulitas rerum nouarum cognoscendarum istos susti-
net, & etiam nutrit. Nam nisi hi duo errores plurimum inter homines
possent, isti proculdubio perirent fame, id quod uel hinc patet, quod
etiam nunc quum eis stulte creditur, semper adeo sunt pannosi, ut uix
per uestes illorum, pediculus citra decidendi periculum possit serpere,
ita uero egeni, ut leporarijs panis longe sit paratior, quam illis. Coniectores uero & somniuendae (quorum ars magis exoleuit) alia utuntur
uia, de quorum imposturis ridiculam uobis narrabo fabellam, cuius &
Cicero meminit. Detulit quidam ad Apa-
Fabula   turium coniectorem, somniasse se ouum
pendere ex fascia lecti cubicularis. Re-
spondit coniector, aurum defossum esse, quod ipsemet defoderat. Fodit
ille, inuenit, non thesaurum, sed auri aliquantum, & circundatum ar-·
gento. Misit coniectori in mercedem, quantulum uisum est de argento.
Quod quum uidisset ille, Nihil ne, inquit, affers de oui uitello? In isto
impostore hoc solum iudico tolerabile, quod fuit facetus nebulo. Equidem in hac scientia somniaria non puto dissentiendum a Cicerone, qui
si deus, inquit, uoluisset nos futura praescire, non hoc nobis dormienti-
bus, sed uigilantibus potius concessiset, id quod tunc uerissimum esse
constabit, ut mihi uidetur, si unusquisque sua diligenter obseruaret
somnia. Nam egomet interdum non solum incredibilia, sed etiam ab
omni ratione aliena, immo prorsus impossibilia somniaui, ex quibus
nescio quae futurorum scientia percipi potest. Quid ex his, quaeso,
perquam ridiculis colligendum est? Somniauit hic unus nuperrime

to study these evil and, in fact, damnable arts, especially since they have nothing in common with astrology or any other liberal art approved of by wise men. Instead, they've chosen some other filthy queen named Imposture. Like their quickly named disciples, these black arts offer no other benefit to those who study them than infamy, poverty, and extreme misery. And it shouldn't disturb anyone that they stumble on the truth now and then. That can happen, the same way that someone who shoots craps all day can throw sixes or the Venus [3] at least once. There's no reason for it. It's just an accident.

"To let you in on their tricks a little, you ought to know that they work hardest at this: to learn the secrets of princes. And for that they have their own spies at court, usually the kind of men who hope for some change in the state of things. And if they can learn or smell out anything this way, then they predict that the more probable is what will happen in the future. But if they ever come up with the truth just once, not by learning but by guessing, then they're maintained and even well fed. The reason is not that people are rational, but that they're ready to believe in new things. For these frauds would no doubt die of hunger if men were not subject to those two errors.[4] That's obvious, for even now when fools believe in them, they're always so ragged that a louse can hardly crawl around on their clothes without fear of falling off. In fact, they're so poor that lepers have more bread than they do.

"But fortunetellers and dream merchants (whose art is somewhat out of date) go about it another way. I'll tell you a foolish story about their tribe, one that Cicero mentions.[5] A certain man told Apaturius the fortune- *A story* teller that he dreamed an egg was hang- ing from his bed slats. The fortuneteller said that meant buried gold (he'd buried it himself). The man dug and found no treasure, but a little gold surrounded by silver. He sent the fortuneteller his pay, as much silver as he thought he was worth. When Apaturius saw it, he said, 'Didn't you bring me any of the yolk?' I think the only good thing about this con man is that he was a rat with a sense of humor. As far as I am concerned, I think we should agree with Cicero [6] about this dreamy science. He said that if God wanted us to know the future, he would have shown it to us while we're awake, not while we're asleep. Everyone will agree with that, I think, if he looks at his own dreams carefully. For I myself have sometimes dreamed not only unbelievable things, but totally irrational, in fact, totally impossible things. I don't know how you can derive any knowledge of the future from them.

Duo somnia ridicula

equum suum frustum placentae deuo-
rasse, & in sequenti die illud idem euo-
muisse. Alter nudum se ambulantem, tam
magnum longumque egessisse stercus, ut cogitetur illud ceu caudam
trahere. Sed uideamus quid aliqui non explosi autores de somnijs som-
niant. Scribit Artemidorus de somniorum interpretatione in haec uerba,
ἁρπαστὸν καὶ σφαῖρα φιλονικείαν ἄπειρον συμαίνουσι. [2] πολλάκις δὲ
καὶ ἑτάιρας ἔρωτα, ἔοικε καὶ ἡ σφαῖρα καὶ τὸ ἁρπαστὸν ἑτάιρα διὰ
τοῦ μηδαμῇ μένειν, ἀλλὰ πρὸς πολλοὺς φοιτᾶν, id est, harpastum &
sphaera (quae pilarum lusoriarum genera sunt) certamen infinitum
significant, saepe uero etiam meretricium amorem. uidetur enim sphaera,
& harpastum meretrix, propterea quod nusquam maneat, sed ad multos
prodeat. Equidem in hac interpretatione nihil solidioris doctrinae con-
templari possum, sed inanem potius coniecturam, longo fortasse studio
& tempore acquisitam. Nam haec somnolenta ars, ex quotidiana obseruatione originem traxisse uidetur, quae non tam certa est, quam
saepissime labitur. Non potest enim mea quidem sententia, aut Artemidorus, aut quiuis alius somniorum interpres, ulla probare ratione, unam
& eandem rem, uarium somniorum euentum denotare. Igitur ut mitius
cum istis agamus, relinquamus eis inanem coniecturam, unde & coniectores uocantur, sed tollamus omnem certam scientiam, ne diuinae
potestati somnium aequetur, & quae in deo pars est praecipua, hanc
sibi uendicet indoctus homuntio. Et nec illis credamus somnijs, quae
falso nomine (ut opinor) Danielis circunferuntur, nam nec in his ego
quicquam praeter somnia uideo. quorum unum est illud, Notatur in
illis amicum ei periturum, qui somniat sibi dentem, & praecipue maxil-
larem decidere. Ego contra uidi, post huiusmodi somnium duos recen-
tes amicos acquisitos uni fuisse. Quaerant itaque qui uolunt ueritatem
in somnijs, me comitem non habebunt. Sane non sine causa & ratione
obtinuit consuetudo, ut quoties aliquis friuola, inania, & incredibilia
loquatur, dicamus eum somnia narrare, uel somniare. At dixerit quispiam, quid sentis de somnijs illorum sanctorum uirorum, quibus (ut
in ecclesiastica historia saepe legimus) angeli in somnijs apparuerunt,
& hoc uel illud ex deo monuerunt, quod eis praetermittere religio fuit?
Respondeo, hoc quod ex deo factum fuit, non esse somnio ascriben-
dum, sed purae ueritati per diuinum nuncium allatae. Vnde huiusmodi
diuinae mentis significationes, ab ipsis ecclesiasticis, reuelationes, &
non somnia uocantur, alio & ueriore (ni fallor) nomine. Non me latet
Philosophos, & quidem magnos, aliquid somnijs tribuere, qui etiam
somnia quaedam θεόπνουστα [3] inuenerunt. Sed mihi certum est nolle

---

[2] An error for σημαίνουσι.
[3] The correct form of the word is θεόπνευστα.

"Now I ask you, what can you make of
these crazy things? Just recently a man   *Two ridiculous dreams*
dreamed his horse ate a piece of cake and
the next day threw it up again. Another man dreamed he was walking
along naked and squeezed out a turd so big and long that it dragged
along behind him like a tail.

"But let's see what some authors who are not yet hooted off the stage
dream about dreams. Artemidorus [7] writes about the interpretation of
dreams in these words: *harpaston kai sphaira philonikeian apeiron
sêmainousi. pollakis de kai hetairas erôta, eoike kai hê sphaira kai to
harpaston hetaira dia tou mêdamê menein, alla pros pollous phoitan,*
that is, the *harpastum* and *sphaera* (which are a kind of ball used
in games) signify constant struggle and often the love of whores. For
a whore is like a *sphaera* and *harpastum* because she doesn't stay in
one spot, but rolls around all over. As for me, I can't see any solid
learning in that interpretation, but rather an empty guess arrived at
perhaps by long study. For this sleepy art seems to have originated in
everyday observation, which is more often wrong than right. And I
don't think Artemidorus or any other interpreter of dreams can prove
with any show of reason that various dreams mean one and the same
thing. Therefore, in order to be kind, let's leave empty conjecture to
them; that's why they are called *coniectores* anyway. For our part, let's
support all positive science so dreams won't be put on the same level
as divine power. We don't want an ignorant midget to claim for himself
something that's the particular prerogative of God. And let's not believe
those dreams that are spread around under the false name (so I think)
of Daniel.[8] For I see nothing in them besides dreams. Here's one of
them. They say that one of your friends will die if you dream your
tooth falls out, especially a molar. But I saw someone get two new
friends after a dream like that. So, whoever wants to can look for the
truth in dreams, they won't have me along. Surely there is a good reason we usually say someone is dreaming when he says something foolish, insane, and incredible. But someone will say, what about the
dreams of holy men? As we often read in ecclesiastical history, angels
appeared to them in their dreams and gave them some message or
other from God, and it was a sin for them to ignore it. I say that since
this was done by God, it should not be thought of as a dream, but as
pure truth carried by a divine messenger. That's why ecclesiastics themselves call these indications of the divine mind *revelations* and not
dreams, a different and more exact term, I believe. I realize that philosophers, even great ones, allow something to dreams. They have even
found certain dreams *theopneusta.*[9] But I certainly do not want to

amplius somniare. Et nec Aristoteles ipse potest mihi persuadere aliquid certi incertis somnijs inesse, sed ei opponam Ecclesiasten scribentem, Vbi multa somnia, ibi multae uanitates. At nec Themistius, ipsius Aristotelis sectator, aliquid certi in somnijs uidere potuit. Omnem igitur, o iuuenes, hanc diuinandi & praedicandi futura imposturam contemnite & auertite, praeferentes istis meris nugamentis, illam insignem Aristotelis sententiam & rationem, scribentis, φρονίμων καὶ σοφῶν ταχείαν εἶναι τὴν μαντικὴν, καὶ μόνων, id est, ut dicam breuibus, solos prudentes & sapientes celeriter diuinare. Nam sapientes ex praeteritorum & praesentium coniectura, facile prospiciunt quid sit futurum. Haec itaque sapientissimi uiri sententia, homini tribuit uim ingenij, sed soli deo ueram futurorum praescientiam relinquit. Credite igitur & uos Christo uestro ueritatis praedicatori, immo ipsi ueritati, quum ait discipulis suis, Non est uestrum scire horas & momenta, quae pater meus posuit in potestate sua. Et siqui contrarium aliquid huic diuinae sententiae persuadere conabuntur, hos fugite tanquam pestes, & iudicate nec astrologos, nec astronomos esse, sed (ut imperitum uulgus appellat) extrologos potius, & extrono-

Extrologi Extronomi   mos, quasi omnia quae loquuntur, sint longe extra rationem & legem syderum collocata. & ut aliquid asperius sentiant, torquere in illos illud Demosthenicum telum, μανίαν εἶναι, τὸ παρὰ δύναμίν τι ποιεῖν, id est, insaniam esse aliquid ultra uires conari. Qua in re semper mecum sensit soror mea astronomia. Nae, inquit Astronomia, o soror, ego nulla in re a te dissentio, sed omnia quae a te dicta sunt, confirmo & approbo. Nam istud fallacissimum hominum genus, quod deus malum, male perdat, bonis nostris abutitur, & sua ignorantia adeo omnia peruertit, ut bona pars hominum nunc minoris nos aestimet, quam aliam quamuis pene dicam, artem mechanicam. In causa autem est, quod non nisi indocti, mendaces, egeni, & famelici hoc saeculo nos in ore habent. nam si tales hodie nostri essent sectatores, qualis fuit Democritus, cuius tu paulo ante meministi, praeclare nobiscum ageretur. Sed uix sperare possum hoc unquam futurum, nisi principes & uiri primarij diligentius quam nunc faciunt, literis studeant, & philosophentur. Et non minus uerum est illud, non plures futuros Vergilios, nisi plures dentur Mecoenates. Geometria cum haec dicerentur,

De Geometria   forte astabat. Et quoniam uos inquit, o astrologia & astronomia, causam uestram erudite, simul & eleganter egistis, rogo mihi quoque potestas dicendi,

dream any longer. Not even Aristotle himself could convince me that there's anything certain in the uncertainty of dreams. I would counter him with Ecclesiastes,[1] who writes, 'when dreams increase, empty words grow many.' And Themistius,[2] one of Aristotle's own followers, could not see anything certain in dreams.

"Therefore, boys, despise and avoid all this phony talk of predicting and foretelling the future. Instead of that sheer nonsense, take in this sensible and well-known saying of Aristotle's,[3] who writes *phronimôn kai sophôn tacheian einai tên mantikên, kai monôn,* that is, in brief, only the prudent and wise prophesy easily. By conjecturing from the past and present wise men can easily foresee what the future may be. So Aristotle's saying attributes to man the power of intelligence, but leaves to God alone true foreknowledge of the future. Believe, therefore, in your Christ,[4] the prophet of truth or rather Truth itself, when He says to His disciples: 'It is not yours to know the hour and the moment, which my Father kept in His own power.' And if they try to convince you of anything other than this, run from them like the plague and consider them neither astrologers, nor astronomers, but extrologers and extronomers, as they're known to the ignorant. For it's as though   *Extrology, extronomy* everything they say is located far beyond (*extra*) the system and order of the stars. To give it to them harder, hit them with this from Demosthenes,[5] *manian einai, to para dunamin ti poiein,* that is, it's insane to attempt anything beyond your capability. My sister Astronomy always felt the same as I do about this."

"Right," said Astronomy. "I agree with you entirely, sister; I approve of everything you say. For that conniving breed of men (a goddamn evil I wish God would damn) wastes our money and overthrows everything through its ignorance. It's so bad that nowadays the best people think less of us than almost any other mechanical art. The reason is that no one in this century talks about us except illiterates, liars, beggars, and the half-starved. For if we had followers today like Democritus, whom you mentioned a little while ago, it would go extremely well for us. But I can hardly hope for that, even in the future, unless princes and the leading men of the country study the liberal arts more than they do and become more philosophical.[6] And this is no less true: there will be no more Vergils in the future unless there are more Maecenases." [7]

Geometry happened to be standing there when they were talking. "Dear   *Geometry* Astrology and Astronomy," she said, "you've argued your case with learning and at the same time with

silentibus uobis fiat, ut bonae mentis iuuenes, & doctrinae cupidi, nec me a nobilissimo scientiarum genere degenerasse intelligant. Quare quum ea sim, quae mallem esse quam dici doctrina pulcherrima & utilissima, nolo in meam ipsius laudem ostentabunda multis uerbis uti, sed illorum testimonium de me in medium ad ducam, quos doctissimos & sapientissimos, doctissimi & sapientissimi uiri iudicarunt. Pythagoras igitur, cuius sapientia ipsius saeculum mirifice illustrauit, me adeo probauit & admiratus est, ut dicatur ob inuentas quasdam figuras meas, modo dijs sacrificasse, non uulgariter, sed adhibita illa celebratissima hecatombe, modo ut insanus diu exclamasse, εὕρηκα, id est, inueni. Item Plato, quem a quadam sapientiae diuinitate, diuinum doctissimi uiri appellant, scholae suae inscripsisse traditur, Ἀγεωμέτρητος οὐδεὶς ἐισίτω, id est, nemo geometriae ignarus ingrediatur. Et Xenocrates iuueni cuidam, eiusdem scientiae experti, & ipsius scholam frequentare cupienti, dixisse se lanas non purgare, nimirum hac ductus ratione, quod humano generi nihil geometria magis necessarium sciet. Nam nisi ego omnem aedificandi artem hominibus demonstrassem, uixissent plane ut bruta animalia,[4] omnes sub diuo absque tectis, quod miserrimum eis proculdubio fuisset, a quo mea solius prouidentia liberati sunt. Neque enim oues mihi, licet earum quoque lana homines tegat (ut quaedam alia) anteponendae sunt, nam ego & ouem, & lanam ipsam tego & conseruo. Sed hanc Platonicam sententiam aliqui, & quidem docti, non simpliciter intelligunt, sed ad allegoriam trahunt, ut dicant Platonem, nomine geometriae aequabilitatem, siue aequalitatem omnium rerum intellexisse, ideo quia ab aequalitate geometria nunquam recedit, id quod cum primis est laudandum & expetendum. Nam maxima uis est aequalitatis, & apud deum, & homines. Si enim deus aequum omnium iudicem se non praestaret, tam misera esset bonorum & piorum, quam malorum & impiorum sors, & nec uirtutibus sua solueretur merces, nec punirentur uitia. Apud homines uero, ubi abest aequalitas, ibi adest magna confusio, innumeras ingenerans pestes, ut auaritiam, dolum, fraudem, & id genus alias, quas longum esset recensere. Vnde tum ab ipso Platone, tum ab alijs omnibus, illud Hesiodi Poetae approbatur, πλέον ἥμυσι[5] τοῦ παντὸς, id est, dimidium plus toto, quo Poeta nihil aliud significauit, quam aequalitatem praeferendam esse auaritiae. Porro communitas illa quam Pythagoras in amicitia postulauit, non nisi aequabilitas intelligenda est, astipulante ipso Platone, sic scribente in sexto de legibus, ἰσότης φιλίαν ἀπεργάζεται,

---

4 anialia *1517*
5 An error for ἥμισυ.

grace. But now I ask permission to speak too, if you'll be quiet, so I can tell the bright young men, who are eager to learn, that I have not degenerated from the noble race of sciences. And therefore, since I'm the kind of person who would rather *be* the most beautiful and useful of all the sciences than simply *be called* the most beautiful and useful, I don't want to show off and make a long speech in praise of myself. Let me simply present the testimonials of those who are judged, by the wisest and most learned, to be the wisest and most learned. Pythagoras,[8] then, whose wisdom made his entire age brilliant, liked me and admired me so much that after he discovered certain of my forms he is said to have made a sacrifice to the gods not in any ordinary way, but with that famous hecatomb. Another time he yelled out over and over, like a madman—*eurêka,*[9] that is, I've found it.

"Similarly Plato,[1] whom wise men call divine because of a certain divinity in wisdom, is said to have inscribed on his school *Ageômetrêtos oudeis eisitô,* that is, everyone ignorant of geometry, keep out. And Xenocrates [2] told a certain young man who didn't know much about geometry and wanted to attend his school that he didn't wash raw wool. No doubt he said that because he knew nothing more useful to mankind than geometry. For if I hadn't shown the whole art of building to men, they obviously would have lived like wild animals, out in the open without roofs, which certainly would have been miserable for them. They're free of it only because of my forethought. But that doesn't mean you should think more of sheep than you do of me. Granted their wool also covers you (like certain other things), I shelter the sheep and the wool both. But some men, even some learned ones, do not interpret this saying of Plato's literally. They turn it into an allegory and say that Plato meant by geometry Equitability, or the Equality of all things, since geometry never departs from equality, which makes it particularly praiseworthy and valuable. For equality is the prime force with both God and man. If God were not a fair judge, pious and good men would be just as miserable as the impious and evil. Virtue would not be rewarded and vice punished. And as for man himself, there's great confusion where there's no equality. It produces innumerable plagues, such as greed, deceit, fraud, and similar things which would take too long to enumerate. That's why Plato and everyone else applauded this saying of the poet Hesiod,[3] *pleon hêmisy tou pantos,* that is, half is more than all, by which he meant that equality is better than greed. Besides, that quality of sharing all things which Pythagoras [4] demanded of friendship was nothing but equality. And Plato agreed, for he wrote in the sixth book of the *Laws,*[5] *isotês philian apergazetai,* that is, equality makes friendship.

id est, aequalitas amicitiam facit. Iam uero inter omnes aliarum disciplinarum sectas, magna & diuturna sunt
Dissensio Theologorum   certamina, ut apud Theologos Thomistis
non bene conuenit cum Scotistis, & de
diuae uirginis conceptione longe maxima inter eos est dissensio, quae
aliquibus in locis (non adeo theologice) usque ad arma processit. Cui
malo ut adhiberetur remedium, summus Pontifex imposuit eis silen-
tium, mandauitque ne amplius hac de re disputent. Ideoque quia publice bellum gerere per censuras apostolicas amplius non licet, res agitur pugnis domi & secreto, nec adhuc Benedictini fratres Bononiae
tabulam illam sustulerunt, in qua infinitae & omnes uariae opiniones
hac in re, maiusculis literis inscribuntur.[6] Vt constet scilicet omnibus
Theologiam nobis esse contrariam. Haec de antiquioribus. Nuper uero
reperti sunt nescio qui, qui nouum testamentum maximis ERASMI
nostri laboribus & industria aeditum, & ab omnibus uere doctis ap-
probatissimum, damnare sunt conati, id est, Christum, Euangelistas
omnes, & Apostolos incorruptius & apertius nobis, quam antea loquentes lacerare. Itaque isti non tam Theologi meo iudicio, quam iniquitatis filij uocandi sunt. Porro inter Philosophos non solum magnae, sed
etiam pestilentes, & plane damnandae dissensiones sunt. Vnde prouerbium quoque natum est, Facilius inter horologia, quam inter philosophos conuenire. Nam unus bonus & pius, deum esse credit. Alter per-
uersus & impius, deum esse negat, & atheus potius, quam pius dici
uult. Vnus prouidentiam dei magnis & ueris rationibus astruit, Alter
friuolis argumentis tollit. Vnus de causis naturalibus sapienter & aperte
disputat, & multa clare demonstrat, Alter nihil comprehendi posse contendit, quod ἀκαταληψίαν uocat. Et ut haec fatuitas sit apertissima,
noua producit placita, quibus docet niuem esse atram, & remum in
aquam iniectum, quia fractus apparet, & non est, arguere humanum
uisum hebetem & incertum. Et interrogati aliqua, illico respondent,
ἐπέχω περὶ τούτου καὶ δϊασκέπτομαι, id est, cohibeo assensionem, &
rem consyderandam duco, unde & consyderatorios philosophos quidam
latinorum uocant. Hinc unus in epigrammate, apte in Pyrrhonem mor-
tuum, huius sectae principem iocatur, his uerbis interrogans, κάτθανες
ὦ πύῤῥων, id est, obijstine o Pyrrho? Respondet ille mortuus, ἐπέχω
περὶ τούτου, id est, assentiri nequeo. Porro inter iurisconsultos tam

---

[6] inscribuntur, *1517*

"Now among the various schools in all other fields of learning there are great, everlasting arguments. Among the Theologians, for example, the Thomists don't get along with the Scotists. *Disagreement of theologians* They've argued for a long time about the Immaculate Conception,[6] and in some places it has even come to open war (though not yet in theology). To cure the difficulty, the Pope imposed silence on them and ordered them not to argue about that anymore. And so, since they're forbidden by Apostolic censure to wage war anymore in the open, they fight at home in secret. The Benedictine Brothers of Bologna [7] still don't support the writ in which all the countless, various opinions on the subject are inscribed in majuscule letters. It should be obvious to everyone, of course, that theology is completely different from me. So much for older arguments.

"More recently, there have been some people—I don't know who—who have tried to condemn the New Testament which our Erasmus edited [8] with a great amount of work and industry and which all truly learned men highly approved of. What those people were doing in fact was tearing to pieces Christ, all the Evangelists, and the Apostles, who were speaking to us more clearly and in a more genuine voice than before. I think, therefore, they ought to be called sons of iniquity instead of theologians.

"And as for philosophers, their arguments are not only great, but also unhealthy and obviously damning. That's where the proverb [9] comes from, it's easier to find clocks agreeing than philosophers. For one person, a good and pious man, believes that God exists. Another, evil and impious, denies that God exists and would rather be called an atheist than a pious man. The first one proves the providence of God by great and true arguments; the other raises frivolous objections. The first one discusses natural causes plainly and sensibly and clarifies many things, the other one contends that we're capable of understanding nothing, which he calls *akatalêpsian*.[1] And in order to make his stupidity clearer, he produces new principles by which he demonstrates that snow is black and that human vision is weak and uncertain because an oar thrust in the water looks broken when it's not. And if you question them in some way, they immediately reply *epechô peri toutou kai diaskeptomai*, that is, I withhold agreement and regard the matter as deserving further consideration. That's why some Romans [2] call philosophers *considerators*. Hence in the epigram [3] someone jokes (and rightly so) with Pyrrho, the leader of this sect, who was dead, and asks him *katthanes ô pyrrôn*, that is, 'You're dead aren't you, Pyrrho?' The dead man answers, *epechô peri toutou*, that is, 'I won't commit myself.'

Discordia iurisconsultorum

magna est discordia, ut indoctus omnino habeatur, qui non dissentiat ab altero. Hinc etiam prodierunt illa nimis ingentia uolumina Bartholica & Baldica, Ioannis de Immola, Pauli de Castro cum Saliceto. Et inter illos istorum longe clarior est eruditio, qui Bartholum & Baldum ex diametro (ut aiunt) dissentientes sciunt concordare, quam qui Vlpianum & Paulum puram ueritatem, reiectis strophis loquentes intelligunt. Atqui unus inter istos repertus est, qui lineam transire,

Facetum

& sua egredi palaestra ausus est, nec a suis modo dissentire, sed etiam inter omnes etymologistas discordiam seminare. Is enim dicendi quoque artem professus, ambiuit legationem ad sacratissimum MAXIMILIANVM Caesarem, eloquentiae ostentandae causa. Et quum in sua ad eum oratione, totus in genere laudatiuo uersaretur, coepit & a nomine Maximilianum in caelum laudibus tollere, asserens, & alta uoce tonans, unum hoc nomen Maximiliani, a duobus maximis nominibus compositum, scilicet, inquit ille, maximus a Maximo Fabio, milianus, ab Aemylio Scipione. Vtcunque est, res processit bene, ille laudatus est ab omnibus, & oratio in uulgus est aedita, Etymologistis duntaxat rem improbantibus, non modo quod grammaticis suis rationibus mouerentur, Maximilianum simplicem esse dictionem, sed etiam quod aegre ferunt ex duobus maximis Imperatoribus unum fieri Maximilianum Caesarem, ideo quod is illis etiam quantumuis maximis, longe est maior, nam illorum dignitas temporaria fuit, huius uero perpetua est. Sed hoc fortasse illum iurisconsultum latebat. Praeterea inter medicos perniciosissima est dissensio, de herbarum (quibus maxime utuntur) cognitione, & de confectione illius celebratissimi & salutiferi in primis medicaminis, quae theriace dicitur. Haec ut tollatur, maxime interest humanae uitae. Nam aliqui dicunt theriacem ideo nominatam, quod tyri animalis morsibus medetur, & scribunt tyriacam. Aliqui negant tyrum esse animal, & apud Galenum non tyri, sed theres legendum esse, & ἀπὸ τῶν θηρῶν, id est a feris theriacen uocatam (quibus assentior) & θῆρας a Galeno accipi pro solis uiperis, quod mihi non persuadent, quod nusquam legi apud Graecos θῆρα pro uipera, quibus θῆρ generale uocabulum est omnium ferarum, nec ex sola uipera compositam credo theriacen. Sed hanc quaestionem sorori meae arti medicae, & Linacro eius professori peritissimo discutiendam relin-

"Moreover, there's so much discord among lawyers that they're considered totally uneducated unless they disagree *Discord of lawyers* with one another. And that has produced those excessively huge Bartholican and Baldican volumes by Joannes de Imola and Paulus de Castro along with Salicetus.[4] The most famous and learned among them by far are the ones who know how to reconcile Bartholus and Baldus when they're diametrically opposed to each other (as they say), not those who understand Ulpianus and Paulus [5] and speak the simple truth with no rhetorical flourishes. Yet there was one of them who dared to cross the line and *A funny story* leave his own college of rhetoric. He not only disagreed with his own colleagues, he also sowed discord among etymologists. For he was a professor of rhetoric and tried to get a position as ambassador from Caesar Maximilian [6] in order to display his oratory. Since he used only the rhetoric of praise in his speech before Maximilian, he began with the name Maximilian and praised him to the skies. He thundered in a loud voice and said that this one name Maximilian was made up of two great (*maximis*) names: *viz.*, (he said) *maxim*, from Fabius Maximus and *milianus* from Aemilius Scipio.[7] However it is, it went off well. Everyone praised him, and the oration was published. Only the etymologists disagreed, not only for grammatical reasons (Maximilian is a non-compounded word), but also because they were annoyed that he had made one Caesar Maximilian from two great generals, when he is far greater than they were, no matter how great they were. For their position was temporary; the Emperor's is permanent. But perhaps that point escaped the lawyer-rhetorician.

"Beyond that, there's an extremely unhealthy disagreement among doctors about the knowledge of herbs, which they use a great deal, and in particular about how to make the most famous and healing of all medicines, called *theriaca*. It's of great importance to human life that this argument be ended. For some say *theriaca* got its name from the fact that it's good for bites of an animal call *tyrus*—hence *tyriaca*. Others deny that the word *tyrus* means animal, and they say Galen [8] should read *theres*, not *tyri*, and that *apo tôn thêrôn*, that is, *theriaca* is derived from the word for wild beasts (and I agree). They also say that Galen uses the word *thêr* only for vipers, which is not convincing to me since I've never read in Greek the word *thêr* used for viper. It's the generic term for all wild animals, and I don't believe that *theriaca* is made from vipers alone. But I'll leave that problem to my sister, the Art of Medicine, and Linacre,[9] her most distinguished professor.

quo. Nam quae Philippus Beroaldus in suis in Galenum annotationibus, hac in re scripsit, parum probo. Neque enim tractat fabrilia faber, nec Beroaldus est in sua palaestra. Nicolaum uero Leonicenum, uirum undecunque doctissimum (in cuius morte omnes literae maximam fecere iacturam) aliquid super hac controuersia dignum eruditis auribus, scriptum reliquisse puto. Solebat enim uiuus acutissime de hac re disputare, & communem omnium recentum medicorum, graece non intelligentum, in theriace aegrotis ministranda, opinionem damnare, ideo quod minus recte ab eis conficeretur. Quod cum illi audissent, insurrexerunt in eum gladijs & fustibus, sed quum prodijssent in conspectum, & fustes abijcere, & gladios in uaginas reponere sunt coacti, nam omnia arma cesserunt illius uiri rationibus & doctrinae. Verumtamen (quod mirum dictu est) illi recentiores medici non potuerunt adduci, ut sequerentur quod probarunt, etiam ratione impellente, sed maluerunt uti suo antiquo mumpsimus [7] potius, quam illius, immo ueritatis sumpsimus. Cuius rei causam, quum ego quosdam amicos meos, Leoniceni scholam frequentantes, interrogassem, Nolunt, inquiunt, isti medici aromatarijs esse damno, quorum iactura esset ualde magna, si abijcerent antiquam theriacen, cuius maximam habent copiam, & uterentur hac confectione noua. Et fortasse conuentum est inter illos & medicos, ut (ne fiat) pars lucri diuidatur. Omnem rem nunc inquam ego intelligo, haec faba in te & me, & alios aegrotos cudetur, quos aromatariorum perfidia, & malorum medicorum ignorantia & auaritia impune occidet, & (quod ridiculum est) mortem nostram magna emere pecunia compellemur. Dissentiunt etiam hi in diesi arteriae, motum habitumque febris demonstrantis, uidelicet ridente Auicenna Galenum, diesis inuentorem. Ego tamen ingenium laudo Galeni, qui id tentauit, ideo quod puto posse fieri, ut deprehendatur. sed si Galenus eam re uera deprehendit, illum non imperitiorem musices, quam artis medicae fuisse iudico. Est enim haec res quamsimillima illi subtilitati, quam musici acutissime indagarunt in proportionum suarum inductionibus. Dissident & musici inter se, & quidem subtiliter. Aliqui unius consonantiae suauitatem & perfectionem, aliqui alterius extollentes. tum uero, quod difficilius est, rationem huius rei indagantes, quam haud dubie musici huius temporis non sunt inuenturi, nisi graece docti, ad bibliothecam summi Pontificis accedant, ubi (ut dictum est) multi sunt in re musica optimi libri. Ceterum hoc ausim dicere, nostros Britannos musicos, maxima ingenij subtilitate (si quis acutius rem introspiciat) illas quas uocant proportionum inductiones, inuenisse, & hac una re omnem antiquitatem superasse. Sed e diuerso illud miror, mag-

---

[7] mupsimus *1517*

"Still I don't approve of what Philippus Beroaldus [1] wrote about *theriaca* in his notes on Galen. For this is a case of the workman not using his own tools. Beroaldus is not in his own field. But I think Nicolaus Leonicenus [2] has left something written on this problem fit for scholars to hear. He was the most learned man anywhere, and his death was a great loss to learning. When he was alive, he used to argue brilliantly about this problem and criticize the general opinion of all recent doctors, who didn't know Greek and used to give *theriaca* to the sick although they didn't know how to prepare it properly.[3] When they heard of his criticism, they rose up against him with swords and clubs, but when they came in sight of him, they had to throw away their clubs and sheathe their swords. For all weapons of war gave way to the intelligence and learning of that man. Yet, remarkably enough, these new physicians couldn't bring themselves to follow what they knew was right even when moved by reason. They preferred to use their old *mumpsimus* [4] rather than Leonicenus'—or rather, Truth's —*sumpsimus*. When I asked some of my friends who attended Leonicenus' school the reason for this, they said, 'those doctors don't want to hurt the pharmacists, who would lose quite a bit if they threw out the old *theriaca,* which they have in great supply, and used this new preparation. And (God forbid) perhaps they agreed to give the doctors a cut of the profit.' [5]

"I see the whole thing now," I say. "We're being walked on, you, and I, and all the other sick people. Dishonest pharmacists and ignorant, greedy doctors kill us and get away with it, and (this's the ridiculous thing) we're forced to purchase our own death at great cost.

"Doctors also disagree about the diesis of the artery, showing the fluctuation and state of a fever, with Avicenna evidently laughing at Galen, who discovered diesis.[6] But I still praise the genius of Galen, who felt it, because I think it may still be detected. But if Galen really detected it, I think he knew as much about music as he did about the art of medicine. For this's very similar to the subtle distinctions musicians try hard to make in the inductions of their proportions.[7]

"Musicians also disagree among themselves, and subtly at that. Some extol the sweetness and perfection of one harmony, others of another. Then, with greater difficulty, they search for reasons for their opinion, which they're never going to find unless they know Greek. They can go to the Vatican Library where, as I've mentioned,[8] there're many excellent books on music. Yet I dare say, if one looks into it closely, our British musicians have found with great subtlety of mind those things they call the inductions of proportions, and in that one thing they've surpassed all antiquity. But on the other hand, I'm amazed

nam partem illorum nescire quod sciunt, & scire quod nesciunt. Iam
uero quanta sit inter astrologos & astrono-
Dissensio Astrologorum   mos (quos sicut in consensu, ita & in dis-
sensu copulabo) rixa, demonstrat Plinius
in historia naturali, quum ait, harum artium inconstantiam arguere
ipsas esse nullas. Inconstantia autem apud hos est haec, quod unus
alterius praeceptis non stat, sed hic in omni loco uult praescire futura,
ille nihil tentandum censet, nisi in suo orizonte & climate. His addam
arithmeticos, quorum hic est ἄσπονδος
Dissensio Arithmeticorum   πόλεμος, et implacabile bellum, uter numerus, par an impar, alteri sit praeferen-
dus. Nam unus, numero, inquit, deus impare gaudet. Alter hoc damnat
ut poeticum & tollit ultra sydera, senarij numeri paritatem, ideo quod
deus opus suum diuinum sex diebus (de quo alibi dicetur) compleuit.
Quid de oratoribus loquar? quorum tanta
Oratorum dissensio   est inter se diuersitas, ut ex illis decem
clarissimis graecis, nullus eodem dicendi
genere sit usus, sed hic uehemens & terrificus, ille simplex & suauis,
alius ciuilis & acutus, alius denique aliud (quod maxime approbauit)
dicendi genus delegit. At hi non modo in dicendi generibus inter se
dissenserunt, sed etiam turpiter in fide erga patriam ostendenda. Nam
reperti sunt quidam, qui quum in ardua
Facetum   causa, honorem & commodum patriae
tangente, publice esset orandum, prodie-
runt in publicum, collo & ceruicibus lana obuolutis, ut declararent
populo se anginam (morbum gutturis) pati, & ob id non posse loqui.
Quam technam aduersarij eorum illico odorati, Vos inquiunt, non
anginam, sed argyranchinam patimini, translato morbo in pecuniae
largitionem. quam illi reuera acceperant, ut postea se iactarunt, plus
accepisse ut tacerent, quam alios ut loquerentur. Ad ultimum, de grammaticis (adeo in omnibus & uerbis &
Dissensio grammaticorum   dictionibus dissident) piget loqui. Nam
aliqui admittunt uerba neutralia, aliqui
excludunt. Aliqui diphthongos in scribendo apponunt, aliqui detra-
hunt. Aliqui in scribendis dictionibus duplicibus utuntur literis, aliqui
simplicibus, adeo ut in ipsa quoque litera scribenda, dissensio sit inter

that most of them do not know what they know and know what they do not know.

"And now for the quarrel between the astrologers and astronomers, for I'll lump them together when they disagree just as I did when they agreed. Pliny shows how great it is in his *Natural History* [9] when he says, 'the changeableness of these arts proves that they are nothing.' Their changeableness is this: neither one abides by the rules of the other. Astrology always wants to know the future whereas Astronomy thinks that nothing should be tried except in its own horizon and climate.[1]

Disagreement of astrologers

"Next I'll add the arithmeticians. With them it's a matter of *aspondos polemos* [2] and implacable war whether odd or even numbers are the more valuable. For one camp says, 'God delights in odd numbers.' The other damns that as poetry and praises the proportion of the number six [3] beyond the stars because God completed his divine work in six days (which will be discussed elsewhere).

Disagreement of arithmeticians

"What should I say about orators? They differ so much that not one of the ten most famous Grecian orators used the same style of speaking. One was fierce and terrifying, another simple and sweet, another polite and shrewd, and still another chose another style that he liked best. And they differed from one another not only in their oratorical manner, but also, even more shamefully, in showing loyalty to their country. For there were certain orators who were called upon to speak in public on a difficult subject that had to do with the honor and profit of their country. When they appeared in public, they had their throat and neck wrapped in wool so they could tell the people they had the quinsey (a disease of the throat) and therefore couldn't talk. Their opponents immediately smelled out the trick and said, 'You don't have quinsey, you have silver-quinsey,' [4] changing the sickness into a money-bribe. And they in fact allowed as much since they boasted afterwards that they got more for keeping quiet than others got for talking.[5]

Disagreement among orators

A funny story

"And finally the grammarians. It irks me to speak of them because they disagree about everything, both words and phrases. For some admit neuter words,[6] some throw them out; some put in diphthongs, some take them out. Some use double letters, some single letters. They even disagree on how to write the word *letter* itself,

Disagreement of grammarians

eos, qualis est inter omnes & Aldum solum, in scribenda causa, nam is solus alteram addit s. Sed ut apertius ista intelligatis, nuper quum Paulus Bombasius, & Richardus Paceus de literis disputarent, casu inciderunt in orthographiam. Hic Paceus interrogat Bombasium, qua ratione fit, ut felix, ceterum, questio, scri-

Faceta

bantur a plerisque cum primis doctis, cum graeca diphthongo, & uerbum considero, cum y. Respondit Bombasius se nescire, addit Paceus se ignorare. Nec ullus, inquit, grammaticorum poterit mihi persuadere, ullam dictionem aut uerbum mere latinum, id est, nullo modo ex graeco deductum, admittere graecas diphthongos, uel y. quamquam de considero magis dubito, quod uideo Erasmvm nostrum sic scribere, & Morvm in castigata manu sua Vtopia, deleuisse i, & apposuisse y, in considero. Istud inquit Bombasius, aliquid est, quod illi peritissimi amici nostri sic scribunt, sed quid sit nescio, ego non sic scribo. Sed inter loquendum inquit, Pacee, illud mihi in mentem uenit, felix nullam omnino admittere diphthongum, nam memini me Romae in antiquissimis marmoribus, absque diphthongo scriptum saepius uidisse. Deamo te, inquit Paceus, mi Bombasi, de istis marmoribus antiquis. Quippe quibus ego longe maiorem fidem, quam omnibus recentioribus grammaticis adhibeam. Nam sicut in hoc erratum est, idem in reliquis quoque accidisse potuit, & nihil nobis praeter aliquod antiquum marmor deest, ad intelligendam ueritatem. Nam & marmor docuit Angelum Politianum scribere Vergilium, & non Virgilium, quod in usu quingentis ante annis fuerat. O quam marmoribus debemus. Sed pergamus ad reliqua. Iampridem Paceus grammaticum, in uia publica sibi occurentem, interro-

Quid sit bulla papalis

gat quid sit bulla papalis. Tum grammaticus paulisper apud se cogitans, & suspicatus in re trita aliquid esse scrupuli, Non succurrit, inquit, in praesenti, sed recta ibo domum & uidebo quid sit, in meo Catholicon, & cras hunc nodum tibi soluam. Placet, inquit Paceus. Verum interim tibi (si ita uidebitur) uolo meam opinionem aperire. Dic, inquit ille, libenter audiam. Βουλή,, inquit Paceus, id est, bule Graecis dicitur & consilium, & locus in quo consultatur (qui nunc nouo quidem, sed non inepto uocabulo consistorium uocatur, a

just like Aldus [7] disagrees with everyone else about how to write the word *causa* or *cause*, for he's the only one who adds a second *s*. But to make this clear—recently, when Paulus Bombasius and Richard Pace were discussing liberal education, they hit by chance on orthography. Pace then asked Bombasius why many people and especially learned men wrote *felix, ceterum, questio* with a Greek diphthong and the word *considero* with a *y*. Bombasius said he didn't know; Pace said he didn't either. 'But no grammarian,' he said, 'can persuade me that any purely Latin word or expression, that is, one not derived somehow from the Greek, should have Greek diphthongs or a *y*, although I'm somewhat doubtful about *considero* since I see my friend Erasmus wrote it that way, and More struck out the *i* and put in the *y* in *considero* when he was correcting the *Utopia* in his own hand.' [8]

Funny stories

"Bombasius said, 'that's something that those two expert friends of ours should write it like that, but I don't know why they do. I don't write it that way myself. But while you were talking, Pace,' he said, 'it occurred to me that *felix* should never have a diphthong, for I remember I've often seen it written on ancient marbles at Rome without the diphthong.'

" 'Dear Bombasius, I love you for those marbles,' Pace said. 'God knows, I put more faith in them than I do in all our new grammarians. For just as they made a mistake about this, they could do the same about other things, and we need only an ancient inscription to understand the truth. For it was an inscription that taught Angelus Politianus [9] to write *Vergil* and not *Virgil*, which was the way it was usually spelled for five hundred years before. God only knows what we owe to inscriptions.'

"But let's go on to the rest. A long time ago Pace met a grammarian on the street and asked him, 'What's a papal bull?'

What a papal bull is

"After thinking a little while and suspecting there was something tricky in such an easy question, he said, 'It doesn't occur to me at the moment, but I'll go straight home and look it up in my *Catholicon* [1] and let you know tomorrow.'

" 'That's fine,' said Pace. 'But meanwhile I want to tell you what I think it is, if you don't mind.'

" 'Go on,' he said. 'I'll listen gladly.'

" '*Boulê*,' Pace said, 'that is, *bule*, means in Greek both counsel and the place where the counsel is held. It is now known by the new but suitable term *consistory*, taken from *considendo, sitting together*. But

considendo) sed Latini more suo mutata e in a, bula dixerunt, ut fit a rhetorice & rhetorica. Et quia omnia summorum Pontificum decreta, non nisi suprema autoritate & consilio, tum illorum, tum totius sacri collegij emanant, nec emanare debent, haec omnia decreta, quae in literis apostolicis continentur, signo plumbeo roborata, bulae nominatae sunt, ac si diceres consilia ipsa perfecta, uere sancta, ecclesiastica, & ab ipso Christo proficiscentia. Atque hinc est, quod nulli hominum liceat has infringere, citra periculum animae damnandae.[8] Immo nec ipsis Pontificibus acta decessorum suorum rescindere, nisi nauicula Petri periclitetur, & ingruat bellum, ut nunc est. Nam tunc licet & bulas concessas reuocare, & omnia aliorum acta rescindere, ut decima uel duodecima exigatur ad defendendam ecclesiasticam libertatem, contra Christi & ecclesiae hostes, & iniquitatis & perditionis filios, qui uidentur quotidie pullulare. Sed uos grammatici addentes ignoranter alteram l, & ex bula facientes bullam, effecistis, ut nec illi qui quotidie scribunt bullas, intelligant quid sit. Ita ne? inquit grammaticus, Tu non nos solum, sed etiam ipsos summos Pontifices, ignorantia notare uideris. Non, inquit Paceus, non tam insanio, ut aliquem summum Pontificem, cum infimo grammatico coniungendum putem, immo nec uerbum factum est de Pontifice. Fateor, inquit ille, sed grammatici quoque suum habent acumen. De scriptoribus bullarum es locutus, & licet summus Pontifex non scribat, committit tamen ut scribantur, & qui per alium facit, per seipsum facere uidetur. Quid, inquit Paceus, hoc leguleium est? Studes ne tu legibus inscijs omnibus, sicut grammaticam publice profiteris? Non sum, inquit ille, iurista, sed hoc quod dixi, notaui ut prouerbium, & omnibus in ore. Credo, inquit Paceus, tibi (si Musis placet) de prouerbio, scio tamen non esse Erasmicum.[9] Sed ad rem. Acumen tuum o grammatice, quod mox ostentasti, hebetabo si potero, immo tollam & subuertam. Nam ego nec uolui, nec potui aliquid in summum dicere Pontificem, ideo quod quae audisti omnia, scripta mihi fuerunt sede uacante. Ad hoc, longe est a me alienissimum, ut uel male cogitem de summo (qui nunc uiuit) Pontifice. Quippe quem noui optimum & sanctissimae uitae car-

Laus summi Pontificis   dinalem, maximo omnium consensu, in
                               Pontificem maximum electum, nulla largitione, nulla symoniaca labe interposita, a maximis periculis, dei solius prouidentia conseruatum, inuictissimo Regi meo clarissimum patrem,

---

[8] damnandae, *1517*
[9] Erasmicum, *1517*

the Romans, after their fashion, changed the e to a and said *bula,* as in the case of *rhetorice* and *rhetorica.* And since all Papal decrees do not and should not proceed from anything but the greatest authority and deliberation—sometimes by the Popes themselves, sometimes by the entire sacred college—all the decrees contained in Apostolic letters and confirmed by a lead seal are called *bulls,*[2] as if to say the counsels themselves are perfect, truly holy, ecclesiastical, and derived from Christ Himself. And that's why no one can break them without danger of damning his soul. In fact the Popes themselves cannot rescind the acts of their predecessors without endangering Peter's ship and pro- voking war, as is now the case. For in that event they could revoke lawful bulls and rescind all acts of others.[3] So they could demand a tenth or a twelfth to defend ecclesiastical liberty against all enemies of Christ and the church and against the sons of inquity and perdition who sprout up every day. But you grammarians are ignorant and add another *l* to make *bull* from *bula.* And because of you those who write bulls every day don't know what they are.'

" 'Don't they?' the grammarian said. 'You seem to be branding the Popes themselves as ignorant and not just us.'

" 'No,' Pace said. 'I'm not so crazy that I think a Pope should be linked up with a low-class grammarian. In fact I wasn't speaking about the Pope.'

" 'Granted,' he said, 'but grammarians have some intelligence too. You've spoken of writers of bulls, and though the Pope doesn't actually write them, he nevertheless has them written. And whoever acts through another is regarded as acting on his own.'

" 'What a quibbler you are!' said Pace. 'You study every unknown law just as you teach grammar in the streets, don't you?'

" 'I'm no lawyer,' he said, 'but I've heard what I just said as a prov- erb on everybody's lips.'

" 'I believe you,' Pace said, 'about the proverb (if it please the Muses), but I know it's not one of Erasmus'.[4] But to the subject. That was a sharp point you made a minute ago, but I'll blunt it if I can. In fact I'll pick it up and turn it over. For I would not and could not say anything against the Pope since I wrote everything you heard while the throne was still vacant.[5] For that matter it's the furthest thing from my mind even to think anything bad about the Pope who's now living. For you see I knew him when he was an excellent cardinal who led a most holy life. He was elected Pope unanimously, with no bribery, no taint of   *Praise of the pope* simony about it. He has been saved from great dangers by the providence of God alone. He is the most glorious father of my unconquerable king and in short deserves well from me.'

de me denique ipso optime meritum. Interea dum haec Paceus est locutus, grammaticus uidebatur serio studere & meditari, & tandem euomuit
illud. Scio, inquit, nunc Pacee, quare in bulla altera 1. addita fuit. Quod
bonum, faustum. felixque sit, inquit Paceus, Dic rationem. Sicut, inquit,
religio modo cum una 1. modo cum duabus (teste Seruio) scribitur,
ita potest scribi & bulla. Scio, inquit Paceus, Seruium aliquid tale in
religio notare, causa carminis, sed de latina, non graeca dictione loquitur. Perge, perge ad tuum Catholicon, nam hoc totum, quod tam serio
a tam longo studio & meditatione effutiuisti, nihil est. Tum grammaticus recedens, & apud se sursurrans, Maledicaris, inquit, tu cum tua
bulla, quae me uituperauit in media uia.

Maledicaris barbare   Omnes, inquam, omnium aliarum scientiarum professores, inter se pertinaciter
contendunt. sed geometrae a sua quae omnia potest aequalitate, nunquam recedunt, nec aliquod unquam de illa inter ipsos oritur certamen, sed potius contrarium accidit, ut tum maxime & merito conten-
dant, quum aliquid est inaequale. Nam

Similitudo   sicut in rebus humanis quando sanctarum
legum aequabilitatis (quae isonomia di-
citur) nulla geritur cura, nec pauperi permittitur sua uti mediocritate,
ut diuiti sua effluere luxuria, maximi inter populum concitantur tumul-
tus, ita apud geometras si semel ab aequalitate disceditur, omnia
subuertuntur & pereunt. Nec quemquam in admirationem trahere debet, quod a Plinio meo iuniore scriptum est, nihil esse tam inaequale,
quam aequalitatem ipsam. Is enim illos damnat, quorum numerus est
aequalis, sed non prudentia. Nam de iniqua loquens condemnatione,
his utitur uerbis. Hoc pluribus uisum est, numerantur enim sententiae,
non ponderantur. Nec aliud in publico consilio potest fieri, in quo
nihil est tam inaequale quam aequalitas ipsa. Nam quum sit impar
prudentia, par omnium ius est. Hinc est quod quidam sapientissimi
uiri, reiectis quibusdam alijs scientijs, (quas nominare nolo) me praecipue in ciuitate sua doceri uoluerunt, ut adolescentes aequalitati assue-
scerent, qua in rebus humanis nihil potest esse conducibilius. Quin-
immo & deus ipse, quum uult hominem demonstrare, insigniter bonum
& honestum, ex me sumpta metaphora, templum suum appellat, ut in
scriptura, Templum dei estis uos. Quocirca non est mirum Platonem
dixisse ipsum deum γεωμετρεῖν, id est, esse geometram. Sed de mysticis
meis bonis satis est dictum, aggrediar iam illa quae apertiora sunt,

"Meanwhile, as Pace was saying that, the grammarian seemed to be thinking and meditating seriously and at last vomited this out. 'I know now, Pace,' he said, 'why another *l* was added to *bull.*'

" 'Tell me why,' Pace said, 'and good luck to you.'

"He said, 'Just as *religio* is written sometimes with one *l*, sometimes with two, according to Servius,[6] so also *bulla.*'

" 'I know,' Pace said, 'Servius wrote something like that about *religio* for the sake of meter, but he was talking about a Latin word, not a Greek. Go on, go look it up in your *Catholicon*. For all this that you've babbled out after such long, hard study is worth nothing.'

"Then the grammarian went away mumbling to himself and said, 'Damn you and your bull, shaming me like that in the middle of the street.' *Curses rudely*

"All professors of all other sciences, I say, dispute continuously among themselves, but geometricians never depart from their equitability, which is present in everything, and they never quarrel about it. Rather it's the opposite. When something is unequal, then they argue about it a good deal, and properly so. For just as in human affairs when no care is taken for the equality of the sacred laws (which is *Comparison* called *isonomia*) and the poor are not permitted to make use of their moderate means ôr the rich to pour out their excess, then there are great disturbances among the people. And so it is with geometricians. If one of them ever depart from equitability, everything is overthrown and destroyed. And no one should be surprised at what my dear Pliny the Younger wrote: 'nothing is so unequal as equality itself.'[7] He damns those who are equal in number but not in common sense, for he used those words in speaking of unjust condemnation. Many people are unjustly condemned, because opinions are counted but not weighed. It can't be otherwise in public decisions, where nothing is so unequal as equality itself. For although common sense is unequal, law is equal to all. That's why some wise men rejected certain other branches of learning (which I don't want to name) and wanted to have me in particular taught in their country so that the young people could become used to equality. Nothing could be more useful in human affairs. Yes, indeed. And when God Himself wants to point out a man who's particularly good and honorable, He takes His metaphor from me and calls him a temple, as in the Scripture,[8] 'You are the temple of God.' And so it's no wonder that Plato [9] said God Himself *geômetrein*, that is, is a geometer. But enough's been said about my mysterious properties. Let me go on now to things that are more open and familiar.

& magis trita. Meus alumnus fuit Archimedes ille Syracusanus, quo natura nihil mirabilius fecisse dicitur. Is enim primus omnium quadraturam circuli inuenit, quam Aristoteles omnis doctrinae uberrimus fons, ignorasse se fatetur. Eundem sphaerae quoque inuentorem aliqui tradunt. Sed scientia geometrica praecipue & mirifice floruit, adeo ut pene uires humani ingenij longe superent, quae ab eo facillime omnibus spectantibus, facta fuisse constat. Solebat enim (quod & Titus Liuius notat) omni quantumuis graui mole, in aere ceu pila ludere. Quomodo, nescio qui, his uestris temporibus polliciti sunt maximis Pontificibus, se facile de loco, in quo sita est, in alium transportaturos illam ingentem pyramidem, quae adhuc Romae uisitur, & in cuius summo, urna est affixa, Iulij Caesaris cineres, ut imperiti sed non docti, credunt, continens, quae acus sancti Petri, quod tendat perpetuo in acutum, uulgo nominatur. Sed nullus eorum quod promisit, persoluere potuit, nimirum ob imperitiam doctrinae geometricae, quam magis ostentarunt quam norunt. Sed redeamus ad Archimedem. Quum ciuitas Syracusana ab hostibus obsideretur, naues hostiles miranda arte, id est, geometrica, in ciuitatem nullo negocio traxit. Ego enim illa sum quae machinas aptas ad remouendas & transportandas haud difficulter quammaximas moles, excogitaui. Ego tecta, fastigia, culmina superstruere, lapides adaptare, trabes mira arte ad mensuram (unde nomen mihi est, Latinis enim metiendi scientia uocor) coniungere docui, quibus rebus non solum uniuerso generi humano prosum, sed deum quoque ipsum, & omnes caelites honoro. Quippe quum nullum templum, nulla aedes, nullum sacellum, his nisi me ministra, construatur. Nec solum aedificandi uiam doceo, sed etiam bene aedificandi, adeo ut obstructis artificiose, uel minimis rimis, nunquam in eorum capita possit pluere uel ningere. Quod si aliquando accidit, id non mihi imputandum est, neque bono & perito architecto,

Iocus   sed malo & indocto sacerdoti, qui mauult sacram aedem, una cum sancto, cui est dicata, aequatam uidere solo, quam uel obolum ad eam tempestiue instaurandam insumere. Sane notandum est, Achimedem non minus in me dispexisse diuinitatis, quam Platonem, dicentem deum esse geometram. Nam is capta ciuitate sua, ipsi uitae figuram geometricam anteposuit. Erat enim adeo oculis, animo, & cogitatione, quibusdam suis descriptis in puluere lineamentis intentus, ut nec discurrentes hostes, nec captam ciuitatem senserit. Quum uero repente miles quidam nequissimus astitisset, iussissetque ut sese ad M. Marcellum Romano-

"Archimedes of Syracuse was one of my nurslings, and they say that Nature made nothing more remarkable than he. For he was the first to discover the square of the circle, which Aristotle himself, that rich fountain of all learning, confessed he did not know.[1] Some say that Archimedes also discovered the sphere.[2] But he was particularly good in geometry, for everyone who saw him agreed that the things he did so easily almost surpassed the power of human understanding. As Titus Livius noted,[3] he used to play with all sorts of weights in the air, no matter how heavy, as though they were balls. Similarly, some people in our own time—I don't know who they were—promised the Popes they could easily move a huge pyramid from one place to another.[4] It was the same pyramid you can still see at Rome, with Julius Caesar's ashes in an urn on top—according to the ignorant, but not the learned—the one the people call St. Peter's Needle because it tapers to a fine point. But no one who promised to move it was able to, no doubt because they were unskilled at geometry, which they pretended to know more about than they actually knew.

"But let's return to Archimedes. When the city of Syracuse was besieged by its enemies, he drew the enemies' ships into the city [5] by a miraculous art—that is, by Geometry. For I'm the one who invented machines suitable for removing and transporting such great weights easily. I taught people how to build houses, roofs, and rooftrees, how to fit stones together and join beams in a wonderful way by measuring (which is how I got my name, for the Romans call me *metiendi scientia,* the science of measuring). And in all those things I'm not only useful to the entire human race, I also do honor to God and all the heavenly host. Obviously, since no church, no shrine, no chapel is built without my help. I teach people not only how to build things, but how to build them well, so that they skilfully seal even the slightest cracks, and it can never rain or leak on their heads. But if it ever does, I'm not to blame, and neither is the good and experienced architect. It's the fault of the   *Joke* bad and unlearned priest who'd rather see the shrine leveled to the ground along with the saint it's dedicated to, than spend one penny on repairing it on time.

"Actually, it should be noted that Archimedes saw as much divinity in me as Plato when he said that God was a geometer. For when his city was captured, he valued a geometrical figure more than his life.[6] For he was so absorbed, in sight, mind, and soul, on certain diagrams he had drawn in the dirt, that he was not aware of the enemy running here and there or of the capture of the city. In fact, when some totally worthless soldier suddenly stood in front of him and ordered him to

rum Imperatorem sequeretur, (qui iam iusserat, ut uni omnino Archi-
medi, doctrinae causa parceretur) morari paululum rogauit, donec
rem propositam inuestigaret. Quo contemptu percitus miles, stricto
gladio eum perfodit.[1] Imperatore tamen ita aegre id ferente, ut dicatur
maiorem dolerem de illius morte, quam gaudium de capta urbe conce-
pisse, adeo omnem dignitatem suam, honorem & gloriam nobilissimae
doctrinae post habendam iudicauit. At dixerit quispiam, o Geometria,
quis est qui te hodie profitetur? neglecta uideris ab omnibus fere.
Fateor, inquit Geometria, uel nullos, uel perpaucos his diebus me pro-
fiteri. Atque id merito, ideo quod non intelligunt uel minimam partem
illorum, quae de me antiqui posteris tradiderunt. E quorum numero est
Euclides, cuius ingenij clarissima adhuc extant monimenta. Verum
enimuero illud insigniter est in me spectandum, quod nescientes, im-
prudentesque me homines utuntur, quodque ego (quae mea est erga
humanum genus humanitas) facile passa sum, ut ex singulari scientia
& doctrina, in usum quotidianum, & experientiam conuerterer. Quo

Sententia

factum est, ut uiluerim magis, nam assi-
duitas experiendi, paulatim subtrahit ad-
mirationis incitamentum. At uobis o probi
& studiosi iuuenes, non tam quod est, quam quod esse debet, est considerandum. Nam si omnia bona, quae humana negligentia in deterius
abierunt, penitus negligerentur, perirent nimis cito uirtutes omnes, &
humanum genus a bestijs non differret. Proinde nihil est hominibus
conuenientius, quam ut in id totis uiribus incumbant, ut omnia praeclara, in quibus primum locum obtinet doctrina, restituantur, nec sinant
illa perire bona, quibus solis homines fiunt, & brutorum feritatem

Fructus geometriae,
aequalitatem seruare,
& commode habitare

exuunt. Antiquitus quando tam magna
erat sapientum copia, quam nunc est
inopia, diligenter sunt intuiti, quantum
ego in commune omnibus hominibus prosum, & fructum longe pulcherrimum &
utilissimum ex me prouenientem (de quo paulo ante locuta sum)
maximi fecerunt. Ac ut debitum nomini meo honorem non detraherent,
me inter mathemata primam (absit arrogantia uerbis) numerarunt.
Mathemata autem sunt doctrinae & scientiae per excellentiam nominatae, eo quod sunt clarae, alijs multo certiores, atque omni numero
perfectae. Quum haec nouissima uerba altiori uoce, & rotundo ore pro-

---

[1] perfodit, *1517*

follow him to M. Marcellus, the Roman General, he asked him to wait
a little while until he had investigated the problem before him. And
although the General had ordered his men to spare the one and only
Archimedes because of his learning, the soldier became incensed with
his contempt and drew his sword and ran him through. But the General
took it so hard that he said he felt more sorrow over the death of that
one man than pleasure over the capture of the entire city. For he considered that his own reputation was of less importance than the honor
and glory of noble learning.

"'But,' someone might say, 'who teaches you today, Geometry?
Almost everyone seems to neglect you.'

"That's true," said Geometry. "No one, or almost no one teaches me
these days. And rightly so, for they don't even know the little things
about me the ancients handed down to posterity. Euclid was one of
them.[7] There're glorious monuments of his intellect still standing. Yet,
you have to note one thing about me in particular: ignorant, unknow-
ing men make use of me, and I'm so kind to the human race that I
readily let them transform me from an extraordinary science and field
of learning into something used every day and learned by experience.
In that way I cheapened myself even more, for constant use little by
little takes away the inducement to won-
der. But you studious and upright boys   *A wise saying*
should consider not what is, but what
ought to be. For if all good things that have fallen into a worse state
through human indifference were completely neglected, all virtues
would quickly perish, and men would be no different from beasts.
Therefore, there's nothing more suitable for men than to strive with all
their might to restore all those glories, the most important of which is
learning. They should not let them be lost, for it's through them alone
that they become men and put off the
wildness of beasts. In ancient times, when   *Benefit of geometry, to preserve*
the number of wise men was as great as   *equality and to be housed*
the dearth of them is now, they carefully   *properly*
considered how much good I did to all
men in general, and they prized highly the handsome and useful benefit that I afforded (which I spoke about a little while ago). And not to
detract from the honor due my name, they counted me as the first of
the branches of mathematics. But I don't want to brag. The branches
of mathematics, however, have been called the sciences and fields of
learning *par excellence* because they're so clear, much more exact than
the others, and perfect down to the last number."

nunciarentur, prodijt in conspectum Arithmetica. Et quia de numero,
inquit, nonnihil audiui, non possum me
Arithmetica loquitur   continere, quin me quoque aliquid inter
scientias esse ostendam. Est enim mihi
numeralis uel numerandi scientia, latinum nomen, Graece uocor Arithmetica, quo nomine Latini libentius utuntur quam suo. Illud autem
aliud nomen, quo ignari literaturae graecae, immo latinae, Arsmetricam
me uocant, quum nec graecum, nec latinum, sed plusquam barbarum,
& plane ociosum sit, non agnosco. Discant itaque nunc Arithmeticen me
uocari, & praeteritum errorem condonabo. Ac nomine meo recte cog-
nito, de uiribus & potentia mea pauca disseram, ut quomodo ex ungue
totus (quod dici solet) leo cognoscitur, sic & uos ex paucis, quae pro-
feram, animo uidere & complecti reliqua possitis. Considerate igitur, o
optimi iuuenes, nihil esse, siue in diuinis, siue in humanis rebus, quod
ad numeros, ex quibus equidem tota consto, non refertur. Deus enim
ipse, quem siue ut unum, siue ut omnia, siue ut unum & omnia (id
quod est) contempleris, meam ornat unitatem. Vnde quidam philosophi, monada illum nominarunt. hinc etiam illud apud graecos effluxisse
uidetur, ἕν τὸ πᾶν, id est, unum & uniuersum idem esse. Non imperite
igitur senserunt, qui numerum omnia complecti contenderunt, a quibus
Pythagorici non uidentur dissensisse. Vt qui quoties aliquid sanctius &
religiosius affirmare uoluerunt, hoc iureiurando uti sint soliti, μὰ τὴν
ἡμετέραν τετρακτὺν, id est, non ita esse nostrum iuramus numerum
quaternarium. nostrum ideo uocantes, quod ei omnia tribuerent, nimirum quatuor elementorum uim, ex quibus omnia constant, intuentes &
suspicientes. Praeterea in figura quadrangulari, nescio quae admiranda
inuenerunt mysteria, ad sanitatem humani corporis tuendam condu-
centia. Porro ternarium numerum, non solum philosophorum acuta
ingenia laude extulerunt, & caeteris ideo perfectiorem iudicarunt, quod
principium, medium, & finem contineat, sed ipsa quoque diuina & in-
diuidua trinitas, incomparabile illi ornamentum affert. Ad hoc, quina-
rium numerum, quinque nostri humani sensus, & quinque digiti, tam
manuum quam pedum, conspicuum reddunt, sicut & senarim quaedam
perfectio, quae in alijs numeris non repereris. Perficitur enim suismet
partibus in summam ductis, id est, uno, duobus, & tribus. Atque hinc
est, quod deus ipse (ut sacrarum literarum autores tradunt) [2] illa sua
diuina in mundi creatione opera, sex diebus compleuit. Nam in sep-

---

[2] ttadunt) *1517*

When Geometry said these last words in a louder voice than usual and in an orotund style, Arithmetic came in sight. "I just heard you say something about numbers," she said, "and I couldn't
stop myself from showing that I'm of some account among the sciences. For my Latin name is *numeralis* or *numerandi scientia*, the *numerical science* or *science of numbering*. In Greek I'm called *Arithmetica*, a term the Romans use more freely than their own. But I don't acknowledge that other name—*Arsmetric*—that people call me who don't know Greek or even Latin. For it's neither Greek nor Latin; but rather an obviously superfluous barbarism.[8] So let them know that I'm now called *Arithmetica*, and I'll forgive their past mistake.

"Now that my name's straight, I'll say a few words about my strength and ability. And just as you can tell a whole lion from the claw (as they say),[9] so from the few things I mention you'll be able to see the rest in your mind's eye and understand them. Consider, therefore, you fine young men, that there's nothing either human or divine that doesn't have to do with numbers, which is what I'm entirely made up of. For God Himself lends glory to my unity, whether you regard Him as one, or as many, or as one and many, which He is. That's why certain philosophers term Him *the monad;* [1] and hence the phrase *hen to pan* (that is, the one and the many are the same) seems to have been current with the Greeks.[2] The people who contended that everything's made up of numbers were correct, therefore, and the Pythagoreans seem to have agreed with them. Whenever they wanted to affirm something solemnly and religiously, they ordinarily used this oath: *ma tên hêmeteran tetraktyn*, that is, we swear by our quaternary number that this is not so.[3] They called it *ours* because they attributed everything to it; for they were amazed by and truly admired the power of the four elements, which everything is composed of. Moreover, they found in quadrilangular figures no telling what wonderful mysteries [4] helpful in maintaining the health of the human body. Furthermore, brilliant philosophers praised the number three and considered it more perfect than the rest not only because it has a beginning, middle and end, but also because the divine and indivisible Trinity lent an incomparable adornment to it. In addition, our five human senses and our five fingers and toes make the number five noteworthy, just as there is a certain perfection in the number six that you don't find in other numbers. For it's made up of the sum of each of its parts—that is, the numbers one, two, and three. And that's why God Himself (as the writers of the Bible say) completed that divine work of His, the creation of the world, in six days. For the seventh day is for rest, prefiguring that

timo requies dei commendatur, denotans illam sempiternam requiem, omnibus bene, & ex praeceptis Christi uiuentibus, ab immortali deo repositam. Est enim & septenarius perfectus quidem, sed alia ratione. Nam ex ternario toto impari, & quaternario toto pari constat, & ideo pro uniuerso saepe ponitur in scriptura sacra, teste diuo Augustino. sicuti est, Septies cadet iustus, & resurget, id est quotiescunque ceciderit, non peribit. Et, septies in die laudabo te. quod alibi alio modo dictum est, Semper laus eius in ore meo. Huic denique septiformis illa diuina gratia, nihil non tribuit. Item octonarius numerus superbum uendicauit sibi prouerbium, & uult ut omnia dicantur octo. Graece enim dicitur ἅπαντ' ὀκτώ. sed unde hoc adagium ductum sit, ignoramus & nos, una cum ERASMO uiro doctissimo, & prouerbiorum patre. Et donec inueniamus meliora, credamus his quae ipse in aenigmate diuinauit, & interim rideamus una cum illo

Ridiculum   Heliogabalum Imperatorem, qui huic prouerbio omnia tribuens, solebat simul ad coenam inuitare octo canos, octo luscos, octo podagrosos, octo surdos, octo nigros, octo praelongos, & octo praepingues, hoc uno errans, quod magnus princeps, octo quoque morionum, & totidem scurrarum sit oblitus. Est & alijs quoque numeris sua proprietas & in proprietate perfectio. Nam in me, quocunque te uer-

Fructus Arithmetices, semper   tas, nihil, nisi quod uel hac, uel illa
respicere ad perfectionem   ratione perfectum est, uidebis. de quibus in praesentia ideo tacebo, quod Paceus constituit longe plura exactius de numeris scribere, ad quam rem perficiendam, multa iam in collectaneis parata habet. Interim autem illa uobis sufficiant, primo quod in laudibus ipsius dei dictum sit, non a quouis autore, aut quouis libro, sed ab ipso Salomone in libris Sapientiae, non sine magna ratione & mysterio, Omnia in mensura, numero, & pondere disposuisti. Deinde quod nihil potest doctrinam arithmeticam magis commendare, quam quod quoties uiri sapientes & docti uolunt aliquid ex omni parte absolutissimum esse demonstrare, non possunt maiori emphasi & expressius id eloqui, quam quum dicunt, id omni numero perfectum esse. Immo & natura ipsa docet quanti ego aestimanda sum, quippe quae omnibus hominibus cupiditatem mei, id est, perfectionis, ingenerasse uidetur. nam pueri adhuc, quum per aetatem rationem iam gustant, ad altiora tendentes, a me incipiunt, & citra praeceptorem discunt (ut Flaccus ait),[3] ludere par impar. Quanta uero

---

[3] ait,) *1517*

eternal rest reserved by immortal God for all those who live good lives according to the precepts of Christ. There's also a certain perfection in the number seven,[5] but for another reason. For it's made up of the number three, which is completely odd, and the number four, which is completely even, and so it's often used in the Bible as the universal number. Witness St. Augustine: ' "A just man falleth seven times and riseth up again," that is, no matter how often he falls, he will not perish. And "Seven times a day I praise thee," which has been said elsewhere in a different way: "His praise shall continually be in my mouth." ' And finally, divine grace, which is sevenfold,[6] adds no little bit to this number. Similarly, the number eight claims a proud proverb for itself and wants everything to be called eight. For it's said in Greek *hapant' oktô;* but where this proverb came from I don't know and neither does Erasmus, that extremely learned man, the father of proverbs. And until we find a better explanation, let's believe what Erasmus surmised[7] and laugh with him at the Emperor Heliogabalus, who swallowed the proverb whole, and used to ask to dinner at the same time eight old *Something stupid* men, eight men with one eye, eight men with gout, eight deaf, eight black, eight tall, and eight very fat men. He was wrong about only one thing, that great Prince. He forgot to have eight clowns and the same number of fools.

"Other numbers also have their own properties and in their properties their own perfections. For wherever you turn you'll see nothing in me that's not *Benefit of arithmetic, to* perfect for one reason or another. But I'll *contemplate perfection always* be quiet about them for the moment since Pace has agreed to write much more in a more precise way about numbers.[8] And in preparation for it, he has already taken many notes. Till then these should be enough for you: first, that Solomon himself in the Books of Wisdom,[9] and not just any author in any book, said, 'Thou hast arranged all things by measure and number and weight,' and he said it not without great profundity and mystery. Second, that nothing can recommend the field of arithmetic more than the fact that whenever wise and learned men want to show that something is perfect in all of its parts, they can't express it more clearly or emphatically than by saying that it's perfect in all of its numbers.[1] Yes, indeed. Nature herself teaches how valuable I am. In fact, the desire for me—that is, the desire for perfection—seems to be innate in all men. For when they're still boys, at an age when they enjoy counting, they yearn for something better and begin with me, and as Flaccus says, they learn to play odds or even without a teacher.[2] The strength of the desire for

perfectionis uis (cui ego dominor) sit, hinc patet, quod nullus unquam
modo ingenium haberet, nisi in rebus optimis & excellentissimis eam
quesiuit. Nam in malis, uel uilibus rebus eum querere, stulti, immo insani est. Vnde Alexandri Magni iudicium uehementer est laudandum,
qui unum manu certissima & nunquam aberrante, grana ciceris in
acum inserentem, non nisi modio ciceris donabat, nempe deridens tan-
tam in re tam parua & humili perfectionem, quod Plato quoque fecit
in illo auriga, qui eo spectante, nunquam aberrauit ab orbita. Cauete
ergo o studiosi adolescentes, ne fidem Lycurgo illi Lacedaemonio
adhibeatis, hoc uno plane insanienti,
Arithmetica contra Lycurgum quod me, ceu turbulentam, e ciuitate sua
legumlatorem eijciendam censuit. Nam is adeo erat
legum formulis, controuersijs, & litibus
districtus, ut me ne summo quidem digito unquam attigerit, & nihil
omnino praeter suas odiosas leges sciuerit. Nec tam ratio illum quam
inuidia ad istam iniuriam mihi inferendam concitauit. Semper enim
mihi meam perfectionem inuidit, & quod uno modo, sicut res diuinae,
semper me habeo.[4] A quibus longissime ipsius leges abesse uidentur.
Nam modo uetus lex habet locum, modo noua conditur, modo anti-
quata in multorum hominum perniciem profertur. Inuidit mihi & simplicitatem, nam apud omnes gentes bis duo conficiunt quatuor sine
controuersia, sed iurisperiti Lycurgi discipuli, in singulis oppidis &
ciuitatibus, unius quantumuis paucorum uerborum legis, innumeras
excogitarunt interpretationes, & illa semper praeualet, quae citius
loculos est oneratura. Vnde & inter Germanum Theologum & iurisconsultum iampridem (ut audiui) maxima
Contentio inter Theologum orta est contentio, in aula principis, Theo-
& Iurisconsultum logo in haec uerba prorumpente. Istum,
inquit, uersipellem, omnium legum cor-
ruptelam, & spoliatorem paupertatis, non pudet laborare, ut mihi ante-
ponatur, & principem adeat, me excluso, qui sacra imbutus Theologia,
nihil aliud tracto quam bibliam, & diuinos libros, Christum & eius Apostolos semper in ore habeo, & uerbum dei ad populum praedico. Ad haec
iurisconsultus, toruo uultu, & colaphos minitanti similis, Tace, inquit,
in malam rem o Scotista, quid damnas leges, earumque peritos? tu ille
es qui corrumpis populum, non nos. tu Curios simulas, & bacchanalia
uiuis. Spoliare populum uocas, mercedem magnorum capere laborum.
De tuis sunt qui spoliant populum, qui postquam indixerunt bellum

---

[4] habeo, *1517*

perfection (which I control) is obvious in this: that no one would ever have any talent unless he searched for it in the best and finest things. To search for it in bad or worthless things is stupid, or rather, crazy. That's why we should praise very highly the judgment of Alexander the Great.[3] When someone stuck pea seeds in the eye of a needle with a steady hand that never shook, he gave him nothing but a peck of peas for his reward, obviously making fun of such perfection in such a small and insignificant thing. Plato [4] did the same thing in the case of the charioteer who never swerved from the track while he watched him.

"Take care, therefore, O students. Do not put your faith in Lycurgus the Lacedaemonian,[5] who was obviously crazy in this one thing. He thought that I should *Arithmetic against Lycurgus the Lawgiver* be thrown out of his country as though I were a troublemaker. He was so taken up with lawsuits, controversies, and litigations, that he never touched me even with the tip of his finger. He knew absolutely nothing except his own odious laws, and he was driven to inflict that injury on me not so much by reason as by envy. For he always envied me my perfection and also the fact that I always behave the same, just like something divine, and his laws seemed to be far removed from that. An old law is in force at one moment, then a new one is established, then an antiquated one is dug up to ruin many people. And he envied me my simplicity, for all nations completely agree that two times two makes four. But the disciples of Lycurgus, experts in law in separate towns and cities, think up innumerable interpretations of a single law, no matter how few words it has, and the one that prevails is always the one that fills his pockets the quickest.

"That's why (as I've heard) there was a great argument a while back between a *Argument between a theologian and a lawyer* German theologian and a lawyer in a prince's court. The theologian burst out: 'That double-dealer,' he said, 'that corrupter of the law and robber of the poor, he's not ashamed to work against me. He gets to see the Prince when I'm not allowed to— me! full of sacred theology! I treat nothing but the Bible and divine books. I always have Christ and His Apostles on my lips, and I preach the word of God to the people.'

"At that the lawyer, with a wild look, as if he was going to hit him with his fist, said, 'Shut up, you goddamn Scotist! Why do you damn the law and its practitioners? You're the one who ruins the people, not me. You pretend you're a Curius [6] but your life is an orgy. What you call robbing the people is simply the reward we receive for our hard work. You're the ones who rob the people. After you've declared war

pecuniae, amplissimas sunt consecuti diuitias. & ut suam manifestam
faciant hypocrisin, quia prohibitum est pecuniam tangere manu,
dimissa manica tecta, uel in linea fasciola, uel sudario capiunt, si desit
scilicet minister, cui licet eorum nomine, etiam nuda manu ingentem
colligere thesaurum. Vnde Pontifex Maximus iampridem prudentissime
(ut omnia) fecit, qui etiam a mendicantibus, decimam colligendam
decreuit. Quid tibi cum principe est agendum? Princeps nec syllogis-
mos tuos, nec questiunculas Scoticas nouit. Sine me adire, nec de
Christo, nec de Apostolis nunc est loquendum. Agitur causa utilitatis
imperatoriae, ignarus es rerum, nescis uti foro, importunus esset accessus tuus. Hic theologus, non tam uerba quam uerbera timens, erat pene
extra se. Tum circunstantes, audaciam & uerbositatem iurisconsulti,
omni praeferentes Theologiae, coeperunt ironice consolari Theologum,
& illi praesertim, qui opera iurisconsulti, in fraudulenta lite indigebant.
O domine frater, haec aequo animo ferenda sunt.[5] Hic est magnus uir,
hunc princeps amat, quod ipsius utilitati (cuius ratio semper habenda
est) semper studeat. Tum Theologus derideri se, & ludibrio esse omnibus non ignorans, retrocessit, & murmurans apud se filios perditionis &
satanae, atque omnem psalmum Deus laudem, in illos recitans, coniecit
se in angulum. Sed ad rem redeundum est. Qui fieri potest, ut ego nisi
per inscitiam, ceu turbulenta male audiam? quippe quum e contrario
maximorum dissidiorum, in omnibus locis tollendorum, sim studiosis-
sima, nam saepissime (quod scitis) in ciuitatibus, & alibi, grauissime
de re pecuniaria, praesertim inter mensarios, dissensiones oriuntur. Nec
prius sedantur, quam hic aut ille alta uoce clamet, Producantur libri
rationum, conferantur, computentur.[6] Quod simul atque iuste factum
est, e uestigio omnis lis dirimitur, nisi si qui sunt, qui malunt pugnare,
quam soluere, cum quibus mihi nihil est commune. Ego itaque non
turbelas in ciuitatibus concito (ut Lycurgus putauit) sed sedo potius,
& omnia placo. Nec immerito libri mei,
Libri rationum libri rationum nominantur, ideo, quia
quantum ratio postulat, tantum unicuique

---

[5] sunt, *1517*
[6] computetur. *1517*

on money, you pile up great wealth. And, to make plain your hypocrisy, since you're forbidden to touch money with your hand,[7] you take it with a long sleeve covering your hand, or in a linen neckerchief, or handkerchief. But that's only if the attendant's not there who's allowed to collect the huge treasure for you with his bare hands. That's why the Pope [8] acted very prudently a while ago (as always) when he decreed that tithes should be collected even from beggars. What business do you have with the Prince? The Prince doesn't know anything about your syllogisms or your Scotistic quibbles. Let me approach his Highness. This is not the time to talk about Christ or His Apostles. When it's a question of Imperial business, you don't understand anything; you don't know how to handle affairs of state.[9] It would be unsuitable for you to approach him.'

"With that the theologian was almost beside himself with fear, not of what he said, but of physical violence. The bystanders preferred the boldness and verbosity of the lawyer to any theology, and they began to console the theologian ironically, especially those who needed the lawyer to help them in fraudulent lawsuits. 'O brother *domine*,' they said, 'you ought to bear all that with a calm mind. This is a great man; the Prince loves him because he's always on the lookout for ways to help him (and that's always something that has to be taken into account).'

"Then the theologian went on back, knowing that he was a joke and a laughing stock to everyone. And mumbling to himself 'sons of perdition and the Devil,' and reciting the whole psalm *Deum Laudem*,[1] he threw himself in the corner.

"But to return to the subject. How can I have a bad reputation, as if I were a troublemaker, except through ignorance? On the contrary, I'm extremely eager to remove great disagreements everywhere. For as you know serious quarrels occur most often, in cities and elsewhere, over money matters, especially among bankers. They no sooner sit down than one or another of them yells out in a loud voice, 'Let's see the accounts. Compare them and add them up.' As soon as that's properly done, the whole dispute is solved on the spot, unless they're the sort of people who would rather fight than settle things, and with them I've nothing in common. So I don't stir up trouble as Lycurgus thought; rather I settle and smooth over everything. My books are called *libri rationum*,[2] account books, for a good reason. It's because whatever amount of reckoning or reason (*ratio*) is needed, that's the amount I give to every single one.

Account books

tribuo. Ad haec, quanto usui ego quotidie in uniuersum omnibus sim, non est opus multis uerbis commemorem. Nemo est qui non libentissime scire cupit sua expensa & accepta, & qui per fortunas suas potest, unum aliquem in arithmetica expertum, etiam mercede conducit. cui si oblata merces exigua uidebitur, illico qui conducit, blandis uerbis ultra mercedem, montes quoque auri pollicetur, quorum tamen (quia animus uerbis non respondebat) nihil unquam est praestiturus, sed fidelem ministrum, sectatorem meum, iuxta uulgatum prouerbium, tanquam perpetuario utitur asino, nisi si cui foecundior afflarit fortuna. Ceterum huic plerunque tota cura domestica committitur, propterea quod honesti & frugi homines habentur, qui mei sunt periti. Magni autem mercatores & mensarij, nisi tales multos domi nutrirent, longe facilius, citiusque quam nunc faciunt, decoquerent. Sed de his quae domi fiunt, satis est dictum. Si peregre tibi eundum sit, a nullo xenodochio, aut itineraria [7] mansione prius abire permitteris, quam uoceris ad calculum, & tunc nisi habeas aliquem mei callentissimum, maxima exhibebitur tibi molestia, ut taceam damnum. Hac in re non possum non laudare diligentiam Germanorum hospitum, qui

De gypso Germanorum   gypsum in loculis semper ad supputandum paratam habent, nec fere unquam aliud agunt, id quod hinc patet, quod mensas illorum semper gypsatissimas reperies. Hi & ludentes gypso utuntur. Haec enim notat quod lucri est, & quod perit. Comedunt denique & bibunt ad gypsum, nam omnes qui exhauriuntur canthari uini (qui multi sunt) caelo, ut ipsi aiunt, ita postulante, gypso signantur, itidem & fercula. Quo fit, ut ad gypsum quoque soluatur, & gypsus recipientem laetum, numerantem uero tristem reddat. Vt dicam in summa, nullus illic habetur frugi homo, qui non habet gypsum in crumena, & si gypsus errat, mauult alieno damno errare quam suo. Verum non omnes in numerandi ratione gypso utuntur, nam apud hos calculi sunt in usu, apud illos aenea nomismata, apud alios calamus, describens figuras numerarias, quod genus nunc laudatissimum habetur, sicut apud Priscos ratio illa numerandi per digitos, quae posteriore aetate adeo exoleuit, ut aeque uobis atque Paceo cognitam esse nunc iudicem. Illud solum, o iuuenes addam, ut diligenter attendatis, omnem perfectionem ex me procedere. quam ut omnes uos cum in me, tum omni alia doctrina & scientia assequamini, deum immortalem precor. Quum in hunc modum Arith-

---

[7] iteneraria *1517*

"In addition, I need only a few words to mention how useful I am to everyone in the world every day. There's no one who doesn't want to know his expenses and income, and anyone who can afford it can hire someone who knows quite a bit about arithmetic. If the pay he's offered seems too little, the man who hires him will quickly promise him in winning words mountains of gold besides his pay. But he'll never pay him anything because what he intends to do doesn't agree with what he says. He uses my faithful servant, my follower, like the everlasting ass in the popular proverb,[3] unless fortune smiles on him more favorably than it has. Besides, the fellow who knows arithmetic has almost all the responsibility of the household because people who know something about me are considered honest and thrifty. And if great merchants and bankers didn't keep many people like that in their houses, they would go broke much more easily and much more quickly than they do. But that's enough about domestic affairs.

"If you have to travel, you won't be allowed to leave the hotel or inn until you've called for the bill. And then unless you have someone with you who knows quite a bit about me, you'll have a great deal of trouble, not to mention the money you'll lose. In this connection I can't praise enough the carefulness of the German innkeepers, who always have a piece of chalk in their pockets to total things up.[4] They hardly do anything   *The Germans' chalk* else, and that's why you'll always find their tables covered with chalk. They also use chalk to play games with, marking down how much is won or lost. And finally they eat and drink according to chalk. For every tankard of wine they drink is chalked up (and there're many since, as they say, heaven itself requires it), and they do the same thing with their food. You could even say the check is paid with chalk, and it's chalk that makes the one who gets the money happy and the one who pays it sad. In short, no one's thought to be thrifty in Germany unless he has chalk in his pocket. And if the chalk makes a mistake, he'd prefer the other party to lose the money instead of himself. But everyone doesn't use chalk to keep his accounts, for some of them use pebbles, others pennies, and others reed pens which they use to jot down the figures, and that's the method most people prefer nowadays, just as the ancients used to count on their fingers, which in later times became so obsolete that I suppose you know as much about it as Pace.[5]

"I'll add only this, boys: note carefully that I'm the source of all perfection, and I pray to immortal God that all of you will pursue perfection not only in me, but also in all other learning and science."

metica [8] perorasset, ecce nobilissima Rhetorica, Vix tandem, inquit, &
mihi meus erit dicendi locus, quanquam

De Rhetorica   nec meus quidem, utpote ultimus, quandoquidem possem iure optimo primum
mihi uendicare. Verum tam aliena sum ab omni fastu & ostentatione,
tantaque modestia praedita, ut aequissimo animo feram, omnes has
scientias in semetipsis explicandis & ornandis, bonis meis, id est, arte
dicendi & eloquentia usas esse. Nulla etenim laus maior mihi tribui
potest, quam quod sine me nemo potest laudari recte, uel Phaedra
Romano eruditissimo uiro iudice, qui per

De Phaedra   summam omnium auditorum admirationem, tot Maximorum Pontificum laudes
eloquentissimis orationibus funebribus, lamentabiliter flens decantauit,
longe tutius existimans laudare mortuos, quam uiuos uituperare. Sunt
& huic rei testimonio plurimae in excellentes uiros & mulieres lauda-
tiones, uel (ut graeco uerbo utar) encomia edita, quorum nomina per
me solam aeternitate memoriae sunt donata. neque id adeo mirum.
Quis enim (nisi ego propitia ad sim) scit non modo non laudare, sed
uel unam hominum auribus dignam proferre sententiam? Quis docet
quid & quomodo dicendum sit, praeter me? Quis potest uel aliquid
boni persuadere, uel mali dissuadere, nisi quem ego ita facere docui?
Testes sunt apud Latinos quidem Cicero & Quintilianus, qui meorum
erga ipsos beneficiorum memores (eorum enim nomen apud omnes
illustrissimum reddidi) praeclaros ediderunt libros, commendationem
& laudem mei maxima parte continentes. Apud Graecos uero Aristoteles
ille orbis doctrinae, tum uero alij plurimi, quos studiose omitto, & praecipue Hermogenes, in cuius animo (ut poeticum testatur epigramma)
ipsae Musae aedibus suis expulsae, domicilium sibi delegisse dicuntur.[9]

Iocus de Ideis   Nimirum eum fortasse tantopere admirantes, quod quomodo Plato in rebus
diuinis & aeternis, ita is in rebus meis
ideas inuenerit. Est & hoc quoque uobis, o iuuenes, penitius intuendum,
quod patrum uestrorum temporibus, quibus omnia melius & prudentius
regebantur quam nunc, summa rerum in maximis imperijs penes solos
erat oratores, ut regnantibus Atheniensibus penes celeberrimum illum
Demosthenem, ut alios nouem taceam, Romanis uero, Ciceronem. quorum non solum eloquentia admirabilis, sed etiam praestantissimum
ingenium, doctrina excellens, uita honestissima, mores denique lauda-
tissimi fuerunt. Et cui unum ex his deest, hunc ego in oratorem non

---

[8] Arithmetice *1517*
[9] dicuntur, *1517*

When Arithmetic wound up her oration like that—behold, noble
Rhetoric! "I see I finally got my chance
to speak at last," she said, "although this   *Rhetoric*
is hardly mine—that is, the last place—
since I could claim by all rights the first. But I'm so far above all pride
and ostentation and endowed with so much modesty that I can bear
without getting upset all these sciences using my personal possessions
in showing themselves off and tricking themselves out, that is, my eloquence and art of speaking. For I've no greater praise for myself than
the fact that no one can be praised properly without me. Even Phaedra,[6] an extremely learned citizen of
Rome, thought so. To the great amaze-   *Phaedra*
ment of his entire audience, he used to
keep repeating the praises of a host of popes over and over in extremely
eloquent funeral orations, weeping woefully all the while, since he
thought it was safer to praise the dead than criticize the living. To
support my claim, there are many published praises, or (to use the
Greek word) *encomia*, of excellent men and women. I alone give their
names to eternal memory, and that's not surprising. For unless I'm
there to help him, who knows how to produce a single opinion deserving to be heard, let alone how to praise something? Who teaches what
to say and how to say it except me? Who can persuade a person to do
something good or dissuade him from something bad unless I've taught
him how to do it? Among the Romans, certainly, Cicero and Quintilian [7] are witnesses of this. They remember my benefits towards them
(for I've made their names illustrious among all men), and they've
published famous books containing in great part commendation and
praise of me. Among the Greeks there's Aristotle,[8] a world of learning,
and indeed many others whom I intentionally omit, and especially
Hermogenes.[9] The Muses themselves are said to have made their home
in his soul (as the poetic epigram says) when they were driven out of
their own shrines. They probably admired him so much because he discovered the Ideas of things in rhetorical
matters just as Plato did in divine and   *Joke about the Ideas*
eternal things.

"You should also seriously consider this, boys. In your father's time,
when everything was done better and more intelligently than it is now,
orators alone managed great kingdoms. Demosthenes, for example, that
famous man, ruled Athens, not to mention the nine others,[1] and Cicero
ruled Rome. They were not only remarkable for their eloquence, they
were also outstanding for their intelligence, superior learning, upright
lives, and laudable morals. I don't admit anyone lacking in those things

admitto. Nec dubito quin eadem illis autoritas, nostra quoque tribue-
retur aetate, si non minor daretur opera literis, quam indulgetur uoluptatibus, nec maior corporis quam animi cura gereretur, adeo ut hodie
quid sit orator, uix intelligatur. Nam ubi inueniuntur hodie uiri boni, &
dicendi periti? Sed dixerit hic aliquis, Si non reperiuntur, quomodo ab
eis nos regi uis? Fateor esse perpaucos, quia tu uis, quantum in te est,
esse nullos. Nam hac uestra tempestate, non modo eloquentia, uerumetiam aliae artes sunt consimiles alicui uili quidem, sed rarae rei. quam
si semihoram, plus minus, conspexerimus, in posterum nunquam uidere
curamus. Quid commemorem, nihil unquam in rebus humanis praeclare simul & utiliter, nisi me duce & autore factum. Nam ut prudentis-
simi uiri scribunt, non aliter quam eloquentia & erudita uoce effectum
est, ut illi primi incredibiliter rudes & agrestes homines, illis rusticis
exutis moribus, induerent ciuiliores. non aliter, ut in coetus quae ciui-
tates uocantur, coirent, quam quum uehementi ducerentur persuasione.
non aliter, ut aequas leges admitterent, eisque parerent, quam quum
magnis ualidisque rationibus mouerentur. Sed alia omnia studiose per-
transibo, ut quaedam altiora & diuina tangam. Considerate igitur apud
uos, non solum homines eloquentia usos esse, ad persuadenda omnia,
quae sibi necessaria uiderentur, sed nec Christum ipsum aliud ad fabri-
candam fidem suam, quum in terris esset, instrumentum tractasse, ut
qui non solum sancta, sed etiam erudita uoce, in diuulgandis suis diuinis praeceptis, sit usus. Vnde Iudaei, respondentis illius prudentiam (ut
euangelium tradit) sunt admirati. quod neutiquam fecissent, si inepte
respondisset. Quod si prudenter, sicuti fecit, est locutus, scitote hoc
esse eloquenter loqui. Est enim prudentia, una de eloquentiae comitibus, nec quicquam ab ea est alienius quam imprudentia. Porro est in
diuo Paulo, graece scribente (quem etiam ciuitate Romana ERASMVS
noster nuper donauit) eloquentia, si non fucata, apta tamen, tum rei,
tum personae, in [1] Augustino uero & Hieronymo, magna & uehemens.
Quamobrem uestrum est, si homines sequi in amplexanda eloquentia
recusabitis, saltem ipsius Christi redemptoris nostri, & pientissimorum
sectatorum eius, inhaerere uestigijs, & eloquentiam existimare, omnium
aliarum scientiarum lumen quoddam esse lucidissimum. Nam quid
potest uobis prodesse scientia, quam proferre nescitis? proferre autem,
pronunciare, & eloqui ego doceo. Et si cui haec desunt, is in doctorum

---

[1] In *1517*

to the degree of orator. And I don't doubt we could have more of them in our own time if more people would devote themselves to works of literature instead of indulging in pleasure. They take more care of the body than they do of the soul, and the result is that they hardly know what an orator is like these days. For where can you find men today who are both good and know something about public speaking? [2]

"But at this point someone might say, 'If you can't find them, how can you want us to be ruled by them?' I admit there're very few of them but that's because, as far as you're concerned, you wish there were none. For in this age of yours, not only eloquence, but also all the other arts are like some worthless, but rare thing. If we look at it for a half an hour, more or less, we don't care if we ever see it again. Why should I remind you that no one ever did anything glorious and at the same time useful in human affairs unless I was the leader and thought it up? For, as wise men write, the first unbelievably crude and savage men became more civil and stripped off their rough ways thanks to nothing but eloquence and a trained voice. They came together in groups called *states* only when they were led to it by forceful persuasion. They agreed upon just laws and obeyed them only when they were moved to it by strong and valid arguments.

"But I intentionally pass over everything else in order to touch on something higher and more divine. Consider, therefore, among yourselves that not only men used eloquence to argue for anything that seemed necessary to them, but that Christ Himself employed no other instrument in building His faith when He was on earth. The voice He used in revealing His divine precepts was not only holy, but trained. That's why the Jews marveled at His wisdom in answering them (as the gospel says) [3]—which they wouldn't have done if He had answered them awkwardly. And if He spoke wisely—as He did—that's the same as speaking eloquently. For good sense is one of the companions of eloquence, and nothing is further away from it than stupidity. Besides, in St. Paul, writing in Greek (our friend Erasmus recently made him a Roman citizen),[4] there's a certain eloquence, not ornate, but suitable both to the subject and the speaker, whereas in St. Augustine and Jerome the eloquence is great and powerful. And so, if you don't want to follow men and embrace eloquence, you at least ought to stick to the footsteps of our Saviour Christ and His righteous followers and consider eloquence as a kind of brilliant light to all other fields of learning.

"For what good is knowledge to you if you can't articulate it? But I teach how to articulate it, pronounce it, and make it sound good. And if a person can't do that, he's not to be counted as one of the learned.

numerum referendus non est. nam libentius cum indocto homine colloquor, quam cum his qui duabus horis uix tria balbutiunt latina uerba, & ea male cohaerentia, in quorum ore omnis uilescit doctrina, & deturpatur. Qui & illi intolerabili uitio sunt obnoxij, quod malunt errorem suum defendere quam emendare, dictitantes eloquentiam, uel non magni faciendam, uel non necessariam. Aduersus hos, diuturnum & magnum gerit bellum, Andreas meus Ammonius, qui incredibili sua eloquentia, in toto orbe Christiano, hoc nomen merito est assecutus, ut dicatur omnium illorum esse excellentissimus, quicunque sunt a secretis principum latine scribendis, uel iudice Paceo. Attente igitur, o iuuenes, paucis auscultate. Quibus, queso, rebus dignoscitur hominum doctrina? Profecto his duabus, uel uerbo, uel scripto, uel utroque. Si uerbo, isti nesciunt loqui. Si scripto, minus sciunt scribere. Sunt ergo prorsus indocti, nisi mutam aliquam, & occultam habent doctrinam. Quae si est, reijciendi sunt in Comicorum κωφά πρόσωπα, id est, mutas personas, qualis est apud Terentium Dromo, qui nihil loquitur, praeter ita & non, uel aliquid his simile, in morem istorum qui sunt apud uos albimitrati patres, quoties latine conantur loqui. Commodum haec dixerat Rhetorica.[2] Et ecce Grammatica irata, furibun-

Loquitur grammatica   daque irruit in medium, parumque abfuit, quin in faciem Rhetorices inuolaret.

Ita ne, inquit, o loquacissima Rhetorica, tractor, tum a te, tum alijs scientijs omnibus? Est ne mei inter uos facienda mentio? sed spreta, contemptaque extrudor foras, & ceu morbosa ouis reijcior a grege? Dic mihi, inquit Rhetorica, tu quae nam es? Istud, inquit Grammatica, auctarium est iniuriae iam illatae, quod

Colloquium Rhetoricae &   nec me cognoscere uult, & nomen meum
Grammaticae   nescire se fingit. Quid tibimet garris?

inquit Rhetorica, age dic nomen. Omittendum esset, inquit Grammatica, quod scis, dicam tamen. Sum Grammatica. Hoc, inquit Rhetorica, non sciebam, sed ita esse praesagibat animus, idcirco quod dudum docuisse uideris, uel   μῆνιν ἄειδε θεά, id est, iram Achillis, uel furias Aiacis Oilei, tu quoque irata & furibunda. Mandrabuli more, inquit Grammatica, iuxta prouerbium res mea succedit, nam huic etiam ludibrio sum. Absit, inquit Rhetorica, mihi qui-

---

[2] Rherorica. *1517*

I'd rather speak with an unlearned man than with these fellows who babble hardly three Latin words in two hours, and those incoherent. In their mouths all learning is debased and defiled. They're the ones who're guilty of the unforgivable sin of preferring to defend their mistake rather than amend it. For they say that eloquence doesn't make for greatness, or else is not necessary. My dear Andreas Ammonius [5] has waged a great war against them for a long time. By his unbelievable eloquence he has earned this fine reputation throughout the entire Christian world: he's said to be the best of the Latin secretaries to princes, no matter who they are, especially in Pace's opinion.

"Therefore, boys, pay attention and listen a little. I ask you, what are the real marks of human culture? Actually, two things: speech, or writing, or a combination of both. If speech, these fellows I'm talking about don't know how to talk. If writing, they know even less. They're absolutely ignorant, therefore—unless they have some silent, occult learning. If they do, they ought to be thrown in with those *kôpha prosôpa* of comedy, that is, the silent characters, like Dromo in Terence,[6] who says nothing but *yes* and *no* or something like that, just like the priests with the white hats [7] in your country whenever they try to talk Latin."

Rhetoric had just finished saying that when, lo and behold, Grammar ran out in the middle of the stage, furious and rav- *Grammar speaks* ing, and all but flew in her face. "Is that right," she said, "you rhetorical blowhard? I'm manipulated, am I, sometimes by you, sometimes by all the other sciences? So I don't even need to be mentioned along with you? Am I to be scorned, despised, kicked out, and cut off from the flock like a sick sheep?"

"Tell me," said Rhetoric, "who are you?"

"That," said Grammar, "is adding insult *Conversation of Rhetoric and* to injury. She doesn't want to recognize *Grammar* me and pretends not to know my name."

"What are you running on about?" said Rhetoric. "Go on, tell us your name."

"That's not necessary," Grammar said, "since you already know it, but I'll tell you anyway. I am Grammar."

"I didn't know that," said Rhetoric, "but I had an inkling that's who you were because you seem to have just taught either *mênin aeide thea*, that is, the wrath of Achilles, or the madness of Ajax Oileus, you're so furious and raving."

"I get on like Mandrabulus in the proverb," [8] Grammar said. "I'm just a laughing stock to you."

dem ludibrio non es, sed scis quid mihi risum mouit? Qui potero, inquit
Grammatica, scire quod tu cogitas? neque enim diuina sum uates, aut
spiritum aereum nutrio in ampulla. Illud, inquit Rhetorica, mihi in
mentem uenit, quod Grammatici fere nihil praeter grammaticam
sciunt, & uix illam. ut Papias, scribens puppas imagines quasdam esse
terribiles. Ille qui scripsit Catholicon, id est, uniuersalem dictionarium,
in quo nihil continetur. Isidorus etymologista, qui uerborum proprie-
tates docens, nihil proprie loquitur. Et ut de Graecis quoque aliquid
dicam, quis unquam inter illos nobis reddidit rationem, cur nomina
neutri generis pluralia, cum uerbo numeri singularis coniunguntur?
quo modo loquendi nihil est apud Graecos tutius. Cui rei absimilia non
sunt apud Latinos, nomina terminantia in um, & in a. in us, & in um. ut
Margaritum & margarita, gladius & gladium. Ego igitur quod a Grammaticis discere nunquam potui, cupio ab ipsa nunc doceri Grammatica.
Quare unice te rogo, hunc gryphum mihi explices. O lepidum caput,
inquit Grammatica, duo duntaxat sunt mihi mysteria, & ea tu tibi
reuelari uis, atque id importune. Neque enim nunc est mihi ocium, ut
quae cum iuuenibus longe utiliora tractanda habeam. Tantum tamen
dicam, non deesse, qui hunc loquendi modum ad atticismum trahunt.
Atticismum autem interdum pro soloe-
Iocus de Atticismo   cismo aiunt accipi. Et siquid interim
amplius hac in re intelligere cupis, lege
Apollonium grammaticum, apud quem (nisi mea me fallit memoria)
de hac locutione aliquid reperies. Dij meliora, inquit Rhetorica, mallem me in Timaeum Platonis relegares. Huic ne sphingi uis me alli-
gare? Nam is in grammatica, aenigmata plane scribere uidetur, & est
inter Grammaticos σκοτινὸς, id est, tenebrosus, sicut inter Philosophos [3]
Heraclitus ille, cuius nomen melius quam scripta, quum extarent, intel-
lexerunt omnes. Valeat itaque iste, nolo lucem querere in profundis
tenebris, quinpotius tenebras in tenebris. Immo malo rem mea sponte
nescire, quam ut ille nescire me doceat. Iste & Theodorus Gaza coniun-
cti sunt a chalcographis in uno codice, sed Theodorus, & merito, est
praepositus, ut clarior, apertior, & omnibus utilior. & is sciens prudens-
que praetermisit hanc questionem, tanquam subtilem magis quam
necessariam, & tacite innuit sequendam esse consuetudinem. Merito,

---

[3] Philolophos *1517*

"Not at all," said Rhetoric. "I'm not making fun of you, but do you know what *does* make me laugh?"

"How can I know what you think?" said Grammar. "I'm no holy prophet; I don't keep an airy spirit in a bottle." [9]

"I realize that," said Rhetoric. "Grammarians hardly know anything else but grammar, and they scarcely know that—like Papias,[1] who wrote that dolls are certain terrifying images, or the person who wrote the *Catholicon*,[2] that is, *The Universal Dictionary* that has nothing in it, or Isidore the Etymologist,[3] who taught the properties of words and said nothing properly. And to mention something about the Greeks— who has ever explained to us the reason why neuter plural nouns take singular verbs, which is quite common in Greek? And Latin is not very different with nouns ending in *um* and in *a*, in *us* and in *um*, like *margaritum*, and *margarita*, and *gladius* and *gladium*. Therefore, since I've never been able to learn anything from grammarians, I want to be taught now by Grammar itself. That's the only reason I ask you to explain to me what this *gryphum* [4] is."

"Ah, you're a smart one," said Grammar. "There're only two things I don't know, and you want me to explain them to you—and you ask me rudely, besides. But I don't have the time right now, since I've got far more useful things to talk over with the boys. Nevertheless, I'll say this much: there're some people who attribute this manner of speaking to Atticism. They say an Atticism, however, is occasionally taken for a solecism.[5] Meanwhile, if you want to know anything more about this, read   *Joke about Atticism* Apollonius the Grammarian.[6] Unless my memory deceives me, you'll find he says something about that manner of speaking."

"God forbid," said Rhetoric. "I'd rather you refer me to Plato's *Timaeus*. You don't want to tie me to that sphinx Apollonius, do you? For he clearly seems to write in riddles about grammar. Among grammarians, he's *skotinos,* that is, full of dark conceits. It's the same way Heraclitus [7] was among philosophers; everyone knew his name better than his works when they were still extant. So good-by to him. I don't want to look for a light in deep shadows, or rather for shadows in shadows. No, I'd rather not know a thing of my own free will than have him teach me not to know it. Printers have bound him and Theodorus Gaza [8] together in one volume, but they placed Theodorus first, as they should have, since he's clearer, plainer, and more useful to everyone. Since Gaza is a wise and prudent man,, he passed over this problem as if it were more subtle than necessary, and he implied that one should follow usage." [9]

inquit Grammatica, Theodorum meum, uirum doctissimum probas,
quem omnes docti certatim laudant, sicut & meum Thomam Linacrum.
Nam & is grammaticam latine scribere, non est dedignatus, & quidem
diligentissime simul & eruditissime. Quid ais? inquit Rhetorica, Linacrum quem tuum appellas, non bene nosti. Est enim is summus medi-
cus, & par orator, ut tum experientia, tum libris felicissime editis, manifestum fecit omnibus, & te non nisi aliud agens, & ἐν παρέργῳ, id est,
horis superuacaneis aggressus est. ac quidam ex amantissimis eius persaepe sunt mirati, quod quum natus sit ad altissima quaeque, non
recusauerit ad ista infima descendere, ut contenderet cum Tryphone, uel
nescio quo alio grammatico, de quibusdam minutijs casus uocatiui.
Contendit tum ille feliciter, quia uicit. sed mallem uictoriam fuisse
illustriorem, & similem illi quem Patauij

Laus Thomae Linacri olim reportauit. Nam quum in gymnasio
Patauino, professionis artis medicae, ei
(ut nunc moris est) darentur insignia, publice non sine summa laude
disputauit, & seniorum medicorum aduersaria argumenta acutissime
refellit, tum [4] Iuuenis quidam perquam eruditus, coepit contra argu-
mentari. Sed Aquila, tace, inquit, o bone iuuenis, uidesne & consyderas
hunc, nos seniores te, longo interuallo

De Aquila medico & eius equulo procul a se reliquisse, & in disputando
superasse? Aquila autem erat omnium
Italicorum medicorum sine controuersia, tunc princeps, cum aetate
(peruenit enim ad Galeni, id est, centesimum fere aetatis annum) tum
doctrina & experientia. Sed uulgus (quod iocosum est) aetatem magis,
quam literas argumentum fecerunt doctrinae eius, ideo quod dicebatur
ab omnibus, non solum ad tuendam sanitatem suam, quaedam optima
& secretiora medicamina excogitasse, sed etiam equuli sui gradarij,
quem impense amabat. Nam & is uicesimumnonum aetatis annum atti-
git. Ac fidelis equulus diligenter obseruans domini erga se beniuolen-
tiam, & charitatem, decreuit ei in amore respondere. nunquam enim est
passus, ut ueheretur ab altero, priusquam pheretro impositum, uideret
uehi ad sepulchrum. & tunc nescio quas lachrymas emisisse dicitur, &
intra annum perijsse, ut scilicet physicorum rationes comprobaret,
asseuerantum canes & equos sagaces esse, & ad humanam rationem
proxime accedere. Tum Paceus iunior, & nouarum rerum intelligen-
darum cupidior, interrogauit defuncti seruum, bene sibi notum, quibus
medicaminibus dominus ipsius usus fuerat ad equuli ualitudinem tuen-

---

[4] Tum *1517*

"You're right to approve of my dear Theodorus," said Grammar. "He's an extremely learned man, one whom all learned men sincerely admire, the same way they do my dear Thomas Linacre.[1] For he didn't disdain to write a grammar in Latin,[2] and he wrote it carefully and at the same time learnedly."

"What are you talking about?" said Rhetoric. "You don't know the person you call your 'dear Linacre' very well. For he's a great doctor and an equally great orator, as he has made clear to everyone by his practice in the one case and by the books he has edited [3] so well in the other. He came to you only when he had nothing else to do and *en parergôi*, that is, in his spare time. And some of those who loved him best were often amazed that, although he was born to higher things, he didn't refuse to descend to the lowest level of all to argue with Tryphon or God knows what other grammarian about some minute points of the vocative case.[4] He always argued well because he won, but I wish the victory had been more glorious, like the one he once gained at Padua. For when he was given the insignia of the medical profession at the *Praise of Thomas Linacre* University of Padua (as is the custom now), he carried on a public debate—not without great praise—and very brilliantly refuted the arguments of his opponents, the older doctors. Then a young person who was extremely learned began to argue on the other side. But Aquila [5] said, 'Be quiet, my dear young man. Don't you *Dr. Aquila and his little horse* realize that this fellow has left us far behind and overcome us in debate, although we're older than you?'

"At that time, Aquila was easily the foremost doctor in Italy, both in age (for he had reached the age of Galen,[6] that is, almost the hundredth year of his life) as well as in learning and experience. But the people—and this is funny—made his age rather than his writings a proof of his learning. For everyone said he'd discovered some wonderful, secret medications to preserve not only his own health, but also that of the little pacer he loved so much. As a matter of fact it lived to be twenty-nine years old. And when the faithful horse saw how kind and affectionate his master was toward him, he decided to return his love. So he never let anyone else carry Aquila until he saw him placed on a bier and carried to his grave. And then, they say, he shed God knows what tears and died within a year. He thus clearly confirmed the arguments of the scientists who say that dogs and horses are intelligent and come very close to human reason. Then young Pace, who was eager to learn new things, asked one of Aquila's servants whom he knew well what medicine his master used to keep his horse healthy.

dam. Dicam, inquit ille, libenter quae scio. Nam omnia mihi nota non fuere. Quae autem scio, haec sunt, Bellaria persaepe comedenda, & uinum Cretense bibendum exhibebat. Miror profecto, inquit Paceus, nam hoc modo uidetur equulum lautius & delicatius nutrisse, quam te. Ah, ah, ah ille, & abiuit. Tum Grammatica, Quae de Linacro, inquit, retulisti, magna sunt, & laudabilia, & ob id mihi quamgratissima. sed fabella haec, quam de equuli sanitate interseruisti, bene ne an male nescio, nihil aliud sibi uoluit, quam ut ego illorum, quae supra dixisti, obliuiscerer. nam tu superbissime unum meum damnasti Grammaticum, & eum antiquum, perinde quasi nullus ex tuis sectatoribus reprehendi possit. Dic mihi, quid de illo tuo (qui iactauit se oratorem, & omnes Grammaticorum libros, in latrinam conijciendos) sentiendum est, interpretante ex graeco παρὰ τὴν ἔισοδον, apud Hesiodum, quum iuxta ingressum uertendum sit. Nam si is

Ridiculum uel summis (quod aiunt) labris grammaticen gustasset, e uestigio nouisset τὴν articulum foemininum, non posse cum nomine masculino coniungi, nec deceptus literarum sono, ingressum peruertisset Hesiodum. Istud autem non est in mysterijs literarum errare, qualia sunt illa, quae tu mihi reuelanda proposuisti, sed in rebus minimis, ut sunt articuli, & nomina, in quibus uix pueris errare licet, & si errent, uapulant. Hic inquit Rhetorica, Subsiste o Grammatica, captam te nunc, & irretitam habeo. Nonne statim in principio tibi aperte dixi, Grammaticam nihil praeter grammaticam scire? Dixi certe, & tu hoc nunc comprobasti. nam si aliquid ultra grammaticam scires, non crederes istum, qui tam turpiter errauit, oratorem esse, praesertim quum oratoris definitio illa sit non incognita, ut dicatur uir bonus, & dicendi peritus, & iste nec bene, nec perite sit locutus. Nescio, inquit Gram-

Grammatica nihil habens matica, quid de bono & perito uiro nu-
respondendum, conuertit garis. sed hoc unum certum scio, nemi-
sermonem ad alia nem de tuis unquam fuisse perfectum. Nam & Quintilianus tuus fatetur, neminem unquam fuisse perfectum, sed esse posse. Hoc idem sentit & Cicero, tamen stultus scripsit de perfecto oratore. Sed te mi Rhetorica, per omnes illos deos, deasque, quos Demosthenes tuus in concione

" 'I'll gladly tell you what I know,' he said. 'For I didn't know everything. But I do know that he often gave him candy and macaroons to eat and Cretan wine to drink.'

" 'I'm certainly amazed at that,' Pace said. 'The horse seems to have been fed more luxuriously and more delicately than you were.'

" 'Ah, ah, ah,' he said and went away."

Then Grammar said, "What you said about Linacre is great and praiseworthy and therefore extremely pleasing to me. But this story you stuck in about a horse's health—God knows whether for a good reason or a bad—serves no other purpose than to make me forget what you were talking about before. For you've arrogantly passed sentence on one of my grammarians, one of my ancient ones, as though none of your followers had any faults. Tell me, what about the one who claimed he was an orator [7] and said that all books by grammarians ought to be thrown in the toilet? He translated *para tên eisodon* from Greek as *near Hesiod* [8] when it should have been
near the entrance.[9] For if he had had just   *A stupid thing*
a thin layer of grammar,[1] as they say, he
would have known on the spot that the feminine article *tên* can't take a masculine noun,[2] and he wouldn't have been fooled by the sound of the letters and turned *entrance* into *Hesiod*. That, however, is not a mistake in the mysteries of literature, like the ones you proposed to reveal to me, but in little, tiny things like articles and nouns, which schoolboys are hardly allowed to make a mistake about. And if they do, they're beaten."

At that point Rhetoric said, "Wait a minute, Grammar. I've got you now; you're caught. Didn't I say to you right at the beginning 'Grammar knows nothing but grammar'? Certainly I did, and now you've just proved it, for if you knew anything besides grammar, you wouldn't believe that the fellow who made such a rotten mistake was an orator, especially since the definition of an orator is well known,[3] that is, someone who's a good man and an expert at speaking. But this person spoke neither well nor properly."

"I don't know why you want to make
jokes about a good man and an expert   *Grammar, who has nothing to*
speaker," Grammar said, "but I know this   *say to that, changes the*
one thing for sure: not one of your fol-   *subject*
lowers has ever been perfect. For even your dear Quintilian [4] admitted that no one has ever been perfect, although people are capable of it. Cicero [5] also thought the same thing, though the fool turned around and wrote about the perfect orator. But I beg you, dear Rhetoric, by all the gods and goddesses that your dear Demosthenes [6] called on in

inuocauit, oro, nunc me missam facias, mihique ut mea agam negocia, sicut tu perfecisti tua, concedas. nam ingenue fateor, me non tantum eloquentia ualere, ut te loquacissimam uincere possim. Loquacem ne, inquit Rhetorica, me uocas? Ignoscas queso, o Rhetorica, grammatice loquenti, & non animo, sed uerbis erranti, nam peritam dicendi dicere uolebam. Vale ergo R. Vale & tu G. Tum

Oratio grammatices ad iuuenes   Grammatica, conuerso ad iuuenes sermone, Non me latet, inquit, o optimi iuuenes, quam arduum, quamque difficile mihi erit, aliquid excogitare & inuenire, quod uel uobis satisfacturum, uel mihimetipsi profuturum sit. Posteaquam tot, tantasque scientias, sua bona, quamfacundissime & copiosissime potuerunt, declarantes & extollentes audistis, nihil denique humanum aut diuinum omittentes, quo sese excellentiores reddere, & uobis omnia persuadere potuerint. Verumtamen quum in hoc non minima pars prudentiae, mea sententia, sita est, ut tam etsi magna merito admiremur, & suspiciamus, non tamen deceat parua, quae ad illa ueram & rectam uiam commonstrant, contemnere, uestrae fuerit humanitatis, me sicut alias fecistis, attente audire. Praesertim quum honestatis & utilitatis uestrae, non minorem quam illae, curam geram, & nihil dictura sim, nisi quod maxime ad id conferat, de quo loqui est institutum. Doctrina utique comparanda, qua nihil in rebus humanis uos magis ornare poterit, siue nunc quum iuuenes estis, siue olim, si in uiros (quod deus uobis det) creueritis. Diligenter igitur, quaeso, animaduertite, & notate quantum auxilij ego benignissime praesto, ad hoc diuinum doctrinae donum consequendum. Principio enim ego sum, quae literarum figuras, & nomina doceo, deinde concorditer in syllabas connecto. Neque unquam fama auditum est, aliquam inter meas literas discordiam ortam esse, nisi apud Lucianum inter s, & t. Cui certamini

Iocus de s. & t.   non literae meae (ut sunt modestissimae, & suo quaeque loco contentae) originem praebuerunt, sed Atheniensium superbia, & dominandi cupiditas, qui ut multas

Thalassa Thalatta   gentes bellis uexarunt, & sua eis eripuerunt, ita etiam meam literam s, sua possessione, & praecipue toto maris dominio, expellere sunt conati. Sed spero (magna iudicum aequitate confisa) rem bene compositum iri nam adhuc sub iudice lis est. Sane proba haec mea ancilla s, omnium

his speeches, to let me go now and get on with my business like you did yours. For I frankly admit I'm not eloquent enough to overcome your long windedness."

"Are you calling me longwinded?" said Rhetoric.

"I beg your pardon, Rhetoric. I was speaking grammatically and didn't mean it. I made a mistake in the words, for I meant to say I couldn't overcome your *skill in speaking*. So good-by, R." [7]

"Good-by to you too, G."

Then Grammar directed her speech to the boys: "I am aware, my good sirs, how *Grammar's speech to the boys* hard and difficult it will be for me to think up and discover something that will either satisfy you or be of use to me, myself. Besides, you've heard many great sciences explaining and extolling their own attributes as eloquently and fully as they could. They omitted nothing in the end, either human or divine, that might make themselves more outstanding and persuade you of everything they said. But yet, in my opinion, there's quite a bit of good sense in the fact that, although we marvel over great things, as we should, and accept them, nevertheless we shouldn't scorn the little things that point out the true and straight path to the others. It will be kind of you to listen to me as carefully as you did to the others, especially since I care about your reputation and advantage as much as they did and since I'm not going to say anything that doesn't contribute a great deal to the subject under discussion.

"You must by all means obtain learning. Nothing human can adorn you more, either now while you're still young or later when (God willing) you've grown into men. I beg you, therefore, consider carefully and observe how much help I'm kind enough to offer you in attaining this divine gift of learning. For in the first place I'm the one who teaches the forms and names of letters. Then I put them together harmoniously in syllables. And no one has ever heard of any discord among my letters, except in Lucian [8] between the letters S and T. And it wasn't my letters that started that trouble (they're very modest and quite content with their own station in life), but *Joke about S and T* rather the Athenians' pride and their desire to rule. [9] Just as they harassed many nations in war and deprived them of their possessions, so they tried to drive my letter S away from her own property and especially *Thalassa, thalatta* from all her control over the sea. But I hope (trusting in the great justice of the judges) that it's about to be settled properly, for the case is still in court. Surely this good maid

literarum fuit infortunatissima. Nam & quidam indoctus sacrificus Anglicus, eam possessione sua annis triginta expulit, nec puduit illum tam longo tempore mumpsimus legere, loco sumpsimus. Et quum moneretur a docto, ut errorem emendaret, respondit se nolle mutare suum antiquum mumpsimus, ipsius nouo sumpsimus. Item syllabarum doceo quantitates, ut sonorius, suauius, & doctius pronuncientur omnia. Qua in re damno ualde illum sacrificum Gal-

De sacrifico Gallo.
male pronunciante

lum, qui inter preces sacras dicendas legit, quesúmus domíne, peruerso accentu. Quod quum audisset alter, bonarum literarum non ignarus, Tu, inquit, non placas deum istis tuis precibus, sed potius ad iram prouocas, tam barbare omnia pronunciando. Tum ille, Nos Gallici, inquit, non cúramus de quantítate syllábarum, haec quoque omnia peruerso proferens accentu. At tu, inquit alter, nihil aliud studere uideris, nisi ut unum altero peius pronuncies, tu es Musis plane inimicus, sed dabis poenas (mihi crede).[5] Nam Budeus, cuius eruditissimas & purgatissimas

De Budeo uiro eruditissimo

aures, ista tua imperitia offendet, curabit te tanquam barbarum e ciuitate expellendum. Huc accedit, quod nisi ego, ut sum amica omnibus, uniuerso generi humano ancillas meas quinque uocales prostituissem, nullus unquam uel uerbum protulisset, nec illud

βεκ, primum verbum a
puero prolatum, & Phoenicum
lingua panem significat

primum βεκ, occasionem praebuisset historiae conscribendae. Immo nec tuus, o Rhetorica, Demosthenes unquam in concione tonasset, Philippum Macedonem πανοῦργου καὶ ὄλεθρου, id est, uersipellem, & humani generis pestem, sed tandem uere suam. Postremo ego ex syllabis conficio dictiones & uerba, ex quibus omnis constat sententia & oratio. Atqui ex his omnis percipitur doctrina. Vnde initio illi sapientes uiri uulgo, Grammaticos solos literatos uocabant. Sed hoc in loco, ut omni respondeatur obiectioni, illud uos monebo, neminem unquam extitisse, qui non ex uerbis collegerit omnes sententias, excepto uno Thoma Moro nostro. Nam is e contrario, ex sententijs colligit uerba, &

De Moro

praecipue in graecis intelligendis, & transferendis. Ceterum hoc non est a gram-

---

[5] crede) *1517*

servant of mine, the letter S, was the most unfortunate of all letters. For a certain boorish English priest [1] drove her away from her own property for thirty years, and he was not ashamed at having read *mumpsimus* instead of *sumpsimus* for that long a time. And when a learned man advised him to correct the mistake, he replied that he didn't want to change his old *mumpsimus* for some new *sumpsimus*.

"I also teach the quantities of syllables so that everything can be pronounced more sonorously, sweetly, and learnedly. And on this point I strongly condemn the French priest [2] who read the sacred prayers saying *quesúmus domíne*, with the accent on the wrong syllable. When someone who knew something about good literature heard him, he said 'You won't please God with these prayers of yours. You'll probably make Him angry, you pronounce everything so barbarously.'

A French priest with a bad pronunciation

"Then he said, 'We French don't care about the quantity of syllábles,' with all the words accented on the wrong syllables in this case too.

"The other one said, 'You don't seem to care about anything except pronouncing one word worse than the other. You're obviously no friend of the Muses, but believe me you'll suffer for it. For Budé,[3] who has an educated and sensitive ear, will be shocked at this ignorance of yours and will see to it that you're driven from the city like a barbarian.'

Budé, an extremely learned man

"And so it happens that if I weren't everyone's friend and didn't prostitute my maid servants, the five vowels, to the entire human race, mankind would never have brought forth a single word, and that first *Bek* [4] would not have given the occasion for the writing of history. In fact, Rhetoric, your dear Demosthenes [5] would never have thundered at Philip of Macedon in a speech *panourgou kai olethrou*, that is, deceiver and ruination of the human race, though in the end he was Demosthenes' own ruination.[6]

Bek, the first word uttered by a child, meaning bread *in Phoenician*

"Finally, from syllables I make words and phrases. From them arise all speech and discourse and from that all learning. That's why in the old days wise men everywhere usually called only the grammarians learned. But right now, in order to answer all your objections, I'll remind you that there's never been anyone who didn't arrive at all his sentences from words, except one person, our Thomas More.[7] For he, on the contrary, arrives at words from sentences, especially in understanding and translating Greek. Now that's not

More

matica usquequaque alienum, sed paulo
plus quam grammaticum, id est, ingeni-
osum. Est enim Moro ingenium plus-
quam humanum. Doctrina uero non excellens modo, sed & uaria, adeo
ut quocunque te uertas, nihil nescire uideatur. Quantum autem graece
sciat, testis sit Incredulus, quem Paulus
Bombasius ualde laudat. Porro facundia
non incomparabilis tantum, sed & duplex,
cum in sua, tum in aliena lingua, id est,
latina. Iam adeo non uulgariter facetus est, & urbanus, ut leporem
ipsum ei patrem, & facetiam matrem fuisse iudices. Et interdum, hoc
est, quando res postulat, bonos imitatur cocos, & omnia acri perfundit
aceto. Habet & nasum, quum uult, etiam inter nasutissimos, quem tam
artificiose etiam detrahit, ut eo detracto, nullum faciei desit lineamen-
tum. In philosophia nulla secta est, quam non aliqua ex parte probat,
& ut quaeque maxime excellit, ita eam maxime admiratur. Sed uni
praecipue (quod faciunt fere omnes) se addixit, id est, Democriticae.
De illo autem Democrito loquor, qui omnes res humanas risit, quem
non modo diligentissime est imitatus, uerum etiam una syllaba supe-
rauit. Nam ut ille humana omnia ridenda censuit, ita hic deridenda.
Vnde Richardus Paceus, Morum amicissimum suum, Democriti filium,
uel successorem, per iocum appellare solet. Is denique magnum bellum istis indixit, qui nec uera, nec uerisimilia,[6] atque a personis suis
alienissima loquuntur. Quale contigit, quum audiret duos Theologos
Scotistas, ex his qui grauiores habentur, & pulpita conterunt, (quique
in te, o Colete, satis non indocte modo, sed etiam impie insurrexerunt,
quum diceres salutarem pacem, pernicioso bello longe esse praeferendam).[7] Quum audiret inquam, serio affirmantes inter se, Arcturum
regem (quem aliqui natum negant, aliqui nunquam obijsse, sed nescio
quo disparuisse contendunt) togam sibi ex Gigantum barbis, quos in
praelio occiderat, confecisse. Et quum Morus interrogasset illos, qua
ratione hoc posset fieri, tum senior, composito in grauitatem uultu,
Ratio, inquit, o puer, est aperta, & causa euidens, quod scilicet cutis
hominis mortui mirifice extenditur. Alter hanc rationem auditam, non
solum approbauit, sed etiam ut subtilem & Scoticam, admiratus est.
Tum Morus adhuc puer, Hoc, inquit, semper antea aeque mihi incog-
nitum fuit, atque illud est notissimum, alterum ex uobis hircum mul-

Mori descriptio

Incredulus, Luciani dialogus, a
Moro uersus

---

[6] uerisimilia. *1517*
[7] praeferendam.) *1517*

completely alien to grammar, but it's a
little more than grammatical—it's genius.   *Description of More*
For More's intelligence is more than
human. In fact his learning is not only outstanding; it's also varied, so
that wherever you turn he seems to know everything. But let *The
Doubter* [8] be a witness to how much he
knows in Greek. Paulus Bombasius praises   *Incredulus, a dialogue of*
it highly. Moreover, his eloquence is not   *Lucian's translated by More*
only incomparable but dual: it functions
in his own tongue as well as in a foreign language, that is, Latin. Again,
he's not so vulgarly witty and urbane that you'd think politeness was
his father and wit his mother. And every now and then, whenever the
occasion demands, he imitates good cooks and pours sharp vinegar
over everything. He has a nose [9] when he wants one, in fact, one of the
nosiest noses of all, which he can draw in so skilfully that he does it
with a perfectly straight face. There's no school of philosophy he
doesn't approve of in part. Whatever each one particularly excels in,
that's what he particularly admires about it. But he likes one in particular (like almost everyone else), and that is the school of Democritus.[1]
Naturally I'm speaking of the Democritus who laughed at all human
affairs.[2] More not only imitated him very carefully, he even surpassed
him by one syllable. For just as Democritus thought that everything
that pertains to man was *ludicrous,* More thought it was *ridiculous.*[3]
That's why Richard Pace as a joke calls his dear friend More the son or
successor of Democritus. And finally, More declared all-out war on
those who don't tell the truth, or things resembling the truth, but
things foreign to their own nature. That was the case when he heard
two Scotist theologians, the kind who're considered to be heavyweights
and beat the pulpit to pieces—in fact, the kind who rose against you,
dear Colet,[4] not only stupidly, but also irreligiously, when you said
that a healthy peace was far better than a deadly war. When, I say,
More heard them seriously maintain among themselves that King
Arthur (who some say was never born, some say never died, but con-
tend that he somehow or other disappeared) made a coat for himself
out of the beards of giants he killed in battle; and when More asked
them how he could have done that, the elder composed his face gravely
and said, 'The reason, my boy, is clear and the cause evident. Obviously
it's because the skin of a dead man has a wonderful stretch to it.'
When the other one heard that reason, he not only approved of it, he
admired it since it was subtle and Scotus-like.

"Then More, who was still a boy, said, 'I never knew that before
either, but, this is very well known: when one of you milks a billy-

gere, alterum cribrum subijcere. Quod dictum quum perciperet illos non intellexisse, ridens sibi, & eos deridens, abiuit. Hoc unum (quod dolenter refero) Morum meum persequitur infortunium, quod quoties peritissime & acutissime loquitur inter uestros leucomitratos patres, in sua ipsorum, quam ipse quoque callet scientia, toties illi eum damnant, & puerilia omnia quae dicit, nominant. non quod reuera eum damnandum censeant, aut aliquid puerile audiant, sed quod mirabile ingenium ei inuideant, & alias, quarum ipsi ignari sunt, scientias, quod denique puer (ut ipsi uocant) sapientia senibus longe antecellit. Sed haec hactenus de Moro, ad rem meam iam reuertar. Literatos (ut dixi) antiqui solos Grammaticos nominarunt, & eos literatos esse interpretati sunt, qui aliquid diligenter & acute, scienterque possint aut dicere, aut scribere. Sed quidam postea inuidentes mihi, introduxerunt nescio quas differentias, inter eruditum & literatum, literatum & literatorem, ut meo nonnihil detraherent honori. quod reuera ne pili quidem faciendum est.

Sententia contra inuidos

Cui enim non est manifestissimum, inuidos nec ex iudicio, nec ex animo quicquam damnare, sed ut omni reiecta ratione, suo inani & detestabili satisfaciant appetitui. Quocirca quum ex his quae supra dicta sunt, manifeste patet, ex nudis literis perueniri ad syllabas, ex syllabis ad dictiones & uerba, ex his ad perfectas sententias, atque hinc ad omnem doctrinam, quis est qui tam desipit, ut me fundamentum omnium doctrinarum non credat? Alioqui semper hesurus in minimis, quum posset gnarus mei ad magna penetrare. Quo fit, ut aliqui affecti tedio suae negligentiae, omne literarum studium penitus relinquant. & qui in doctos uiros euadere potuissent, fiant egregij aleatores, uel alicui alij id genus infami arti totos se dedant. Imitamini igitur, o iuuenes, bonos architectos, quibus quoties aliquid aedificandum committitur, primum omnium hanc curam agunt, ut fundamentum ualidissimum iaciatur, nimirum probe scientes, quicquid male iacto fundamento superstruitur, facillime corruere. Quod & illis eueniet omnibus, qui ad doctrinam aliquam peruenire contendunt, nisi prius a me bene & diligenter erudiantur, & regulas meas pari modo intelligant, memoria teneant, & ad manum semper paratas habeant. Damnandus est igitur delirus ille Philo Iudaeus Apella, qui dixit geometriam ἀρχὴν καὶ μητρόπολιν, id est,

goat,[5] the other one stands by and catches it in a sieve.' When he saw they didn't understand what he said, he went away smiling to himself and laughing at them.

"There's one unfortunate thing that dogs my dear friend More, and I refer to it sadly. Whenever he speaks learnedly and brilliantly before your white-topped fathers [6] on their own subject, which he also knows extremely well, they always criticize him and term everything he says childish. But they really don't think he should be criticized nor did they hear anything childish. They're just jealous of his extraordinary talent and the knowledge he has of things unknown to them. In short they're jealous that a boy (as they call him) far surpasses old men in wisdom. But that's enough about More. I'll return now to my own business.

"The ancients, as I said, called only grammarians learned, and they considered that people were learned if they could either say or write something clearly, carefully, and learnedly. But later on some people who were jealous of me introduced God knows what differences between the erudite and the learned, and the learned and the grammarians, in order to detract considerably from my reputation. But that shouldn't matter a bit. For it ought to be clear to everyone that envious people condemn things from neither their minds nor their hearts. Instead, they abandon all reason to satisfy their own hollow, detestable desires. Therefore, since its *A wise saying, against the envious* clearly evident from what was said above that bare letters lead to syllables, syllables to words and phrases, and words and phrases to complete sentences, and thus to all learning, is there anyone foolish enough not to believe that I'm the foundation of all learning? If so, he's always stuck at the little things, when he could go on to something greater if he knew me. And that's why some people are disturbed by the tediousness of their own negligence and abandon all studies entirely; and those who might have gone on to be learned men become excellent gamblers, or else they give themselves over completely to some other kind of unsavory occupation. Therefore, boys, you should imitate good architects. Whenever they're given something to build, they take care of this first of all: to lay a strong foundation, for they know right well that anything built on a weak foundation will easily collapse. And the same thing will also happen to all those who try to arrive at a certain amount of learning, unless I teach them carefully first to understand all my rules, remember them, and always have them ready at hand. So that crazy Philo Judaeus Apella [7] is all wrong. He called geometry *archên kai métropolin,* that is, the mother and beginning of all learn-

principium & matrem omnium disciplinarum, quum utrunque ueracius mihi attribuendum sit. Hinc exijt illud amici mei Quintiliani, docentis me omni conuenire aetati, quum inquit, grammaticam iucundam esse senibus, iuuenibus uero necessariam. Idem monet & illud, erudite simul & utiliter, aut a graeca grammatica (ex cuius fonte hausta est latina) incipiendum esse, aut utranque, latinam & graecam coniungendas. Quod & ego perquam necessarium esse arbitror, ut quasi una & eadem opera, duae utilissimae res possint simul perfici. Hic est, o iuuenes, ille fructus, cuius copiam ego uolentibus omnibus uobis, largissime suppeditabo, & ut quam humana & benigna sum, intelligatis, quantumcunque quisque uolet, gratis donabo. Facit Ptolemaeus & Strabo, scribentes de

De Geographia

situ orbis, ut nec Geographiam silentio omnino praeteream, nam horum arte effectum est, ut Taprobana his nostris temporibus a Lusitanis reperiretur. Clara haec quidem, & Lusitano utilis Regi, cui tamen ego Vtopiam non

Vtopia

postposuerim. Nam ut dem huic deesse aromata, qualia mercantur Lusitani, est tamen accessus longe minus periculosior, & abundat & haec incognitis suis delitijs. Sed cui haec Geographiae scientia cordi est, uel mundum peragret oportet (quod nimis arduum, difficile, & sumptuosum est) uel Strabonem perlegat, aeque longum & latum atque ipse est orbis, Graece tamen, quia translatio est corruptissima, nisi si cui haec breuior uidebitur uia, ut has contempletur orbis descriptiones, quas Mappas mundi uulgo uocant. Sciat tamen & has ex illorum quos nominaui doctrina, profectas esse. Disciplina quoque militaris, apud Priscos clara fuit, sed

Disciplina militaris

hodie ab omni schola tam est aliena, ut stultum fortasse de ea loqui iudicetur. Tantum tamen ut miles, qui in Christi uerba iuraui, dicam longe esse consultius, ut bella (si qua esse debent)

Seria de bello

prudentia doctrinae comite potius, quam gladio conficiantur. Nam qui semper ad atroces conflictus sunt parati, nihil aliud agere uidentur, nisi ut strenuos se praebeant homicidas. Qui uero sanguinis immaniter effundendi est abstinentior, primum parcit suis.[8] Deinde clementia, qua in hostem utetur, diuinam prae se fert misericordiam, sine qua, nulla humano generi, animae in hoc salo miseriae semper periclitantis, salus est speranda. Vnde Demonactis philosophi,

---

[8] suis, *1517*

ing, whereas both those titles can more truthfully be attributed to me. For example, there's the remark of my friend Quintilian,[8] to the effect that I'm suitable for all ages, when he said that grammar was pleasant for old men, but really necessary for the young. He also said this,[9] learnedly and at the same time usefully: one should either begin with Greek grammar (from which Latin is derived) or else join Latin and Greek together. And I think that's extremely necessary since it accomplishes two useful things at the same time by one and the same operation, as it were. That, boys, is the benefit which I'll generously supply to all you who want it; and to show how humane I am and kind, I'll give each of you as much as he wants for nothing.

"Ptolemy and Strabo, who described the regions of the world in their works, are the reason I shall not pass over geography entirely in silence.[1] For through the art of these men the Portu- *Geography* guese discovered Ceylon [2] in our own time. That's certainly a famous place and useful to the King of Portugal. Nevertheless, I wouldn't put it in front of Utopia.[3] For granted Utopia doesn't have the spices the Portuguese *Utopia* buy, still, the way to it is far less danger- ous, and it is full of its own unknown delights. But whoever takes the science of geography to heart either has to travel all over the world (which is extremely unpleasant, difficult, and expensive) or he has to read through Strabo, which is about as long and as broad as the earth and is a world in itself—and in Greek too, since the translation is extremely corrupt.[4] But that's what you have to do, unless this seems shorter: to study the sketches of the globe called colloquially maps of the world.[5] But you ought to know that they also proceed from the learning of those two men I've already mentioned.

"Military training was also renowned among the ancients, but it's so foreign to *Military training* all the schools today that you'll probably think I'm foolish to talk about it. But I'll say this much, speaking as a soldier who has sworn on Christ's words, that if you have to have wars, it's much better to settle them with the good sense of learning rather than with *Discourse on war* a sword. For those who are always ready for savage conflicts show only that they're violent murderers. In fact, whoever goes easy in the hideous spilling of blood, first of all spares his own men; and then the mercy he shows to the enemy is an image of the divine mercy without which there can be no hope for the salvation of man's soul, which is constantly in danger in this sea of misery.

quantumuis Ethnici (cuius uitam nos latinitate donauimus) laudandam & obseruandam iudicamus. Qui quum Athenienses, ad imitationem quorundam Barbarorum, admissuri essent in ciuitatem gladiatorium illud singulare certamen, Nolite, inquit, o

Insignis sententia contra
crudelitatem

ciues mei, hanc crudelitatem prius intro-ducere, quam misericordiae aram sitis demoliti. Artes sibi uendicarunt, & Physio-gnomones, & Metoposcopi, quorum illi

Physiognomia Metoposcopia

ex totius corporis formae inspectione, naturam cuiusque iudicant, hi uero ex

sola fronte contemplanda. Sed has artes ego minime ueras existimo, ut-pote coniectura magis (ut de somnijs scripsimus) & longa obseruatione, quam ulla certa ratione nitentes. Et constat inter peritos, Pythagoram non ultra coniecturam, Physiognomia esse usum, quum mores naturas-que discipulorum, de totius corporis filo atque habitu sciscita-retur. Vnde non solum incredibile dictu est (ut ait Plinius) sed etiam (ut mea fert opinio) impossibile factu, quod Appion grammaticus scriptum reliquit, Alexandrum quendam, tam indiscrete imaginum simi-litudines pinxisse, ut quidam Metoposcopus ex his dixerit futurae mortis annos, aut praeteritae. His addo & Chiromanticam, & artem il-lam χαλαζοφυλάκων, id est, speculatorum

Chiromantia

& obseruatorum futurae grandinis, quos Seneca, Cleonis illius semper μετὰ τὰ

πράγματα σοφοῦ, id est, sero sapientis, publice praepositos fuisse tradit, ineptiam cum istorum, tum omnium qui eis credebant, libro quarto naturalium questionum, egregie depingens & deridens, quod quisque pro se, monentibus istis, alius agnum immolaret, alius pullum, quasi protinus illae nubes grandinosae alio declinarent, quum gustassent ali-quid sanguinis. Omnes itaque has quatuor artes in unam societatem collectas, tanto ueris artibus inferiores esse iudico, quanto uerae & cer-tae rationi, instabilis & fallax cedit coniectura. Quamobrem a sententia mea longe est alienum, ut in his bonae horae male collocentur, & tem-pus teratur. His ita dictis, festinantem me ad quaedam seriora, corri-

That's why we think Demonax [6] the philosopher (whom we have given life to in Latin) should be praised and kept in mind, although he was a pagan. When the Athenians imitated certain barbarians and were about to introduce those strange gladiatorial contests into the city, he said, 'Fellow citizens, don't let in this cruel thing until you've taken down the altar of Pity.'

Notable saying against cruelty

"The arts of physiognomy and metoposcopy put in a word for themselves. The former judges a man's nature by inspecting the shape of his entire body,

Physiognomy and metoposcopy

the latter by studying only his forehead. But I don't think these arts are valid at all since they depend more on guessing [7] (as we noted concerning dreams) and long observation than on any certain knowledge. And those who know agree that Pythagoras was not above guessing and used physiognomy when he would learn the character and nature of his disciples from the outline and appearance of the entire body. That's why, according to Pliny,[8] it's not only incredible to say but also (I think) impossible to do what Apion the Grammarian describes in his book, where he tells of a certain Alexander who painted such lifelike portraits that another man named Metoposcopus could tell from them the year of death, whether past or future.

"To physiognomy and metoposcopy I append chiromancy [9] and the art *chalazo-phylakôn*, that is, the art of observers

Chiromancy

and investigators of future hailstorms. Seneca [1] said they were Cleon's public appointees, the Cleon who was always *meta ta pragmata sophou,* that is, wise after the fact. He thus portrayed their absurdity in the fourth book of his *Natural Curiosities* and made fun of them and everyone who believed in them. For when these weathermen advised them to, everyone sacrificed something for himself—one person a lamb, another a chicken—as if the clouds full of hail would immediately go someplace else as soon as they tasted some blood.

"And so I think all these four arts joined together in one bunch are inferior to real arts, just as uncertain and wrong guesses give way to true and certain reason. That's why I don't think you should spend good hours on them and waste your time."

When I said all that and was hurrying on to something more serious, a deformed little woman grabbed me and held onto me. "Who are you?" I said.

"I'm Dialectic," she said. "Aren't you going to mention me?"

Modern Dialectic

Dialectica recens

puit difformis quaedam muliercula, & detinuit: Quae nam es? inquam. Sum Dialectica, inquit illa. Fiet ne de me ulla mentio? Est, inquam ego, una Dialectica tertia pars Philosophiae. Hanc ego quia a Philosophia non separo, in Philosophiae laudibus complexus sum. Sed tu fortasse illa es, quae restrictiones & secundas intentiones inuenisti, in quibus ego fateor me nihil scire, nam ingeniolum meum non capit, quo pacto ratio ualida, & nunquam non libera, possit restringi. De intentionibus uero, hanc animi esse scio, in contemplanda altius rerum natura, illam uocis (ut apud Musicos) aliam denique aliarum rerum, sed haec una est semper, & sola, nec secundam admittit. Ipsissima, inquit illa, sum, non tamen omnino odi Sortem & Platonem. Vah, inquam ego, uerba tua manifestam te fecerunt, nam Socratem restrinxisti in Sortem. Abi hinc sortilega, mihi tecum nihil est commune. Sic recessit illa, deflens suam sortem.

De praeceptis ad doctrinam incitantibus

Postquam de scientijs omnibus, ut audisti mi Colete, disseruimus, non alienum iam fuerit a re instituta, aliqua (qualiacunque erunt) compendiaria tradere praecepta, quibus iuuenes magis ad doctrinam consequendam incitentur. Quandoquidem (ni fallor) persuasum habent, nihil esse in rebus humanis, quod bonis literis, & praeclarae eruditioni, ex quibus omnis uirtus originem ducit, possit conferri aut aequari. In quam rem eleganter scribit Plinius nepos. Quid publice, inquit, laetius, quam clarissimos iuuenes, nomen & famam ex literarum studijs petere? Ex quibus uerbis hoc quoque obiter est notandum, quod publice utilissimum aperte testatur, non modo inferioris conditionis iuuenes, sed etiam clarissimos, nomen sibi & gloriam ex doctrina petere, quod longo distat interuallo, ab illius cornigeri generosi opinione, quam in praefatione strenue irrisimus. Ceterum in hac parte meo, qualecunque est, utar iudicio, & non multis uerbis iuueniles animos delassabo, (Nam si omnia quae in hanc rem dici possent, scribere uellem, in nimis magnum uolumen opus cresceret),[9] sed pauca paucis perstringam, quo libentius, faciliusque imbibant, & si utilia uidebuntur, imitentur. Primum igitur iuuenibus cauendum censemus, ne ullam temporis, nimis cito fugientis, & irreuocabilis horam male collocent. Nam ex tempore, quod frustra, inaniterque teritur, nihil fructus percipient, praeter pudorem & poenitentiam, quodque clare cognoscent, quicquid sibi in hac breui & caduca placet uita, praeter uirtutem (cuius sedula suppeditatrix est doctrina) hoc totum breue esse somnium, & simillimum bullae in aqua turgescen-

---

[9] cresceret,) *1517*

"One part of dialectic," I said "is the third part of philosophy. Since I don't make a distinction between it and philosophy, I included it in my praise of philosophy. But maybe you're the one who invented restrictions and second intentions,[2] which I confess I don't know anything about. For with the little bit of brains I have I don't understand how reason can be restricted since it's always strong and free. I know there's one intention,[3] or rather intensity, in the soul when it contemplates deeply the nature of things; there's an intention or tension, of the voice (as among musicians); and finally there's the intention of everything else. But this new intention is always single and solitary and doesn't admit a second."

"That's me," she said, "in the flesh. But I don't hate Sortes[4] and Plato completely."

"Aha," I said, "your words give you away, for you've abbreviated *Socrates to Sortes*. Go on, get out of here, you *sortilegia*, you fortune-teller. I have nothing in common with you." So she went away bewailing her *sortes*, I mean her lot.

Now that we've discussed all the sciences, as you heard, dear Colet, it may not be off the subject to mention at random some short precepts to stir on the boys to pursue learning more than they do. For unless I'm mistaken, they're persuaded that nothing in human affairs is comparable to good learning or distinguished erudition, which are the source of all virtue. Pliny the younger[5] wrote elegantly on the subject. "What is more fortunate for the state," he said, "than for young men of distinction to seek fame and glory in the pursuit of learning?" It should be noted in passing that he clearly says it's extremely useful for the state to have not only young men of the lower classes seek fame and glory for themselves in learning, but also young men of distinction. That's a far cry from the opinion of that noble horn-blower we laughed at so hard in the preface.[6] Yet in this part I'll rely on my own judgment, such as it is, and not bore young minds with many words; if I wanted to write everything that could be said on the subject, my book would grow too big. But I'll touch lightly on a few things in a few words so they can take it in free and easy, and if it seems useful, they can follow it.

In the first place, then, we think young people should watch out and not waste any time; it passes too swiftly and irrevocably. For they derive no benefit except shame and repentance from time that's wasted and spent in vain. And they should clearly realize that whatever seems good to them in this brief and fleeting life except virtue (and learning is her diligent assistant)—all that is a brief dream and like a bubble in

Precepts that move one to learning

tis, quae simul atque exorta est, euanescit. Quod si uolunt tempus bene
& honeste consumere, nec melius profecto, nec honestius id facere possunt, quam in bonarum disciplinarum studijs, quae ob hoc solum bonae
dicuntur, quod bonos uiros reddant. Istud uero ut facilius assequantur,
& ab incepto non desistant, nec in hac literaria militia desertores fiant,
in primis fugiendam iudicamus improborum & malorum hominum consuetudinem, sciantque a Demosthene, Oratorum Graecorum principe,
cum eleganter, tum uere dictum esse, τοιοῦτός ἐστιν ἕκαστος, ὥσπερ
ἥδεται συνὼν, id est, talem quemque decet esse, quales sunt illi, quorum consuetudine oblectatur. Cui assentitur Dauid quoque noster,
diuino afflatus spiritu. Cum bono, inquit, bonus eris, & cum peruerso
peruerteris. Et quod diuus Paulus scribit, Bonos mores corrumpunt
colloquia mala, potuisset etiam uerti, consuetudines malae (quae uul-
garius conuersationes appellantur) nam utrumque significat apud
Graecos ὁμιλία, sed sensus est idem. Etenim tantum proculdubio hinc
prouenit mali, & praecipue iuuenibus, quorum aetas est infirmior, & ob
id facile huc uel illuc impellitur, ut haud sciam an sola improborum,
malorumque & peruersorum hominum consuetudo recte uocetur Ilias
simul & Lerna malorum, & si quod aliud adagium sit, cum plurimas,
tum maximas calamitates denotans. Siquidem haec est uere illa pestis,
quae omnes ad unum bonos mores subuertit, utpote omne utile &
honestum studium damnans, ut teterrimae indulgeatur uoluptati,
omnem fidem expellens foras, ut introducatur mera perfidia, omne ius
in profundas conijciens tenebras, ut iniuria lucidissime in aperto splen-
deat, simplicitatem ceu rem perditissimam uilipendens & detestans, ut
fraus in altissimo throno collocetur.[1] Et ut summatim dicam, omnium
uitiorum irritamenta excogitans, ut omnis prorsus uirtus e medio pella-
tur. Ab hac igitur iuuenes liberati, sumant sibi in exemplum illos doctos uiros, qui superioribus aetatibus floruerunt, & nullos in toto orbe
reperient, plus existimationis & honoris unquam consecutos, quam illi,
nec qui de genere humano melius sunt meriti. Hi enim non uerbis
modo uitia fugienda docuerunt, & uirtutibus inherendum, sed re ipsa
singularia bene & honeste uiuendi exempla omnibus praebuerunt. Vnde
Rhetores in personis laudandis, cum alia multa, tum praecipue doctrinam & gesta hominum obseruanda tradunt, haud quaquam inepte doctrinam etiam gestis praeferentes, quasi nihil, ubi doctrina desit, recte
geri possit. Atque hinc euenisse satis constat, illos antiquos principes &
reges clariores, & doctrinae fuisse cupidissimos, & nihil aeque appetisse,
atque ut doctos uiros, magna mercede conductos, nutrirent, existiman-
tes se solidam gloriam tum demum assecuturos, si sapientem, id est

---

[1] collocetur, *1517*

swollen waters that vanishes as soon as it appears. But if they want to spend their time properly and honorably, they can't do it better or more honorably than in the study of good fields of learning, which are called *good* for this reason alone: because they produce good men. In fact in order to pursue it more easily and not stop at the beginning and become deserters in this army of learning, we think first of all that they should avoid the company of dishonest, evil men.[7] They should also know that Demosthenes,[8] the prince of Greek orators, said elegantly and truly *toioutos estin hekastos, hôsper hêdetai synôn,* that is, a man is known by the company he keeps. Inspired by the Holy Spirit, our David[9] also agrees with him. "With a good man," he says, "you will be good, and with a bad man, you will be bad." And what St. Paul writes,[1] "bad conversations ruin good morals," might have also been translated, "bad customs," which are called colloquially *conversations,* for in Greek *homilia* means both. But the meaning is the same either way. For no doubt this is the source of much evil, and especially to the young, who are inexperienced and therefore more easily inclined this way or that. In fact, I don't know but what you should call the companionship of dishonest, evil, and corrupt men the *Iliad* as well as the Lerna[2] of evil—or anything else you can think of denoting many great misfortunes. Surely this is the destructive force that destroys all good habits at once, inasmuch as it condemns all useful and honest study in order to indulge in loathesome pleasure. It drives all faith out of doors, so it can bring in pure faithlessness. It casts all justice into deep darkness, so that injustice can shine brightly in the open. It despises and detests simplicity as a thing corrupt, so it can enthrone deceit on high. And, in short, it thinks up provocations to all vice, so it can drive all virtue completely from our midst.

Young men, therefore, who are free from all that, should take the learned men who flourished in former times as patterns for themselves. They'll find no one in the whole world with more character and honor than they had and no one who deserves better of the human race. For these men not only taught in words alone that we should shun vice and cling to virtue, but they also furnished everyone with examples of proper and honest living in their own actions. That's why rhetoricians say that when we praise people we should note particularly how learned they are and how they act, along with many other things. And not at all foolishly they prefer learning to deeds, since nothing can be done properly without learning. And it's generally agreed that that's why those ancient princes and famous kings desired learning very much and wanted nothing more. They all wanted to maintain learned men, brought together at great cost, for they thought they'd finally get

doctum uirum domi, a quo erudirentur, familiarem haberent. Quod si
nostra quoque aetate fieret, praeclarius proculdubio cum rebus humanis ageretur. Nam quanto maior principum est sapientia, tanto felicior
est populorum conditio, necnon illorum
Sententia   securior malorum, quae ex publica re per
imprudentiam male administrata, nimis
multa obueniunt. Istud hoc nostro saeculo, raro & paucis accidit, &
nemini certe illustrius, quam ERASMO
De Erasmo   nostro. cuius doctrina tam admirabilis est
& multiplex, ut Pontifices Maximi, omnes
Cardinales, omnes Reges & principes, uno consensu, de eo certare
uideantur. nec immerito. Nam apud quemcumque hic orbis doctrinae
erit, is uiuam habebit imaginem, quam omnibus suis stemmatis longe
possit anteferre. Verum quod risum mihi mouit, ERASMVS ipse dixisse
fertur, nihil sibi hoc certamine, longo tempore infelicius accidisse. Nam
dum illi strenue certarunt, ipse [2] misere eguit, propterea quod huius
tempestatis homines libentius admirantur doctos, quam nutriunt. Sed
quoniam huiuscemodi de doctrina ERASMI nostri mentio est oblata, non
possum illud literis non commendare, neminem esse in tota Italia, siue
doctus sit, siue indoctus (quorum ille iudicio & ratione, hic uero fama
& nomine mouetur) qui non summa admiratione & laude illius doctrinam prosequatur, excepto uno titulo tenus archiepiscopo, professione
non Theologus, sed Scotista. Is enim
Erasmum defendit Paceus   nuper me audiente, dixit se in sinu ha-
contra Scotistam   bere unum, ut uocabat, rotulum, ERASMI
errores in sacra Theologia continentem,
& coepit strenue auram uerberare, hoc est, in ERASMVM nostrum absen-
tem inuehi, ac si fuisset in sua corona & palaestra. Tum ego insaniam
hominis, cum ex gestibus, tum ex uerbis dispiciens, (ridebimus, inquam
apud me) profer, quaeso o bone uir, istum tuum rotulum, & doce nos
istos errores, ut possimus eos fugere. Nam & nos ex illis sumus, qui
permulta legimus Erasmica, etiam theologica, nec unquam huiuscemodi potuimus deprendere errores. Ideoque quia tu Theologiae (ut
iactas) professor es, a te ualde cupimus doceri, & sententiam tuam si
meliorem Erasmica ostenderis, pia mente (ut Christianos decet) seque-
mur, & bono zelo (ut uestris utamur uerbis) instigati, tanquam nec
Platonis, nec Socratis, sed ueritatis amici, una tecum damnabimus

---

[2] ipe *1517*

the glory if they had a wise man, that is to say, a learned man, in the house as their close companion to teach them. If that were done nowadays, no doubt our age would be more distinguished. For the greater the wisdom of the prince, the better the condition of the people, and the more secure from the many evils which come *A wise saying* from having public affairs badly handled through stupidity.

In our century it's rarely done. Few people are given preferment and certainly no one more gloriously than our dear friend Erasmus.[3] His learning is so admirable and extensive that the popes, *Erasmus* the cardinals, kings and princes with one accord seem to fight over him. And they should. For whoever has that world of learning in his household will have a living image which he can rate far above all his ancestral portraits. In fact what Erasmus himself is reported to have said makes me laugh.[4] He said nothing more unfortunate than this competition had happened to him for a long time. While they struggled so hard for him, he was poor and miserable because men nowadays marvel at the learned more willingly than they take care of them.

But since I've mentioned our dear friend Erasmus in this way, I can't help but add that there's no one in all Italy, learned or unlearned, who doesn't honor his learning with the greatest admiration and praise (the learned through their own reason and judgment, the unlearned through his fame and reputation). Everyone in Italy, that is, except one person, an archbishop,[5] at least in title; in profession, not a theologian, but a Scotist. For I recently heard him say he had in his pocket a little black book, as he called it, full of Erasmus' *Pace defends Erasmus against* errors in sacred theology. And he began *a Scotist* to flail about wildly, that is, attack our dear Erasmus, who wasn't even there, as though he was in his own circle and school. I despised the man's insanity, not only his actions, but also his words, and I said to myself, let's have a laugh.

"Let's see that little black book, my good man, and show us the mistakes so we can steer clear of them. For I'm one of those people who's read quite a bit of Erasmus, as well as theology, and I couldn't ever find any mistakes like that. So, since you're a professor of theology (as you keep on saying), we want very much to be taught by you, and we'll follow you piously (as Christians should) if you give us something better than Erasmus. And (to use your own words) 'incited by true zeal,' we'll damn Erasmus too, as friends not of Plato, nor of Socrates, but of truth."

ERASMVM. Non domine Ambassiator, inquit excandescens Scotista, non uolo nunc proferre, dominatio uestra non est Theologus, ego sum doctus sciatis, ego legi Pisis.[3] Ego uolo trahere istum haereticum ad concilium generale. Hic unus ex circumstantibus interrupto sermone, Quod legisti, inquit, Pisis, nihil penitus fuit, sed ego in Germanicis hypocaustis te inter bibulos egregie declamantem audiui, & uociferando superasse ipsum stentorem. Sed ego, bona uerba queso, inquam, o Scotista. Ego nec Theologus sum, fateor, nec Philosophus, immo nec doctus. Et quod plus est, fateor me hoc solum scire, quod nihil scio, & hoc uno sum sapientior te. Quod autem ad generale concilium Erasmum uis trahere, non est opus trahatur, quippe sua sponte & libenter uenturus, ideo quod generalia concilia, eo eiusque similibus potius quam tui uehementer indigent. Sed dic mihi, Nouisti ne Erasmum? Noui, inquit, & uidi, est magnus ribaldus. Quare, inquam, tunc rotulum tuum non protulisti?

Barbare & incongrue loquitur Scotista

Ita non, inquit, uolui plura colligere, & facere librum. Res non ita habet, inquam ego, nam Paulus meus Bombasius, uir cum primis eruditissimus, longe aliam causam mihi retulit, affirmans te, Erasmo praesente, non modo non rotulum tuum, sed nec teipsum ausum esse proferre. In quo solo ego ingenium tuum laudo, ne uidelicet una te cum tuam proferres singularem ignorantiam & stultitiam. Qui enim fieri potest, ut tu, aut quiuis alius, Erasmum haereticae impietatis possit damnare, qui euangelio, id est, ipsi Christo, Paulo uestro in euangelium segregato, Hieronymo & Augustino, atque alijs scientiae uestrae luminibus fixus, pertinaciter adhaeret, nec ab his uel transuersum unguem recedit, id quod in omnibus operibus eius est manifestissimum. Et hi adeo ei memoria non excidunt, ut etiam in Adagijs illorum sit memor, ut Pauli, quum ait, Noli aduersus stimulum calcitrare. Quod prouerbium tibi etiam, și sapis, est discendum. Tum Scotista Theologiae oblitus, Adagijs, inquit, quid est hoc? est ne nouum Erasmi opus? Tibi, inquam, omnino nouum, quia ne nomen quidem intelligere uideris. Quid, inquit, in aerem circunspiciens, & contorquens labia, quasi

Perplexe loquitur

Adagijs studiose incongrue ponitur

---

[3] Pisis, *1517*

"No, my lord Ambassador," said that
inflamed Scotist. "I don't want to give it   *The Scotist speaks incongruously*
to you now. Your lordship is no theolo-   *and ungrammatically*
gian, but I'm a learned man, you know.
I've read Pisis.[6] I'd like to drag this heretic before a general council."

At that point one of the bystanders interrupted him and said, "What
you read in Pisis wasn't very deep. But I've heard you spouting forth
splendidly with the drinkers in German pubs, louder than Stentor." [7]

"Come on, give us a kind word, old Scotist," I said. "I'm no theologian, I admit, and no philosopher. In fact, I'm not learned. And what's
more I admit I only know this: that I know nothing. And in that one
thing I'm wiser than you. But you want to drag Erasmus before a general council. There's no need to. He'd go willingly since general councils need him and people like him much more than they need people
like you. But tell me, you don't really know Erasmus, do you?"

"I know him," he said, "and I've seen him before. He's a big
hellraiser."

"Why don't you show us your little black book, then?" I said.

"No indeed," he said. "I want to collect
more notes and make a book."   *He speaks confusedly*

"That's not true," I said, "for my friend
Paulus Bombasius, who's as learned as they come, gave me a very different reason. He said that when Erasmus was around, you didn't dare
show yourself or your little black book. And for that one thing I praise
your intelligence, that is, you had sense enough not to exhibit yourself
and your remarkable stupidity at the same time. How is it that you or
anyone else can condemn Erasmus as an irreligious heretic? For he
sticks closely to the Gospel, that is, to Christ Himself, to your dear friend
Paul [8] 'set apart for the gospel of God,' to Jerome and Augustine, and
all the other luminaries of theology. He clings to them obstinately and
doesn't depart from them even the width of a fingernail,[9] which is obvious in all his works. He's so far from forgetting them that he remem-
bers them even in the *Adagia,* like St. Paul, for example, when he says,
'Don't kick against the pricks.' [1] That's a proverb you'll learn too, if
you're wise."

Then the Scotist forgot about theology and said, "*Adagias?* What's
them? They're not some new works of
Erasmus' [2] are they?"   *Adagiis is carefully*
misused
"It's completely new to you," I said,
"since you don't even understand the
title."

"What?" he said, peering about in the air and squeezing his lips

blateraturus aliquid, Non domine, non est cura de uerbis. Quid ais, inquam ego, insanis ne? Est ne omnis scriptura uerbum dei? Est ne deus ipse uerbum? Haec tu si non curas, negligis, si negligis, tu haereticus es, non Erasmus, qui nihil praeter haec praedicat. His ita dictis, nihil habens respondendum, aspexit astantes suos ministros. Et Ioannes inquit submissa uoce, per deum iste ambassiator deridet me, & uidetur esse scientificus, quod si sciuissem antea, de Erasmo nullum dixissem uerbum. Sed faciliter me uindicabo, nam uolo abire & emere istum

Istum

nouum opus Adagijs, & cercare plures falsitates, & omnes portare meis confratribus, qui una mecum insurgent contra utrunque. Scriptum est enim, Insurget gens contra gentem. Huic egredienti & grauiter irato, obuiam sit Bombasius meus, domum meam ingrediens, sed ne uerbum quidem ei locutus, (delicatissimarum aurium suarum, ne barbarie offenderentur, curam gerens),[4] recta ad me in cubiculum peruenit. Quid tibi, inquit, cum isto Scotista? Disputauimus, inquam, de lana caprina. Non decet, inquit, te cum istis disputare, quia sunt indocti. Hoc morbo, inquam, & ego laboro.[5] Vetus dictum est (ut nosti) pares cum paribus, sed non tam disputaui quam irrisi illum, & uix tandem ridendo extrusi foras. Sed unde digressi sumus, redeundum est. Labor, dixerit aliquis, in doctrina comparanda multus est, & uia ad illam aspera. Est & in nugis labor, est in uoluptatibus, quas (ut Plutarchus ait) etiam difficilius ferimus quam labores, & ipsum corpus humanum, ocio citius turpi marcessit, quam conteritur labore, immo labore plerunque uiget. Nullum denique est uitium, ut dicam breuibus, quod labore uacat. Ad quod suauiter & eleganter allusit Sophocles, quum ait, πόνος σὺν πόνῳ πόνον φέρει, id est, labor labori laborem addit. Verum si in rebus optimis, & soli uirtuti innitentibus, (qualis est doctrina, immo quarum est princeps) labor hominibus uidetur maior, quum ita natura comparatum sit, ut omnia praeclara in arduo collocentur, non labor modo, quo temetipsum temere deterres, intuendus est, (sorte illius Romani, haud quaquam studioso homini deprecanda, cui nihil puero quidem feriae unquam obtigerant) sed fructus etiam, qui ex huiusmodi laboribus prouenit, perpendendus. Tur-

---

[4] gerens,) *1517*
[5] laboro, *1517*

together as if he were going to blabber something. "No, my lord, words don't matter."

"What are you talking about?" I said. "Are you crazy? The entire Bible is the word of God, isn't it? God Himself is the Word, isn't He? If you don't care about these things, you neglect them. If you neglect them, you're the heretic, not Erasmus. For he deals in nothing but words."

After I said that, he had nothing to reply but looked at his servants standing around and said in a low voice, "By God, John, this here Ambassador is making fun of me and seems pretty smart. If I'd known that before, I wouldn't have said a word about Erasmus. But I'll get back at him easy, because I want to go out and buy this here new work *Adagias* and look for more mistakes and take them all to my colleagues. *Same as above* They'll rise up with me against both him and his work. For it's written, 'Nation will rise against nation.'"[3]

As he was going away completely enraged, my dear friend Bombasius, who was on the way to my house, met him, but Bombasius didn't say a word to him. He wanted to take care of his delicate ears, so they wouldn't be hurt by his ignorant language. He came straight to my bedroom. "What were you doing with that Scotist?" he said.

"We were arguing about goat wool,"[4] I said.

"You shouldn't argue with people like that," he said. "They're too ignorant."

"Even I've got a touch of that," I said. "There's the old saying [5] you know, 'like to like.' But I actually laughed at him more than I argued with him and finally had a hard time driving him away with laughter."

But let's go back to the point where we began this digression. Someone said there's a lot of work in acquiring knowledge and that the way to it is hard.[6] There's also work in foolishness as well as in pleasure, which Plutarch [7] says we have a harder time putting up with than work. And the human body itself languishes more quickly in shameful ease than it does in work. In fact, it usually thrives on work. And finally, to put it briefly, there's no vice that's void of work. Sophocles alluded to this smoothly and elegantly when he said,[8] *ponos syn ponôi ponon pherei*, that is, work adds work to work. But if the work on things that are best and that depend on virtue alone (like learning, for example; in fact it's the most outstanding), seems harder, you must not only consider the work and thereby discourage yourself unnecessarily, for nature has so ordained that all admirable things are invested in hardship. If you do, you'll be like the Roman [9] who never had any holidays even when he was a boy. He's a good model for learned men. But you must also consider the benefit produced by work of that kind.

pissimum est (mihi crede) detrectare uel fugere laborem, quando ad magnam uirtutem consequendam laboratur. Siquidem natura ipsa manifeste indicat, non magis bruta animalia ad corporis laborem, quam homines ad utrunque, & corporis & animi laborem natos, nec uitam longam esse posse, siquis totum se a laboribus corporis subtrahat. Hinc manus, hinc pedes, hinc omnia membra ad laborem corporis habemus a natura aptissima, quibus etiam ad laborem prisci illi sapientes sunt usi, ut Cincinatus ille, qui ex aratro totus puluerulentus, dictator Romanorum designatus fuit. Sed quantum labor animi, corporis labori excellit, hinc est perspicuum, quod illam diuinam uim ingenij largitus est deus benigne ad laborem animi, membra uero ad laborem corporis, quae & ipsa reguntur ingenio. Laborem igitur animi sequatur & persequatur studiosus iuuenis (sciatque hunc ocium fuisse Scipionis, qui nunquam minus ociosum se esse dictitabat, quam quum ociosus esset, nimirum nactus occasionem, ut labori animi uacaret).[6] Et quum in doctum uirum euadere serio cupit, initio quidem laboribus se addicat, oportet. sed hi labores in honestissimam desinent uoluptatem. Item puer in scholis prima discens rudimenta, molestiae aliquid patitur, quae tum augetur maxime (ut hoc quoque in transcursu notem) si imperitum sortitus sit paedagogum, quales olim scio apud nos fuisse multos, & nescio an adhuc supersint. Nam is si uidet puerum ad discendum tardiorem, non nisi uerberibus agendum censet, & indoctus homo, uerbera plus posse quam naturam credit, ignorans illud saepissime usu uenire, ut tardiora ingenia melius contineant, & ad frugem peruueniant maiorem, quam illa praematura. Hinc Fabius, Illud, inquit, ingeniorum praecox genus, nunquam temere peruenit ad frugem. Hinc & Cleanthes, magni nominis Philosophus, comparatus fuit a praeceptore uasi angusti oris, quod melius continet, quam in id facilius infunditur. Sed in scholis, inquam, puer aliquid molestiae patitur, uerum quum in uirum creuerit, & prouectior aetate, rem penitius intuetur, molestiam illam omnem, maiori uirtute compensatam uidet, & in gaudium usquequaque adeo conuersam, ut nihil magis doleat, quam quod maiorem non sit passus. Iusta nimirum trutina rem expendens, quod dura, aspera, & salebrosa montis radix, ipsum in mollissimum, amoenissimum, & floridissimum cacumen perduxerit. ubi tanta rerum, & quidem pulcherrimarum, uarietate allicitur, ut etiam si uellet, descendere non possit, adeo uirtus doctrinae est tenax sui. Socrates aetate sua unicum sapien-

---

[6] uacaret) *1517*

Believe me, it's a rotten thing to slip out from under work or run away from it, when it makes you have more virtue. In fact, nature itself clearly shows that brute animals are not any more especially born to work with their bodies than men are to work with both their minds and their bodies. And it also shows that if anyone quits working with his body entirely, he won't live long. That's why our hands, our feet, all our limbs are well suited by nature to physical labor. The wise men of former ages used them for work, like Cincinnatus,[1] who was named Emergency Ruler of Rome while he was still all covered with dust from the plow. But you can see from this how much the work of the mind is superior to the work of the body: God kindly bestowed on the work of the mind the divine power of the intellect, and He gave to the work of the body the limbs of the body, which are themselves controlled by the intellect.

Students, therefore, should pursue the work of the mind, and they should know that that was the way Scipio[2] spent his spare time. He said he was never less idle than when he was idle. He obviously meant he found a time when he was free for work of the mind. And since a student seriously wants to turn out to be a learned man, he must give himself over entirely to work at first. But the work finally ends up in honorable pleasure. So also a boy first learning the rudiments in school undergoes some difficulty, which is increased considerably (if I may mention this in passing) if it's his luck to have an inexperienced teacher[3] like the ones I know we used to have a lot of—and probably still do. For if one of them sees a boy who's slow at learning, he thinks the only thing he can do about it is beat him.[4] An ignorant man thinks beatings can do more than nature itself. He doesn't know that it's often the case that slower minds retain things better and produce better fruit than those that are premature. That's why Fabius says,[5] "A precocious kind of mind never comes to maturity easily." And that's why Cleanthes,[6] a philosopher of great renown, was compared by his teacher to a vase with a narrow mouth, which retains things better, but is not filled very easily. Of course, a boy in school has to put up with some trouble. Yet, when he grows up to be a man and is a little more mature, he'll consider it more deeply and see that the trouble he had is compensated for by an increase in virtue and that it's completely transformed into inward happiness. The only thing he'll be sorry for is that he didn't suffer more. And no doubt he's weighed it carefully, because the hard, rough, rugged foot of the mountain finally brought him to the level, delightful, flowery summit.[7] He finds so many things there, such various beauty, that he can't go down even if he wants to, the virtue of learning is so engrained in him. Socrates,[8] who was a unique pattern

tiae specimen, monuit iuuenes utilissime, ut crebro semetipsos in speculis contemplarentur, & si turpiores uiderentur, ornarent se doctrina, sin pulchri, pulchritudinem doctrina augerent. Est enim haec doctrinae uis, ut humilia tollat in excelsum, excelsa uero diuinis aequet. Sicut & hoc quoque *Sententia* habet, ut si tibi prosperior sit fortuna, longe clariorem te reddat. Si uero aduersis obruaris, maxime te consoletur, id quod ego saepius sum expertus. Ad hoc, quia utilitas in rebus humanis plurimi aestimatur, considerandum & inspiciendum est iuuenibus, quot olim, quotque nunc sunt, quos obscuro loco natos, doctrina nobilissimos & illustrissimos reddidit. Et illa demum uera est nobilitas, quam uirtus facit, magis quam clara, longaque generis series. quae questio olim iam ab eruditissimis uiris disputata fuit. Et qui contra senserunt, hi fuere qui omnium bonorum morum corruptelam, in genus humanum inuexerunt. Non enim temere dictum est, non uirtutibus ex no-*Sententia* bilitate, sed nobilitati ex uirtute, honor accedit. Quum ergo ex his satis manifestum esse arbitrer, quanta sit doctrinae excellentia, quamque omnibus uotis sit necessario expetenda, ad alia huc respicientia stilum conuertam. Nam quoniam superius monuimus, improborum & malorum hominum consuetudinem fugiendam, consequitur hoc, ut doceamus quorum consuetudine iuuenibus studiosis est utendum. Immo uetus illud prouerbium hoc docet breuiter, pares cum paribus. Iuuenes itaque literarum studijs dediti, non nisi doctis & honestis uiris familiariter utantur, horum domos frequentent, hos consulant. Siquid dubitant, totis denique uiribus laborent, ut ostendant se discere uelle, & nihil aeque atque doctrinam ex animo petere. Nam si huiuscemodi indolem, & discendi cupiditatem, in adolescente conspexerit, ut quisque est doctissimus, ita libentissime eum erudiet, & currenti (ut aiunt) calcaria addet. Istud mihi primum quidem contigit Patauij, quum iunior literis humanioribus incumbere inciperem, ex Cuthberto Tvnstallo, & Gulielmo Latymero, uiris clarissimis, & undecunque doctissimis. quorum *Praeceptores Pacei, Cuthbertus* praeterea tanta est prudentia, probitas *Tunstallus, Gulielmus Latymerus* uitae, morumque honestas, ut uix dici possit, an doctrina magis illorum mores, an mores doctrinam ornent. Deinde uero a Leonico, & Leoniceno, eius-

of wisdom in his age, advised young men, to good advantage, to look at themselves often in the mirror, and if they seemed somewhat ugly, to make themselves handsome with learning, and if they seemed handsome, to increase it with learning. For this is the power of learning: it raises humble things to the heights, and it
makes things that are already high equal   *A wise saying*
to the divine. And it also has this virtue:
if Fortune smiles on you, learning makes you even more splendid. But if you meet adversity, it's a great consolation—as I've often learned in my own case. Moreover, since most people set a value on utility in human affairs, the young should consider and examine how many people there used to be and how many there are now who were born in obscurity and who have become famous and noble through learning. For true nobility [9] is surely created by virtue, and not by a long and famous line of ancestors. In the old days that question was argued by learned men. And those who disagreed were the ones who corrupted all good customs for mankind. For
it was not said rashly that honor does not   *A wise saying*
come to virtue from nobility, but to nobil-
ity from virtue.

Since, therefore, I think it's clear enough from what I've already said how great learning is and how important it is to seek it with your whole heart, I'll turn my pen at this point to other considerations. For since we've warned you above to avoid the company of wicked and evil men, it follows that we ought to teach you whose company is good for studious young men. In fact that old proverb teaches it in brief: like with like. Thus young men given to the pursuit of learning should associate only with learned and honorable men, frequent their houses, and go to them for advice. If they have any doubts at all, the young men should work with all their might to show they're willing to learn and willing to seek learning with their whole heart before everything else. For if someone sees a disposition like that in a boy and a desire for learning, the more learned the man is the more willing he'll be to teach him and spur on a running horse (as they say).[1]

That first happened to me at Padua when I was a youngster and began to apply myself to the humanities under Cuthbert Tunstal and William Latimer,[2] famous men and
learned in every way. Beyond that, they   *Pace's teachers, Cuthbert*
had so much common sense, such upright   *Tunstal, William Latimer*
lives, and honest characters that you
could hardly say whether their learning added more to their characters or their characters to their learning. After that I studied with Leonicus

dem notae uiris. Item Erasmo nostro uarijs in locis (quod & nunc fit, nam uel libri eius comitantur me, uel ego persequor illos) & Paulo Bombasio Bononiae, ubi magno auditorio laudatissime omnes bonos libros est interpretatus. Nam his solis siqua in me eruditiuncula est, hanc omnem acceptam refero, & ob id in his meis nugis, non ingrati discipuli functus officio, memorem me praeceptorum ostendere uolui, quos uel rusticus apud Aristophanem, honorandos saltem farina censet.

Ex bonis literis, & bonis moribus, perfectio uitae

Ex huiusmodi uirorum, o iuuenes, consuetudine, non solum bonae literae, sed boni quoque mores discuntur, ex quibus duobus tota humanae uitae perfectio conflatur. Ex docto ore nil nisi doctum audietis, quae res ad multa celeriter discenda maxime facit. Nam nescio quo modo saepe accidit, ut quae audimus, modo erudita sint, magis insidant memoriae, quam quae legimus. Nolite igitur hanc, ceu ualidissimum doctrinae acquirendae fundamentum negligere, ne si infeliciter auspicemini, infelicissimus sequatur exitus. Atqui hinc iacto fundamento, opus iam superstruam. Iuuenis sic erga literas, ut supra postulaui, affectus, reuocet in memoriam illa quae in grammatica scripsimus, de graeca coniunctim cum latina discenda. Nullus enim

De literis graecis discendis

proculdubio insigniter doctus esse potest, qui graecae literaturae sit ignarus. quod ut clarius tibi (mi Colete) nuper, quam unquam antea demonstraretur, effecit Erasmus noster sua noui testamenti editione, & annotationibus eidem adnexis. in quibus ita tibi satisfecit (ut in quadam ad eum epistola testaris) ut ad graecas literas discendas, uehementer uidearis ab eo incitatus. Qua in re, iudicio tuo nihil potest esse rectius. nam tantum (mihi crede) doctrinae, quam nunc habes (alioqui adeo singulari, ut & te domi, & patriam nostram foris apud alias gentes mirifice illustret) adijciet graeca literatura, ut eius peritus, te parum antea, aut nihil sciuisse iudicaturus sis. Id quod contigit summo meo amico conterraneo nostro Gulielmo Stokelleio, uiro

Gulielmus Stokelleius

acerrimi iudicij, in Theologicis & Philosophicis excellenti, & plane admirando, & non utriusque modo linguae peritissimo, sed nec hebraicae ignaro. Nam is hoc mihi Romae est ingenue confessus, non mediocriter dolens se annos nimis multos, antequam graece sciret, in imaginarijs quibusdam nugis contriuisse, ut sunt restrictiones, nescio quae, & secundae intentiones, quas ne Vtopiani quidem unquam admiserunt. Hic insurgit, nes-

and Leonicenus,[3] also famous men; with our friend Erasmus in various places (as I still do today, for I either have his books with me or I go and get them); and with Paulus Bombasius of Bologna. In a great lecture hall in Bologna he brilliantly interpreted all good books. I owe what little erudition I have in me to these men alone, and so I want to perform the office of a grateful student in this insignificant little book of mine and remember my teachers. Even the farmer in Aristophanes [4] thought they should at least be honored with corn meal.

My boys, you can acquire not only good learning, but also good character *From good books and good* from knowing men like that. And from *character, the perfection of life* those two things flows the entire perfection of human life. From the mouths of the learned, you'll hear nothing but learning, which will help you considerably to learn many things quickly. For I don't know how it happens, but the things we hear (provided they're learned) stick in the mind better than the things we read. So don't overlook this, for it's the soundest foundation for acquiring learning. If you make a poor beginning, you'll make a worse ending.

And now that I've laid the foundation, I'll begin the building. A boy thus inclined to learning, as I've postulated above, should remember what I've written in the section on grammar about learning Greek along with *On learning Greek* Latin.[5] For it's obvious that no one can be very learned if he doesn't know anything about Greek literature. Our dear Erasmus made that clearer to you recently (dear Colet) than it had ever been before in his edition and notes to the New Testament. He so satisfied you with it (as you say in one of your letters to him) [6] that you seem to have been passionately inspired to study Greek yourself. And you couldn't be more correct, for believe me, Greek literature will add so much to the learning you now have (already so remarkable that it distinguishes you wonderfully at home and our country abroad, among other nations) that once you've learned it, you'll think you knew little or nothing before. That's what happened to my great friend and our fellow countryman William Stokesley,[7] a brilliant theologian and *William Stokesley* excellent philosopher—completely admirable—who not only knows Greek and Latin, but also something about Hebrew. For he told me frankly at Rome that he was pretty sad he'd wasted so many years in imaginary nonsense before he learned Greek. He meant the restrictions (God only knows what they are) and second intentions [8] that are not allowed in Utopia.

cio quis, contra me, Asseueras ne tu, inquit, omnes indoctos esse & fore, nisi qui graece sciunt? Non hoc dico, inquam, immo fateor multos doctos esse posse, qui nec graece, nec latine sciant (si benigna natura uim largiatur ingenij) quales fuerunt Hebraei & Chaldaei, quos tamen tantum superarunt Graeci, quantum Latini cedunt Graecis. Ratio seipsam profert, nec multis utendum est argumentis. Apud Chaldaeos nihil ferme est, apud Hebraeos parum, quod tamen est, bonum est, quia ad uetus testamentum intelligendum nonnihil confert. Apud Latinos uero, quicquid apparet proprium, ut in arte dicendi, & in historia, hoc totum quasi mutuo sumptum est ex Graecis. Nam Ciceronem, quantus est in arte Oratoria (Quintiliano id confitente) fecit Demosthenes & Isocrates. In Philosophia uero, Plato & Aristoteles, quorum alterum diuinum, alterum sapientissimum, ut doctissimos Graecos saepe appellat. Sed Philosophia adeo apud Latinos manca est, ut nihil possit esse eruditis auribus stultius, quam Latinos Philosophos cum Graecis comparare. Quo in genere, nec Ciceronem ipsum (quod eius uenia dictum sit) excipio. Porro in historia sunt Latini octo, uel ad summum nouem probati, quos omnes, meo quidem iudicio, unus superat Thucidides, cui cur tam parum tribuit Cicero, uiderit ipse, longe dissentiens a Demosthene, omnis eloquentiae fonte, quem sua ipsius manu Thucididem octies scripsisse constat. Nempe admiratur (id quod est) maximam eloquentiam cum summa prudentia, pulcherrimis dicendi ornamentis aspersa, coniunctam. Praeterea in Theologia omne nouum testamentum graecum est, atque in id Graeci praeclarissimi uiri, cum alij, tum sancti scripserunt. A quorum hortis, qui sunt apud Latinos praecipui (ut Hieronymus & Augustinus) omnes scientiae suae flosculos decerpserunt. Quid inquis, in causa est? Maxima profecto librorum copia, & eorum non triuialium, sed ab excellentissimis in omni scientiae genere uiris editorum. Vnde igitur hoc malum accidit, ut quod omnes maiores nostri unico consensu approbarunt, nos uix umbram literarum assecuti, & bis per omnia (ut Musico utar prouerbio) ab eis distantes, adeo negligamus, & aliqui etiam damnare audeant, & cornici (sed nimis inepte) oculum effodere. Certe hac in re, tria sunt quae pestilenter nocent.[7] Ignorantia boni, laboris magnitudo, uel potius suspicio laboris magni, atque ob hunc desperatio literaturae graecae consequendae. Quod mihi uel hinc est notissimum, quod uidi quosdam apud

---

[7] nocent, *1517*

At this point somebody or other pops up and says, "You don't mean to say everyone's unlearned unless he knows Greek, do you?"

"I don't say that," I say. "In fact, I admit there can be many learned men who don't know Greek or Latin (if kind nature gives them strong minds)—the Jews and the Chaldaeans, for example. But the Greeks surpassed them as much as they did the Romans. The reason's self-evident, and you don't have to use many arguments. The Chaldaeans have almost nothing; the Jews have a little, but what they have is good because it contributes something toward understanding the Old Testament. Whatever seems to have originated with the Romans—history, for example, and oratory—was all taken from the Greeks as if on loan.[9] For Demosthenes and Isocrates created Cicero, as great as he is in the art of oratory (and Quintilian [1] admits it). In philosophy it was Plato and Aristotle. To Cicero they were the most learned of the Greeks, and he often calls one of them *divine* and the other *the most wise*.[2] But Roman philosophy is so imperfect that learned men think nothing is more stupid than to compare Roman philosophers with the Greeks. And I don't omit Cicero himself (if he'll pardon my saying so). Moreover, in history there're about eight or at most nine good Romans, but Thucydides by himself is better than all of them (at least in my opinion). Just why Cicero had so little regard for Thucydides is his own business,[3] but he differs widely in that from Demosthenes, the fount of all eloquence. For it's well known that Demosthenes copied out Thucydides eight times in his own hand.[4] No doubt he admired great eloquence together with good sense sprinkled with beautiful ornaments of speech (which is what it is). Besides, in theology the entire New Testament is in Greek, and the most famous men of Greece wrote about it—ordinary men as well as saints. From their gardens the most distinguished Latin authors, like Jerome and Augustine, plucked all the flowers of their learning.

What's that got to do with anything, you say? Well, it produced a great number of books. None of them were trivial; they were all written by men outstanding in all kinds of knowledge.

And that's how this difficulty has come about: neglecting everything our ancestors approved of unanimously, we scarcely follow the shadow of learning, and (to use a proverb from music) [5] we're twice removed from them in everything. Some of us even dare to condemn what they approved of and put out the crow's eye [6] (but not very well). There're undoubtedly three things that hurt us badly here: ignorance of what's good for us, the amount of work, or rather, the suspicion of a lot of work, and because of that, despair of learning to read Greek. I know quite a bit about it because I've seen some people wondering quietly

se tacite admirantes quidem, quum audirent aliquem locum, graeca
eruditione tractatum, sed quia puduit illos graece nescire, uerbis id
se non magnifacere ostenderunt. Quo uitio quid potest esse turpius?
Sed non ab re erit, hoc quod dixi, uobis ridiculo quodam exemplo confirmare. Quum Ferrariae olim bonis lite-

Facetum exemplum   ris, non negligenter (quantum ingenioli
mei uena passa est) uacarem, & modo
graeca transferendo, modo latine scribendo stilum exercerem, casu
incidi in Simplicij perquam erudita in categorias Aristotelicas commentaria. Praefationem legere incepi, rem tam suauem reperij, ut prius
auelli non potuerim, quam omnem deuorassem, nec hoc contentus,
cepi illico in latinum transferre, nec destiti ab incepto, priusquam to-
tam latinam fecissem, haud multos post dies accedit ad me Philosophus, uir alioqui probus, & adeo in sua Philosophia recenti eruditus, ut
multi eum in corona disputantum, egregie uociferantem, & (ut fit)
etiam aduersario conuitiantem, admirarentur, ex solo clamore eum
doctum iudicantes. Is mihi ut amico, narrat se principis sui benigni-
tate, assecutum esse stipendium annuum, ad Philosophiam publice do-
cendam, meque unice rogat, ut ea die qua exordium daturus erat,
interesse uellem. Interpretandas autem delegerat, quas dixi categorias.
Gratulor, inquam ego, tibi uehementer, & non solum libentissime inter-
ero, uerumetiam ostendam tibi quaedam, quae ad rem tuam maxime
facient. Amo te, inquit, mi Richarde, rem pergratam mihi feceris. immo
fortasse molestam, inquam ego, si nihil eruditis tuis auribus dignum
audieris. Et hoc unum te rogatum uelim, ne ad meam in transferendo
imperitiam respicias, sed ad rem ipsam animum intendas, quam mihi
uidetur Simplicius eruditissime tractare. Profero Simplicium latine,
(quantum in me fuit) loquentem perlego. Ille attente audit, & ne
uerbum quidem interloquitur, ne legentem me interrumpat, adeo ut
Simplicium omnino mirari uideatur. Perlecta re, quid sentis, inquam.
Oh, inquit ille, (parce & maligne laudans) satis bene, sed haec non
sunt similia his, quibus nos moderni (hoc enim barbaro uerbo usus
est) Philosophi utimur in nostris circulis. Verum est quod narras, inquam ego, nihil a Simplicio, homini simplici & ueritatis amico, magis
alienum quam illa. Sed omittamus hoc, & siquid sit quod tibi satisfacit,
excerpe & utere, ut solent facere docti. sin minus, tua tibi circularia

to themselves when they heard some subject being treated with Greek learning. But since they were ashamed of not knowing Greek, they said they didn't think much of it. And what's more shameful than that?

It won't be beside the point for me to illustrate what I've just said with a ridiculous example. A while ago when I was at Ferrara I tried to cultivate good literature (as much as I could with my little streak of intelligence). As I exercised my pen, sometimes by translating Greek, sometimes by writing in Latin, I came by chance on Simplicius'[7] extremely learned commentary on the Aristotelian categories. I started to read the preface, and I found it so pleasant that I couldn't tear myself away until I'd devoured it all. And not content with that, I began to translate it into Latin on the spot and didn't stop till I'd made it all Latin. A few days later a philosopher came to me. He was on the whole, a respectable man, so well-informed in his new philosophy that many people, when they heard him yelling splendidly in a circle of debaters and (as it happened) attacking his opponent, were struck with amazement, convinced of his learning just from the sound of his voice. He told me confidentially that he'd received through the kindness of his prince an annual stipend to give a series of public lectures on philosophy, and he asked me specially if I'd be there on the day he was going to give the first lecture. Besides, he'd chosen as his subject the categories I've mentioned.

A funny example

"Thanks a lot," I said. "I'll not only be happy to come, but I'll also show you something that'll help you quite a bit."

"I love you, Richard my dear," he said. "It'll be a great favor to me."

"No. Maybe you won't like it," I said, "if you don't hear anything worthy of your learning. But I want to ask you one thing. Don't pay any attention to my awkward translation, but keep your mind on the material itself, which I think Simplicius handles very nicely." So I bring out Simplicius talking away in as good a Latin as I knew. I read it all out loud for him. He listened attentively and didn't say a word, didn't interrupt me, and seemed to marvel at Simplicius. When I was through, I said, "What do you think about it?"

"It's alright," he said (praising me sparingly and maliciously), "but it's not the sort of thing us modern metaphysical-theosophers [8] (he really used that barbarous word) use in our circle."

"That's true," I said. "Nothing could be further from Simplicius than that, for he was a simple man and a friend of truth. But let's skip that, and if there's anything that satisfies you, take it out and use it, as learned men usually do. But if there isn't, your modern circle will be

satis erunt, & praefatio Simplicij a me peruersa, quiescet domi. Orsu, inquit ille, (barbara uerba male latinis connectens) non cupio relegere, sed uellem domi apud me habere. Placet, inquam ego, asporta, & relege, ut melius quam fortasse facis, intelligas, & notes siquid ad rem tuam pertinet, modo ne diuulges, ideo quod plura sunt, in quibus raptim transferendis, parum ipse mihi satisfeci. & est unus aut alter locus, qui mihi corruptus uidetur, quibus tres notulas, ut uidebis, apposui, ut possim celerius inuenire, & nactus opportunitatem, praeceptorem de eorum sensu consulere. Ad hoc, ego non incumbo isti uestrae circulari philosophiae, in qua uos ita estis acuti, ut si quem meum errorem deprehenderetis, illum in uestris circulis proclamaretis, & me una cum Simplicio derideretis. Faciam, inquit, ut mones. & abit. Aduenit dies destinata, principio professioni dando. Accedo una cum alijs. Repletur schola partim doctis, partim indoctis, & qui nihil sciunt, nisi explodere aut exibilare praeceptorem, aut sedilia pulsare. Ego me confero ad locum quampropinquissimum meo Philosopho, & totus attentus in faciem eius inhio, & quasi ex locuturi ore pendeo, ut intelligam quid possit in medium adducere, quod praestaret illi Simplicianae praefationi, quae mihi non modo elegans uidebatur, sed etiam ipsum scopum in Aristotele declarando attingere. Tandem composito in grauitatem corpore simul & uultu (ut fit) incipit. Nihil audio praeter Simplicium. Ausculto sequentibus, nihil adhuc praeter Simplicium, nec sententiam modo, sed eadem quoque uerba. Interea alij qui aderant, magni circulares Philosophi, Vnus, Haec pulcherrima, inquit, sunt. Alius, Haec eruditissima. Tertius, Hic iuuenis admirabilis est. Pergit ille in finem una cum Simplicio. Et (quod ridiculum mihi uisum est) illa loca, in quibus ego egregie erraram, rotundius caeteris pronunciat, nemine non admirante, & rem, & hominem. Quum perorasset, applaudunt omnes, salutant, exosculantur, ut moris est. Ego interea dum haec officia praestarem, tantum non effuse rideo, continui me tamen, & gratulatus sum amico, quod tam feliciter ex aliena semente, id est, graeca, messem sibi fecerit. Post haec quotidie operam do, ut ex discipulis intelligam,

Categoria apud Graecos, &
praedicamentum, &
accusationem significat

quomodo se gerit in reliquis, nihil probatum, nihil laudatum audio, praeter praefationem. Tunc uero incipio eum iudicare omnibus categorijs dignissimum. Sed prosequamur institutum. Siquis naturae

enough for you, and Simplicius' preface, which I've corrupted, will stay quietly at home."

"*Assez,*[9] now," he said (miserably mixing barbarous words with Latin). "I don't want to go over it again, but I would like to have it at home with me."

"As you like," I said. "Take it away and reread it, and maybe you'll understand it better and see if it has to do with what you're up to. The only catch is that I don't want you to show it around because there're many places where I was translating quickly that don't please me. And there're one or two places that seemed to me corrupt. I've put three little marks alongside them (as you'll see) so I can find them quickly and ask a professor what they mean as soon as I get a chance. Besides, I don't want to trouble your philosophical circle, where you're all so sharp, for fear that if you caught any error of mine you'd make it known to the entire circle and make fun of me along with Simplicius."

"I'll do as you say," he said and went away.

Then the day came for the start of the lectures. I go along with the others. The school is filled, partly with the learned, partly with the unlearned, who don't know how to do anything but hoot and hiss at the teacher and beat on the seats. I got a place for myself quite near my philosopher, and I gape at his face, completely absorbed, and hang on his lips, as it were, waiting for them to speak so I can understand what he has to offer all these people that's better than Simplicius' preface, which, I thought, was not only graceful, but actually managed to explicate Aristotle. At last, face and body composed in gravity (as it happens), he begins. I hear nothing but Simplicius. I listen a little more; I still hear nothing but Simplicius, not only the ideas, but the very same words. Meanwhile, one of the others who are there, one of the great circle of philosophers, says, "This is tremendous." Another one says, "Extremely learned." A third, "A brilliant young man."

He goes on to the end, and so does Simplicius. And (what seemed ridiculous to me) he delivered the places where I made a bad mistake more roundly than the rest, and no one failed to admire both the man and his speech. When he came to the end, everyone applauded him, shook his hand, and kissed him, as is the custom. Meanwhile I performed this office: I didn't laugh out loud, but contained myself and congratulated my friend for reaping such a fine harvest for himself from alien corn,[1] that is, from Greek. After that, I took the trouble every day to find out from his students how he did in the rest of the lectures. I heard nothing was applauded, nothing praised, except for the preface. Then I really began to think he deserved all the categories [2] he got. But let's follow our plan.

Category *in Greek means both* predicament *and* indictment

beneficio, absque graeca eruditione, ad aliquam deueniat doctrinam, haec (quod notabile est) haud dubie adiunctis Graecis duplicabitur. Porro si cum Graecis incipias, eris prius insigniter doctus, quam si ea praetermittas mediocriter. Nam Graecarum literarum ignorantia facit, ut multi tantum temporis absumant in minimis, quanto possent in eximie eruditos uiros euadere. Verum esse, & manifestum quod loquor, cum alij complures, tum praecipue ERASMVS noster, hac nostra aetate com-

De Erasmo

probauit. Qui posteaquam Graeca calluit, non modo alios, sed etiam seipsum super-are coepit, adeo ut illorum quorundam, quae antequam Graece bene sciret, edidit, ne codicem quidem nunc extare, libenter (certum scio) uellet. non quod mala illa quidem sint, sed quod haec posteriora, quae graecam sapiunt eruditionem, illis longe antecedunt. Discant igitur qui nesciunt graeca, cum exemplo huius doctissimi uiri, tum utilitatis causa, & currant cum ERASMO stadium, supplantent si possint, & procul a se relinquant. Nam ille (quae eius est modestia) hoc aequissimo feret animo. Vt primum iuuenis satis eruditus erit, id est, adusque legendos omnes bonos au-tores, & stilum exercendum, tunc autorum delectus est habendus, id est, non nisi optimi & approbatissimi legendi. Est enim antiquum dic-tum, non multa, sed multum legendum esse. quo significatur non esse legendos omnes etiam triuiales autores, sed bonos multum, id est, saepe legendos. Quod dictum (ut hoc quoque obiter annotetur) apud Plinium nepotem, in epistola quadam inuersum legitur, etiam in Aldi-cis exemplaribus quae correctissima habentur. sicut paulo post in eadem notum prouocatumque est, pro prouulgato, mendose legitur. Qui autem autores deligendi sunt, ita est (ut idem Plinius ait) pro-uulgatum, ut demonstratione non egeat, & Erasmus de hac re libellum scripsit, & hunc (ut omnia) erudite. Ego

De Plutarcho

de uno tantum Plutarcho hoc monebo, ut nunquam dimittatur e manibus. Nam nunquam legi aliquem (legi autem in utraque lingua plurimos) qui tam multa in omni scientiae genere, tam bene & erudite scripserit, adeo ut is solus satis mihi esse uideatur, ad faciendum hominem doctissi-mum. Non me latet quosdam in illo desiderare facundiam, de quo

If by the benefit of nature someone should arrive at some learning without Greek erudition, it would be a noteworthy thing, but it would doubtless be doubled by the addition of Greek. Besides, if you begin with Greek, you'll be remarkably learned much more quickly than if you pass over it lightly. For an ignorance of Greek makes a lot of people waste enough time on trifles to have made them extremely learned men. Many people in our own time have proved that what I say is obviously true, and especially our dear friend Erasmus. After he mastered Greek, he began   *Erasmus*
to surpass not only others, but even him-
self. And I know for a fact he'd be happy if not one of the volumes he wrote before he knew Greek well[3] were now extant. It's not that they were bad, but that the later ones, which smack of Greek erudition, far surpass them. Those who don't know Greek, therefore, should learn from the example of this most learned man and also have an eye to their own profit. They should run a race with Erasmus, trip him up if they can, and leave him far behind. For he's so gentle, he'd take it calmly.

As soon as a young man is educated enough, that is, as far as reading all good authors and working on his style is concerned, then he has to choose his authors. None but the ones generally regarded as the best should be read. For there's an ancient saying, "Read not many, but much," which means that you should not read all authors, even insignificant ones, but that you should read good authors a number of times. I might note in passing that you can read that saying in a letter of the younger Pliny,[4] where it's turned around even in the Aldine edition, which is considered the most correct. And a little later on in the same letter *notum provocatumque est* is incorrectly read for *provulgatum.* But it's so *provulgatum,* as Pliny says—I mean *clear*— what authors you should choose that they don't even have to be mentioned. Besides, Erasmus[5] wrote a little book on the subject—learned, like everything he does. Yet, I'll mention just one thing about Plutarch alone: never let him out of your hands.
For though I've read many authors in   *Plutarch*
both Greek and Latin, I've never read
anyone who wrote so much about all kinds of knowledge. And he wrote so well and so learnedly that it seems to me that he alone is enough to make a man learned. I realize some people think he lacks

disputare non est huius loci. Sed nullum (mihi crede) eloquentiae
ornamentum ei deest, quod non admirabilis doctrina suppleat. Genera

Genera exercitationum

exercitationum, simul atque ad scribendum deuentum est, sint haec. uel a
teipso argumentum est excogitandum,
uel tractatum ab alijs sumendum. Si tuum uis, fac quamdiligentissime
& elegantissime potes, id tractes ad imitationem antiquorum, adeo ut
tota quidem res, grauis uideatur, uerba uero delecta & ornata, sicut &
figurae suo loco collocatae, ut late patet apud Rhetores. Si alienum
argumentum deliges, accurate sunt notanda, quae ab alijs in eandem
rem dicta fuerunt, & non nisi cum optimis certandum, duabus ex
causis, quod & Plinius Nepos monet. Nam in his si uinces, magna laus
& animi satisfactio, uictorem sequitur, & alitur ad maxima. Sin uictum
se uidebit, pudore afficietur, sequitur tamen & pudorem suum bonum,
quod maiorem curam & diligentiam suadet. Praeterea quum optimos
sequeris, similia inueniendi facultatem tibi paras. Si nudum alienum
argumentum aggredi uis, nec quicquam uidere ex his, quae ab alijs
in id dicta fuere, probo & hoc, (licet iuueni istud sit audacius, sed
ingenium audaciam fortunatam reddere potest).[8] Nam hic tanto minus
est periculi, quanto abest omnis comparatio, & amatur pariter exerci-
tatio. Aliud genus exercitationis est, transferendi aliquid, uel ex Graeco
in Latinum, uel ex Latino in Graecum. Quod Quintilianus, & omnes
Latini praeceptores, caeteris longe praeferunt, hac ratione moti, quod
hinc proprietas, splendorque uerborum, copia figurarum, uis denique
explicandi acquiritur. Item, ut multa sunt quae legentem fallunt, ita
nihil illum qui diligenter transfert. Nam coactus quodam modo,
omnem curam adhibet, ne negligentia, aut imperitia notetur. Atque
hinc est, quod docti multa addunt, multa demunt, multa interscribunt,
multa ex integro rescribunt, ne quid eruditis indignum auribus, in
uulgus exeat. Tertium genus est, quo possis in epistola scribenda
pulcherrime te exercere, & ex hoc pressum illum, purumque sermonem
epistolis accommodatum acquirere. Quod si ab hoc studio aliquam
animi (qui nunquam in unam perseueranter rem intendi potest) remis-
sionem queres, carmine utaris fas est. Non longo (quod nemini conuenit, nisi his qui meri Poetae uolunt esse, quorum opinionem equidem

---

[8] potest.) *1517*

style, but this is not the place to discuss that. Believe me, though, he lacks nothing in the way of rhetorical ornaments that he doesn't make up for by his admirable learning.

When you come to writing, these are the kinds of exercises you should do. You should either think up a topic for your- *Kinds of exercises* self or take it from others. If you want it to be your own, do it as carefully and elegantly as you can, treating it in imitation of the ancients, so that the whole thing seems grave, the words well chosen and adorned, and each figure set properly in its own place, as the rhetoricians say. If you select a subject that's not your own, you should carefully note what phrases were used by others who wrote on the same topic. And you should argue only with the best authors for two reasons, as Pliny the Younger points out. For if you beat them, you'll receive great praise and satisfaction of mind after your victory, and you'll be encouraged to strive for something even greater. If you see yourself beaten, you'll feel ashamed. Yet from your shame you'll receive this benefit: you'll be more careful next time. Besides, when you pursue the best authors, you gradually develop the ability to discover things like those which they found. If you simply want to lay claim to someone else's argument and not see what others have said on the subject, I also approve of that, though it may be somewhat rash for a boy. Yet ability can make rashness successful. For in this case the more unlike, the less dangerous it is, and the exercise is just as enjoyable.

Another kind of exercise is translating something either from Greek into Latin or Latin into Greek. Quintilian [6] and all other Roman teachers easily prefer that method to any other because it teaches propriety and magnificence of language, a store of figures, and, finally, strength of exposition. Similarly, just as many things escape you when you're reading, nothing escapes when you're translating. For you're driven in a way to take every precaution so that you won't be accused of ignorance or negligence. And that's why learned men add a lot and take away a lot and write a lot between the lines, and then write it all over again, so they won't publish anything unworthy the attention of the learned.

A third kind of exercise is to write elegant letters and so acquire the compressed, natural style suitable for letters. But if you want some rest from your studies (for the mind can never remain intent on one thing for long), you might try a song. But don't make it a long one, for they're not suitable for anyone except people who want to be poets. I don't agree with what they believe, and I don't think you should fol-

nec probo, nec sequendam existimo, ideo quod Poetica nimis nuda est, nisi aliqua alia insigni scientia tegatur) sed arguto hoc, & breui, & ad animum duntaxat reficiendum apto, adeo ut lusus potius, quam studij loco habeatur. Nam non aliter a summis uiris carmen est approbatum & admissum. Quale est illud, ne ipse ignorare uidear, quod doceo,

> Quisquis ades iuuenis, clarae uirtutis amator,
> Ista (scias) fugiet, tu nisi doctus eris.
> Virtutes partas auget doctrina, negatas
> Conciliat, studeas, & bene doctus eris.

De his tribus generibus exercitationum tractat Plinius nepos, libro septimo epistolarum, in epistola ad Fuscum, non longa quidem, sed erudita simul, & utili, quam nos hoc loco sumus imitati. Et haec compendiose scribenti, suffecerint ad uiam illis praemonstrandam, qui arti Oratoriae operam sunt daturi. Quomodo autem in Theologica scientia & Philosophia studendum sit, tot tantique doctissimi uiri, quorum praecepta in manibus sunt, tradiderunt, ut malim studiosos iuuenes, qui his scientijs incumbent, monere, illos potius eruditissime scribentes sequantur, quam aliquid a me hac in re expectent, ne sus cum Minerua contendere uideatur. Meo instituto, qui tyronibus in hac militia, non ueteranis scribo, satis erit factum, si monuero, illis qui rhetoricen calleant, ad omnes quas uolent deligere scientias, facillimum patere accessum. Non ut uerba solum, (quod uulgus imperitorum stulte sentit) sed etiam ut in rem ipsam nullo negocio penetrent. Est enim omnium particeps, plus habens in recessu, quam in fronte ostentat. Haec sunt mi Colete, quibus studiosos literarum iuuenes, ad doctrinam amplexandam hortandos, instruendosque putaui. Quae si tibi, uel iuuenibus tuis, qui per te publice erudiuntur, placere intellexero, operam me non lusisse iudicabo. Hoc unum non dubito, quin assecuturus sim, ut si non omnia probare uelitis, multa saltem rideatis. Adiungentur & illa in appendicem, maximam hac nostra aetate omnibus Anglicis occasionem esse datam, ut optimis studijs omnem animum applicent. Quippe quum habeamus Regem nobilissimum, ut potentia, ita etiam doctrina omnes alios Christianos principes longe superantem, & erga omnes doctos adeo affectum, ut de nulla re libentius audiat, quam de doctis & literis. Cuius doctrinae experientiam ego non ex hoc solo habeo, quod audiui eum prompte & expedite lingua loqui Latina, sed etiam quod olim adhuc pene puer, ausus est Erasmvm nostrum, epistola

low it since poetry is fairly bare unless it's clothed in some other knowledge of note.[7] But make it a short, lively song, fit only for refreshing
the mind, and in this way you can regard it as play, not work. For
great men don't approve of and don't allow any other kind of song.
So I won't seem to be ignorant of what I teach, here's an example:

Whoever you are, young man, you lover of pure virtue,
She'll run away from you, you know, unless you're learned.
Learning increases innate virtues, provides the ones not given.
Study, and you'll be a really learned man.

Pliny the Younger [8] treats these three kinds of exercise in his "Letter
to Fuscus," in the seventh book of the *Letters*, not at length, of course,
but learnedly and at the same time usefully. And we've imitated him
here. And that should be enough, in such a brief account, to show the
way to those who're about to begin studying the art of oratory.

So many extremely learned men have handed down rules about how
to study theology and philosophy that I would rather tell students
who're inclined that way to follow those very learned writers instead
of looking to me for advice. I don't want to seem like a pig competing
with Minerva.[9] I write for those who're recruits, not veterans in this
army, and I'll have done enough of what I intend if I've explained to
those who're talented in rhetoric that they have a clear and easy road
open to them in all the studies they wish to choose. It's no trouble at
all for them to penetrate not only to the words (which the ignorant
mob in its stupidity is capable of hearing), but to the very heart of
the matter. For rhetoric participates in all things and has more beneath
the surface than meets the eye.[1]

These are the things, my dear Colet, that I thought young men
who're eager for books should be provided with in order to urge them
to embrace learning. If I see that they please you or the boys who're
educated by you in your school, I'll think I wasn't cheated by my
work. I have no doubt I've accomplished one thing: if you don't
approve of it all, at least you'll have a lot to laugh at.

And I'll add this as an appendix. Englishmen have been given a
great opportunity in our own time to apply themselves entirely to the
finest of studies. Obviously, since we have a most noble King who far
surpasses all other Christian princes in learning as well as in power.
He's so disposed to all learned men that he hears nothing more willingly than conversations about learned men and books. I have proof
of his learning not only because I myself heard him speak Latin quickly
and fluently, but also because one time while he was still a boy, he

sua ipsius manu scripta, prouocare, quae nihil non latinissimum sapiebat, nam hanc mihi ERASMVS Ferrariae legendam olim exhibuit. Solebat enim eam, quocunque ibat, in arcula quadam ceu thesaurum reconditam, secum circunferre. Est praeterea nobis amplissimus pater Thomas Cardinalis Eboracensis, primas Angliae, & magnus totius regni Cancellarius, qui ut inter sapientes est sapientissimus, ita inter doctos doctissimus habetur. adeo ut isti nobilissimo Regi, regnoque suo, longe plus felicitatis accreuerit, quam uotis expetiuit Plato, quum optauit, ut aut omnes principes philospharentur, aut Philosophi regerent. Nobis enim utrunque euenit. Nam hic amplissimus Cardinalis, philosophiae peculiariter est doctissimus. Quanta autem, ut magnus princeps prudentia, habenas istius regni moderatur, sapientissimo rege (cuius uicem in omnibus sine ulla exceptione rebus gerit) id ita uolente, non est opus commemorem. Nam non nobis solum hoc est clarum & perspicuum, uerumetiam uniuerso orbi Christiano notissimum. O quam rara est haec felicitas, quae haud scio an unquam alicui acciderit, nisi nostro Regi, ut unum haberet uirum, cui omnia tuto posset committere, & non minus de sua, quam aliena certus esse fide. Sane nunquam fuit Rex Pyrrhus suo Cynea felicior, quam inuictissimus Angliae Rex, amplissimo patre Cardinale Eboracensi, Achate suo fidelissimo. Huius sapientiam & doctrinam ornat haec quoque naturae pulcherrima dos, nempe amor erga omnes doctos, quibus tam mirifice fauet, ut nullius rei maiorem curam habere uideatur, quam ut illos promoueat in altum, & de eis optime mereatur (tanti aestimans doctrinam, ut nihil ei anteferendam iudicet) e quorum numero, quoniam me non doctum, sed doctrinae studiosum, non reiecit, fuit mihi quasi alter deus. Nam ut deus me uita semel donauit, ita is bis uel ter uitam mihi defendit. ut omittam Regiae maiestatis amplissimam benignitatem, qua huius solius opera & rogatu in me usa est. Non potest igitur amplissima eius paternitas rectius, aut conuenientius de me loqui, quam quum instrumentum a se fabrefactum, me nominat. Potest enim me etiam plusquam instrumentum, in quemlibet usum uertere. Et in quacunque re, mea utetur opera, non minor mea erga eum apparebit seruitus, quam eius est erga maiestatem Regiam incomparabilis fides. non possum enim expressius meam erga amplissimam paternitatem eius, fidelitatem eloqui.

RICHARDI PACEI, SVPREMI BRITANNIARVM REGIS A
SECRETIS, LIBRI DE FRVCTV, QVI EX DOCTRINA
PERCIPITVR, FINIS.

dared to provoke our dear friend Erasmus with a letter written in his own hand. It savored of nothing but the most Latin of Latin, for Erasmus once gave it to me to read at Ferrara.[2] In fact, he used to carry it around with him wherever he went in a little box like hidden treasure.

Moreover, we have our great father, Thomas, Cardinal of York, Primate of England, and High Chancellor of the entire kingdom. Just as he is the most wise among wise men, so also he's the most learned among learned men. Through him, his most noble king and the realm itself have received much more happiness than Plato [3] prayed for when he wished that either all princes would apply themselves to philosophy or that philosophers would rule. And with us, we have both. For this great Cardinal is particularly learned in philosophy. There's no need for me to mention, however, the amount of prudence he uses like a great prince, in controlling the reins of the realm, as our wise king wishes. For the Cardinal takes the king's place in all things without exception. And this is clear and obvious not only to us alone; it is also well known to the entire Christian world. What rare good fortune that is! I don't think it ever happened to anyone before except our King: to have one man to whom he could safely entrust everything and be no less certain of that other person's faith than of his own! Surely King Pyrrhus was never happier in his Cineas [4] than the invincible King of England in the great father, the Cardinal of York, his faithful Achates.[5] And nature's fairest gift, namely a love for all learned men, also adorns his wisdom and learning. He patronizes them so admirably that he seems to have no greater care than to advance them to high places. And he deserves the best from these men, for he values learning so much that he thinks nothing should be preferred to it. Nor did he exclude me from their number, though I'm not learned, but eager to learn. He was like another God to me. For just as God once gave me life, so he preserved my life two or three times, to say nothing of the great kindness of the King's majesty, through which the pains and entreaties of this man alone were put to advantage on my behalf. His gracious fatherhood, therefore, cannot speak of me more correctly or suitably than when he calls me a tool skilfully fashioned by himself. For more than any tool he can turn me to whatever use he wants. However he uses my services, I shall serve him with the same incomparable trust with which he serves the King's majesty. And I cannot speak more clearly of my loyalty to his glorious fatherhood than that.

End of the Book,
THE BENEFIT OF A LIBERAL EDUCATION,
by Richard Pace,
Secretary to the Supreme King of Britain

BASILEAE APVD IOANNEM FROBENIVM,
MENSE VIIIBRI.
ANNO   M.   D.   XVII.

PUBLISHED IN BASEL
BY JOHANN FROBEN
OCTOBER, 1517

COMMENTARY

COMMENTARY

PAGE 5

1. (d. May 6, 1527). Close friend and correspondent of Erasmus. From 1505-1512 he was Public Reader in Rhetoric and Poetry and in Greek at Bologna. In 1513 he went to Rome as secretary to Cardinal Pucci. In August 1517, he accompanied Pucci to Switzerland, where he was sent as Nuncio. It was there he met Pace again. He returned to Rome in 1518 and remained in Pucci's service until September 1524, when he became secretary to Clement VII. He died during the sack of Rome in 1527.

2. After entering Wolsey's employ in 1515, Pace was sent as a secret agent to Switzerland and spent the next few years attempting to raise a Swiss army against France. After the Treaty of Noyon put a temporary cease to hostilities (August 1516), Pace found himself with time on his hands at Constance (Wegg, pp. 65-114).

PAGE 9

3. The spirit of criticism. According to Hesiod, one of the sons of Night (*Theogony*, 214).

PAGE 11

4. *Hypocausto;* literally, *stove room*. The word carries the added implication of *sweat-box* since they were usually over-heated. Note Erasmus' complaints: "When you've shouted [at the door of the inn] a long time, someone finally sticks his head out of the little window of the stove room (where they spend most of their time until midsummer), like a turtle from his shell . . . . Thus there are often eighty or ninety met together in the same stove room: travelers afoot, horsemen, traders, sailors, carriers, farmers, young men, women, the sick and the whole . . . . Glancing around, he [the inn-keeper] silently counts the people in the stove room. The more he sees there, the more energetically he fires up the stove." *Ten Colloquies of Erasmus,* transl. C. R. Thompson (New York, 1957), pp. 15-17.

5. Cf. Sophocles, Frag. 715. Better known in Horace's version: "Dimidium facti, qui coepit, habet" (*Ep.,* I, ii, 40).

6. *Plutus,* 804-805.

PAGE 13

7. This presumably refers to the section beginning on page 121, "Someone said there's a lot of work in acquiring knowledge, etc."

8. For Erasmus' view of Bombasius' critical powers, see the *Adagia*, I. VI. i, where he compliments him on an emendation in the text of Aulus Gellius.

9. Thomas Wolsey (1472 or 1473-1530). Statesman, cardinal, and chancellor to Henry VIII. After the death of Cardinal Bainbridge at Rome, Wolsey became Archbishop of York and virtually ruled England for the next fifteen years. As a result of Henry's divorce proceedings, Wolsey lost the chancellorship and all his honors and privileges. In 1530 he was arrested on the false charge of treason and died on his way to London. Pace entered Wolsey's employ after the death of Bainbridge in July 1514. For further flattery of Wolsey and the King, linking them together, but at the same time indicating clearly the superiority of Wolsey, see below, pp. 139-41.

1. Erasmus, *Adagia*, I. X. xxx: "Scopum attingere. Est voti compotem fieri, aut conjectura rem ipsam assequi."

2. Nicias was defeated and executed by the Syracusans in 413 B.C. A version of Pace's story concludes Plutarch's *Life of Nicias* (30).

PAGE 15

3. Pace seems to have in mind a saying like Chaucer's (Reeve's Tale, A 4054), "The gretteste clerkes ben noght wisest men." The proverb originates in the Tale of the Wolf and the Mare from medieval Aesopean collections, and is not limited to English. For a French version precisely similar to Pace's, see Montaigne's "Of Pedantry," *Works*, transl. Donald M. Frame (Stanford, 1958), p. 98. Frame notes that the same proverb occurs in Rabelais.

PAGE 17

4. Epicurus recorded his main articles of belief in a series of brief notes or maxims which he called κύριαι δόξαι, *Authoritative Opinions* (Diogenes Laertius, X, 138). See also Cicero, *De Natura Deorum*, I, xxx, 85; *De Finibus*, II, 7. Pace seems to attribute the phrase to Diogenes in this paragraph.

5. Erasmus, *Adagia*, I. III. xxvi: "Ilias malorum." See p. 115 below.

6. *Telum torsisti validum quidem, sed quod facile tamen retorquebitur.* Literally, *You hurled a strong spear indeed, but nevertheless it will easily be thrown back at you.*

PAGE 19

7. Erasmus, *Adagia,* I. VI. lxix: "Quae supra nos, nihil ad nos."

PAGE 21

8. John Colet (1467-1519), Dean of St. Paul's and founder of St. Paul's School. One of the leading Platonists of the early English Renaissance. His famous course of lectures on St. Paul's *Epistle to the Romans* was strongly influenced by Pico's *Heptaplus* and other writings of the Florentine Academy. Colet was also known for his work on Pseudo-Dionysius and his sermons at St. Paul's. He died of the sweating sickness in 1519, to be succeeded by Pace himself as Dean. Pace addresses him as the founder of St. Paul's School and a person deeply concerned with education. See J. H. Lupton, *A Life of John Colet* (London, 1909).

9. Founded in 1510 in St. Paul's Churchyard. The school consisted of a large schoolroom, a chapel, and living quarters for the master and his assistant. It was designed to give 153 boys who could already read and write a sound Christian education in Greek as well as Latin. Over the door was the inscription: "Schola catechizationis puerorum in Christi Opt. Max. fide et bonis literis . . . anno Verbi incarnati MDX."

1. William Lily (1468?-1522). One of the earliest Greek scholars in England. After being educated at Magdalen College, Oxford, he went on a pilgrimage to Jerusalem, stayed for a long period at Rhodes with the military order of the Knights of St. John, studied in Italy under Sulpitius and Pomponius Laetus, and finally returned to England where he was formally appointed first high master of St. Paul's School in 1512. His *Grammaticis Rudimenta,* written for St. Paul's, remained a standard school text for almost four centuries.

2. Pace seems to be making a generic rather than a specific reference to Isocrates, who, in both the *Oration Against the Sophists* and in the *Antidosis,* holds up virtuous character and learning as the marks of the true teacher.

PAGE 23

3. A good example of the way in which Pace's learning mingles classical phrases together. For the proverb about Vergil, see Cassiodorus (*Instit. Div. Lit.,* I, 540): "Vergilium dum Ennium legeret a quodam quid faceret inquisitus respondit: aurum in stercore quaero." The second half of the statement is given by Erasmus (*Adagia,* I. V. lii) as from Seneca: "Vt personam malit quam faciem, id est, uideri malit quam esse." Cf. Seneca, *Ep. Mor.* 24, 13: "Non hominibus tantum, sed rebus persona demenda est et reddenda facies sua."

4. Probably during Pace's visit to England in the spring of 1514, not

his return in 1515 after the death of Bainbridge (Wegg, p. 46). Allen doubts that the episode occurred at all since the last date Pace was in England was October 1515, eight months before the letter of Erasmus referred to below was written (June 1516). The conversation Pace reports, therefore, is obviously imaginary (Allen, 2, 255). But the date Pace gives ("duobus annis plus minus") is not meant to be precise, and even if the letter were written later, Pace could simply have thrown the Erasmus allusion in to make the story better.

5. *Et scholam omnino frequentandam censuit.* Literally, *and he thought that they should by all means attend a school.*

6. Allen, 2, 255 (c. June 19, 1516): "Porro liberis, vxori, reliquaeque curae domesticae ego vnicam vxorem meam oppono τὴν κατάρατον πενίαν, quam nec adhuc humeris excutere possum, adeo τὸν μισοῦντα φιλεῖ." See also below, p. 117.

PAGE 25

7. "Sic me servavit Apollo" (*Sat.* I, ix, 78). Horace was saved by the blowhard's running off to someone else, which he attributes to Apollo, patron of poets; or perhaps the blowhard left him at the forum of Augustus, where there was a statue of Apollo (cf. Pliny, XXXV, 5; Juvenal, I, 128). The phrase, however, originally comes from Homer (*Iliad, XX,* 443); Lucilius had also used it.

PAGE 27

8. For the various classical occurrences of this proverb, see A. Otto, *Die Sprichwörter der Römer* (Leipzig, 1890), p. 195. As attributed to Cato it is usually cited as "Litterarum radices amaras esse, fructus iucundiores." Aphthonius (*Progymnasmata,* 23) quotes Isocrates as follows: "Ἰσοκράτης τῆς παιδείας τὴν ῥίζαν πικρὰν ἔφη, γλυκεῖς δὲ τοὺς καρπούς."

PAGE 29

9. *Sermo* CCLXXII, vii, 7 (*PL 38,* 1251); see also *PL 32,* 602; *33,* 724.

1. Vergil, *Aeneid, IX,* 308-10.

2. Psalms, 119:130. The Revised Standard Version reads: "The unfolding of thy words gives light; it imparts understanding to the simple."

PAGE 31

3. See Aphthonius, *Progymnasmata, XIV,* 53.

4. *Progymnasmata, VII,* 33.

PAGE 33

5. Erasmus, *Adagia*, II. IV. lxxvi: "Nodum in scyrpo quaeris, in anxium dicebatur, nimisque diligentem; aut meticulosum, qui illic scrupulum moveret, ubi nihil esset addubitandum." See also Plautus, *Menaechmi*, II, i, and Terence, *Andria*, V, iv, 38.

6. A version of the proverb "Laws catch flies, but let the hornets go free." Cf. Erasmus, *Adagia*, I. IV. xlvii: "Aranearum telas texere . . . ; leges cum aranearum textis comparabat."

7. Author of the first written code at Athens, 621 B.C. According to the *Oxford Classical Dictionary* (s.v. *Draco*), the orator Demades described Draco's laws as written in blood. Aristotle said "there is nothing peculiar in his laws that is worthy of mention, except their severity in imposing heavy punishment" (*Politics*, 1274b, 15-18).

8. Angelo Poliziano (1454-94), famous Italian poet and humanist. The epigram which Pace cites is entitled "In leges extemporale" (*Opera Omnia*, Paris, 1512, II, sig. p₁v).

9. A pun. In Latin *Draco* means *dragon*.

1. Demosthenes, **ΚΑΤΑ ΑΡΙΣΤΟΤΕΙΤΟΝΟΣ Α,** XXV.15 (Reiske 774.7).

PAGE 35

2. I.e., Medieval jurists as opposed to classical. Francesco Accursius (1182-1260), a famous medieval jurist, taught at Bologna and compiled a glossary or commentary on the whole body of law. Dante put him with the Sodomites in the *Inferno* (XV, 110). Domitius Ulpianus (d. 228 A.D.) was one of the last Roman jurists of the classical period. Killed by the Praetorian Guard, presumably because of his severity and plans for reform. Contemporary and colleague of Paulus, he wrote nearly 280 books, published between 211-17. They were the chief source for Justinian's *Digest*, nearly one-third of which was originally written by Ulpian. Julius Paulus (ca. 200 A.D.), Roman jurist and teacher, wrote more than 300 books, among them a long commentary on the *Edict* and an exposition of the *ius civile*. His works were used extensively by the compilers of the *Digest*, nearly a sixth of which is ultimately derived from him. "Gallus" is either a misprint or a mistake for Gaius (second century A.D.), one of the most renowned Roman jurists. Justinian admired him particularly and ordered his standard work, the *Institutes*, to be used as the basis for the imperial *Institutiones*. Scaevola is probably Quintus Cervidius Scaevola (second century A.D.), legal adviser of Marcus Aurelius and the author of six books of *Responsa* and forty books of *Digesta*, which are renowned as the most important work of casuistic literature.

3. This was the John Clerk who was later Bishop of Bath and Wells and who had studied at Bologna, where he received a bachelor's degree in canon law in 1510. He was in Bainbridge's service at Rome with Pace. See George B. Parks, *The English Traveler to Italy* (Stanford, 1954), I, 627.

4. Erasmus, *Adagia*, I. I. i: "Amicorum communia omnia," placed first in all editions of the *Adages*. See also below, p. 59, n. 4.

5. A Greek coin, worth about three cents.

6. *Sat.*, I, iii, 16-17: "quinque diebus / nil erat in loculis." But the allusion does not seem to fit. Horace speaks of a blowhard, Tigellius of Sardinia, who claims he could live (like Thoreau) on very little, but if you gave him a million, he would spend it in a week (*quinque diebus*). Perhaps Pace simply means to imply that he and Clerk spent recklessly too.

7. Erasmus, *Adagia*, I. II. xlvii: "Calcar addere currenti." See also I. II. xlvi (Currentem incitare) and p. 125 below.

8. Xenocrates of Chalcedon, Plato's pupil and head of the Academy from 339 to 314 B.C.

9. Cleanthes, the disciple of Zeno and head of the Stoic school from 263 to 232 B.C. See below, p. 123, n. 6.

PAGE 37

1. See *Tusc. Disp.* V, ii, 5; *De Fin.*, II, xxvii, 86.

2. Cf. Erasmus, *Adagia*, II. V. lxxxvi: "Ipse semet canit." The modern equivalent would be "to blow one's own horn."

3. See Diogenes Laertius,VIII, 33.

4. *Aphorisms*, I, i.

PAGE 39

5. *Hist. Nat.*, XXIX, 18: "Discunt periculis nostris et experimenta per mortes agunt, medicoque tantum hominem occidisse inpunitas summa est."

6. Thomas Langton (d. 1501), Bishop of Winchester and Archbishop-elect of Canterbury. Educated at Oxford and Cambridge, he took both degrees in canon law, becoming chaplain to Edward IV and sometime ambassador. During the seven years he was Bishop of Winchester (1493-1501), he organized the palace school Pace mentions, where students were instructed in grammar and music. Langton was elected Archbishop of Canterbury on January 22, 1501, but died of the plague before the deed was confirmed. Richard Fox succeeded him at Winchester. See the Introduction, p. ix.

7. That is, in canon and civil law.

8. A proverb. Cf. Thomas Becon's *Catchword on Thynges* (1560), p. 531: "As the common saying is, virtue praised increases." Cf. also "praise makes good men better and bad men worse" *Oxford Dictionary of English Proverbs,* ed. W. B. Smith (Oxford, 1935).

9. Edward IV, Richard III, and Henry VII. Langton was consecrated in August 1483, the year of Edward's death.

PAGE 41

1. Cf. Cicero "hoc sonitu [the music of the spheres] oppletae aures hominum obsurduerunt; nec est hebetior sensus in vobis, sicut, ubi Nilus ad illa, quae Catadupa nominantur, praecipitat ex altissimis montibus, ea gens, quae illum locum adcolit, propter magnitudinem sonitus sensu audiendi caret" (*De Re Publica,* VI, xviii). The idea of the music of the spheres is ultimately Platonic, but it soon became commonplace. Cf. Milton, *Nativity Hymn,* 125-32; *At a Solemn Music;* Browne, *Religio Medici,* II, 9.

2. Ancient accounts of the nine muses all go back to Hesiod (*Theogony,* 25 f.)

3. Horace, *Sat.,* II, ii, 77-79:

> quin corpus onustum
> hesternis vitiis animum quoque praegravat una
> atque adfigit humo divinae particulam aurae.

4. Almost all of the examples which Pace cites in this *laus musicae* are taken directly from Philip Beroaldus' *Oratio habita in enarratione Quaestionum Thusculanarum et Horatii flacci: continens laudem musices* (in *Varia Philippi Beroaldi Opuscula,* Paris, 1505, sigs. b₈-c₂). Beroaldus mentions Martianus Cappella as among his own sources. For Themistocles and Epaminondas, see Plutarch, *Them.,* II, 3 and Cicero, *Tusc. Disp.,* I, ii, 4.

5. For Plato, see, for example, Book VII of *The Republic;* Aristotle's fullest discussion is in the *Politics* (VIII, 5, 1939a f.).

6. We have not been able to trace the stories of Xenocrates, Asclepius, and Theophrastus to a specific classical source. All three are recounted in Beroaldus' *Oratio.*

7. Plutarch tells the story of Thales of Crete (not Thales the philosopher, of Miletus) curing the plague at Sparta with music ("De Musica," 42, *Moralia,* 1146C).

8. I Samuel 16:23: "And whenever the evil spirit from God was upon Saul, David took the lyre and played it with his hand; so Saul was refreshed, and all was well, and the evil spirit departed from him."

PAGE 43

9. Cf. Quintilian, *Inst.*, I, x, 13: "De philosophis loquor, quorum fons ipse Socrates iam senex instituti lyra non erubescebat." Quintilian makes no mention of Socrates' age. He is usually believed to have died at seventy (469-399 B.C.), which would make Pace's version of the story somewhat improbable. See also Valerius Maximus, *Factorum et Dictorum Memorabilium*, VIII, 7.

1. Cf. Edward Topsell, *The History of Four-footed Beasts and Serpents* (London, 1658), p. 105: "if they hear any musical pipings, they stand still to their own destruction: for which cause the *Egyptians* decipher a man overthrown by flattery, by painting a Hart taken by musick [In the margin is a reference to Horus Apollo: "*Horus.* An hieroglyphical emblem."]: and *Varro* relateth upon his own knowledge, that when he supped in his Lordship bought of *M. Piso*, the Pastour or Forrester after supper, took but a Harp in his hand, and at the sound hereof, an innumerable flock of Harts, Boars, and other four-footed beasts came about their Cabinet . . .: the like is also reported by Aelianus. . . ." See also Pliny, *Hist. Nat.*, VIII, 114 and Hugh of St. Victor, *PL 177, 64.*

2. (fl. 628-625 B.C.). Son of Cycleus. Spent most of his life at the court of Periander at Corinth. According to Herodotus (I, 23), he was once returning to Corinth from Sicily when he was robbed by the crew of the ship and forced to throw himself into the sea. He put on his singing robes, sang the "shrill strain" in honor of Apollo, and flung himself overboard, "but a dolphin (so the story goes) took Arion on his back and bore him to Taenarus." Arion is also famous for his contributions to the dithyramb and through it to the development of tragedy. The story of Arion and the dolphin is a standard feature of the *topos laus musicae.* Cf. Castiglione, *The Courtier*, I, 47; Spenser, *FQ*, IV, xi, 23; Keats, *Endymion*, 360.

3. Timotheus may or may not be identified with the historical musician of that name (450-360 B.C.). Suidas' *Lexicon* tells the story of Alexander leaping from his seat during a performance, by Timotheus, of an Orthian Nome to Athena. The story's later fame owes much to Dryden's *Alexander's Feast*.

4. Pace may be reshaping the story which Quintilian (I.x.32) tells of Pythagoras: "Nam et Pythagoran accepimus concitatos ad vim pudicae domui adferendam iuvenes, iussa mutare in spondeum modos tibicina, composuisse."

5. For the Cretans and the Spartans see Plutarch, "De Musica," 26, *Moralia* 1140C.

6. Inhabitants of ancient Sybaris, on the Gulf of Tarentus. Famed for their wealthy luxuriousness.

7. Fourth Lydian King (ca. 610-560 B.C.) of the house of Gyges. Famous for his wars against the Medes and Ionians. Cf. Herodotus, I, 17: "This was the manner in which . . . [Alyattes] attacked and laid siege to Miletus: he sent his invading army, marching to the sound of pipes and harps and flutes, bass and treble. . . ."

8. Erasmus' *Complaint of Peace (Querela Pacis)* was first published in December 1517. His earlier anti-war writings include the *Antipolemus* (1507), the *Dulce Bellum Inexpertis* (in the 1515 *Adagia*) and portions of the *Institutio Principis* (1516). See R. P. Adams, *The Better Part of Valor, More, Erasmus, Colet, and Vives on Humanism, War, and Peace, 1496-1535* (Seattle, 1962).

9. Psalms, 68:30.

1. Egidio of Viterbo (d. 1532). General of the Augustinian order; poet, philosopher, theologian, and historian. He had just been made a cardinal by Leo X, on July 1, 1517.

PAGE 45

2. Pace is clearly ironic in this sentence, for Julius II, an extremely warlike pope, was anything but a gentle good shepherd.

3. *De Architectura*, X, x-xii. Vitruvius does not say precisely what Pace attributes to him, however. In chapter xi, on the balista, he says that only those who know something about "the geometrical treatment of numbers and their multiples" ("geometricis rationibus numeros et multiplicationes") can build these machines, but he does not say that it could not be done without the aid of musical theory. The closest he comes to Pace is in his last sentence dealing with the catapult: "Ita cunearum conclusionibus ad sonitum musicis auditionibus catapultae temperantur" (xii, 2).

PAGE 47

4. One of Pace's teachers at Padua. See below, p. 125 and notes. Latimer had been in Italy from 1498-1505 and he presumably returned to Rome in 1511. See G. B. Parks, *The English Traveler to Italy* (Stanford, 1954), I, 467-68.

5. Christopher Bainbridge (1464?-1514), Archbishop of York and English ambassador at Rome (1509-14). He died in Rome about July 13, 1514, supposedly poisoned by his chaplain, Rinaldo de Modena. See the Introduction, p. x.

6. Erasmus notes (Allen, 4, 19) that More taught his second wife, Alice, to play the cithern, lute, monochord and recorders.

7. Erasmus, *Adagia*, I. I. xlii: "Invita Minerva." A more literal translation would be: *and Minerva did not want him to.* See also Puttenham, *Art of English Poesy*, III, xxv.

8. Plautus, *Poenulus*, I, ii, 119; Cicero, *Epistolae ad Familiares*, VII, i, 3; Erasmus, *Adagia*, I. IV. lxii.

PAGE 49

9. For example, Vergil, *Aeneid*, I, 742.

1. Pliny, *Hist. Nat.*, XVIII, 68. Aristotle (*Pol.* I, II), Diogenes Laertius (I, 126), and Cicero (*De. Div.*, I, xlix, 111-12) attribute the story to Thales, not Democritus.

2. In his *Age of Erasmus* (Oxford, 1914), P. S. Allen notes that Pope Julius II, for one, put off his coronation until the stars were propitious (p. 217).

3. *De Divinatione* I, lviii, 132. Cicero is quoting Ennius, *Telamo*, 332-36.

PAGE 51

4. Greek coin, worth about 16 cents.

5. *Historiae*, I, 22. The Loeb series and the Oxford edition of the *Histories* (ed. C. B. Fisher, 1939) read "infidum potentibus, sperantibus fallax" ("untrustworthy for the powerful, deceitful to the ambitious"). Pace may have been quoting from memory, or he may have doctored the text to suit his own purposes; at any rate, his reading is not listed as a recognized variant in any of the standard editions.

6. Cicero, *De Divinatione*, II, xxiv, 51.

7. Prophets who claimed to be possessed by a familiar spirit or *python*.

8. The particular kind of divination which Pace refers to here is obscure, but see L. Thorndike, *History of Magic*, 2, 32 and 3, 607. The practice is alluded to again on p. 95.

9. By "recent," Pace means non-classical. *Alchemy* is derived ultimately from an Alexandrian Greek formation (first recorded c. 300 A.D.), which probably goes back to an Egyptian original. The art was apparently first practiced in Egypt. For the "obscure" etymology, see the *Oxford English Dictionary*.

1. Aulus Gellius, *Noctes Atticae*, XIV, i, 34. Gellius ascribes the quotation to Accius, the early Latin dramatist, whose works survive only in fragments.

2. We have not been able to locate the specific proverb to which Pace refers. For the opinion on alchemists, see Chaucer, *Canon Yeoman's Tale*. Alchemists never live well because all their money is spent on fruitless

experiments; necromancers never die well because, as with Faustus, the devil claims his own in the end.

PAGE 53

3. The best throw in playing astragal or huckle-bone. The *Oxford English Dictionary* cites *MS Ashmole 788*, fol. 162: "The game of Astragals . . . When all ye fower boanes shal shew seuerall sides this is the most fortunate cast & is called Midas or Venus take all Cock-all." See also Erasmus' colloquy on huckle-bone, trans. C. R. Thompson (Chicago, 1965), pp. 432-440.

4. The structure of the Latin makes it clear that the two errors are "non scientia, sed coniectura . . . non humana ratio, sed credulitas rerum novarum."

5. *De Divinatione*, II, lxv, 134, but Cicero does not give the name of the soothsayer. He calls him merely a *coniector*. See also Erasmus, *Adagia*, IV.III.li: "Nihil de vitello."

6. *De Divinatione*, II, lxi, 126.

PAGE 55

7. *Oneirocritika*, I, 55 (Leipzig, 1805, ed. Nic. Rigaltius and Io. Iac. Reiskius).

8. Cf. *Interpretationes somniorum Danielis prophete reuelate ab angelo misso a deo et primo de diebus lune etc.* [Deft, Christian Snellaert, ca. 1489-90]. The list of dream significations is organized alphabetically. Two of the significations are close to Pace's version: "Dentem vltimum vel penultimum maxille perdere significat mortem proximi parentis," and "Dentes plures perdere significat mortem amici." He seems to have combined the two into one dream. There were a great many editions of this popular dream manual, usually referred to as the *Somnia Danielis*, in the late fifteenth and early sixteenth centuries.

9. That is, "inspired by God." See Plutarch, "De Placitis Philosophorum," 5 (*Moralia*, 904F).

PAGE 57

1. Ecclesiastes, 5:7.

2. Themistius (317?-387) taught at Constantinople. His commentaries on Aristotle were translated by Barbaro in the late fifteenth century, but the first edition of the Greek did not appear until 1534. See his paraphrase on the *De Anima*, IV, (E), 165.

3. See Erasmus, *Adagia*, II.III.lxxviii, "Qui bene conijicet hunc uatem."

After giving the Aristotle passage (*Eud. Ethics,* VII, 14, 1248a), Erasmus translates it as does Pace: "prudentium atque sapientium hominum celerem esse diuinationem, & horum tantum."

4. Mark 13:32. The Revised Standard Version reads: "But of that day or that hour no one knows, not even the angels in heaven, nor the Son, but only the Father." See also Matthew 24:36; Acts 1:1.

5. Demosthenes xxi.69 (ΚΑΤΑ ΜΕΙΔΟΥ).

6. A common idea in the Renaissance, going back at least as far as Plato's philosopher king in the *Republic.* Cf. below, p. 141, and *Utopia,* Book I.

7. Cf. Martial (8, 56, 5): "sint Maecenates, non deerunt, Flacce, Marones."

PAGE 59

8. "We are told by Apollodorus the calculator that . . . [Pythagoras] offered a sacrifice of oxen on finding that in a right-angled triangle the square on the hypotenuse is equal to the squares on the sides containing the right angle. And there is an epigram running as follows:

> What time Pythagoras that famed figure found,
> For which the noble offering he brought."
> (Diogenes Laertius, VIII, 12)

9. Pace seems to have confused Pythagoras with Archimedes, who yelled εὕρηκα after he discovered the principle of the displacement of water and a means thereby of testing (by specific gravity) the proportion of gold and silver in Hieron's crown.

1. The story of the inscription is probably apocryphal. It is recorded by Johannes Tzetzes (fl. 1150) in his *Chiliades* (ed. T. Kiessling, Leipzig, 1826), VIII, 972-75. See below, p. 73, n. 9.

2. Cf. Diogenes Laertius, IV, 10: "To some one who had never learnt either music or geometry or astronomy, but nevertheless wished to attend his lectures, Xenocrates said, 'Go your ways, for you offer philosophy nothing to lay hold of.' Others report him as saying, 'It is not to me that you come for the carding of a fleece.'" Cf. Erasmus, *Adagia,* IV. VII. xxxix: "Lanam in officinam fullonis. Qui praepostere rem gerunt, ueluti si quis theologo committat puerum in grammaticis rudimentis instituendum, lanam in officinam fullonis ferre dicitur."

3. Cf. Hesiod, *Works and Days,* line 40: "πλέον ἥμισυ παντός." In the *Adagia* (I.IX.xcv, "Dimidium plus toto") Erasmus cites the Hesiod passage. Cf. also Diogenes Laertius, I, 75.

4. Diogenes Laertius, VIII, 10. See also above, p. 35, n. 4.

5. See Plato, *Laws*, VI, 757a.

PAGE 61

6. The Immaculate Conception was denied by St. Bernard, Aquinas, and Bonaventure, but supported by Duns Scotus in a series of disputations at Paris. For More's discussion of the matter see *St. Thomas More, Selected Letters*, ed. Elizabeth F. Rogers (New Haven, 1961), p. 133 and note.

7. The writ to which Pace refers is probably the constitution "Grave nimis" published by Pope Sixtus IV on September 4, 1483, which threatened with excommunication all those of either opinion who accused the opposite opinion of heresy. We have not been able to explain Pace's gossipy allusion to the Bolognese Benedictines.

8. Erasmus' *Novum Instrumentum* was first published in 1516. For some of the attacks made on it, see Allen, *Eras. Ep.*, 2, 371, 490.

9. A variant of the proverb "They agree like the clocks of London." Cf. Thomas Nashe, *The Return of Pasquil* in *Works*, ed. R. B. McKerrow (London, 1910), I, 84: "The Preachers of England begin to strike and agree like the clocks of England, that neuer meete iumpe on a point together." But see also Pope's *Essay on Criticism*, 9-10:

> 'Tis with our *Judgments* as our *Watches*, none
> Go just *alike*, yet each believes his own.

1. Cf. Cicero's use of the expression 'negaret quidquam esse quod comprehendi posset' for the Greek adjective ἀκατάληπτον (*Academica*, II.18), and his earlier discussion of the proper Latin equivalents (cognitio, perceptio, comprehensio) for the noun κατάληψις (II.17).

2. E.g., Aulus Gellius, *Noctes Atticae*, XI, v, 1-3. Gellius makes it clear, however, that he is speaking only of skeptic philosophers: "quos Pyrronios philosophos vocamus."

3. A variant of Julianus' epigram in the *Greek Anthology* (VII, 576): A. "Are you dead, Pyrro?" B. "I doubt it." A. "Even after your final dissolution, do you say you doubt?" B. "I doubt." A. "The tomb has put an end to doubt." Pace probably distorted it for his own purposes, making Pyrro's answer, ἐπέχω περὶ τούτου, match that of the philosophers who have just been mentioned.

PAGE 63

4. Leading members of the school of law that overthrew the *glossators* under Accursius and that was itself overthrown by the humanists under Cujas. They flourished particularly in the fourteenth and fifteenth centu-

ries. Baldus (b. 1327), the most famous jurist of his day, taught at the University of Piacenza and the University of Padua, along with Bartol Saliceti. Bartolus of Sasso Ferrato (fl. 1314-27) was a student of Cino da Pistoia, poet and jurist, and himself the teacher of Baldus. Joannes de Imola (d. 1436) was an important commentator on the *Decretals*. Cf. Rabelais, II, x: "you have obscured it [a legal judgment], and made it more intricate, by the frivolous, sottish, unreasonable and foolish reasons and opinions of Accursius, Baldus, Bartolus, de Castro, de Imola . . . , and those other old Mastiffs, who never understood the least law of the Pandects."

5. See above, p. 35, n. 2.

6. Maximilian I, Holy Roman Emperor from 1493 to 1519. The lawyer turned rhetorician to whom Pace refers was Jason Maynus (Giasone Maino), d. 1519. He delivered his oration on March 16, 1494 and it was printed shortly thereafter. See the Paris, 1505, edition, *Orationes Praelectiones et Praefationes et quaedam mithicae Historiae Philippi Beroaldi . . . . Atque vna Iasonis Maini Oratio*, sig. Aaa₁v: "Tibi nomen Maximiliano parens indidit: non sine quodam diuino instinctu vt Plato attestatur: Quod duo significat Maximum / & AEmilianum. Ambo romani militarium copiarum praestantissimi duces ac triumphales viri. Maximus enim Fabius romanum imperium pene desolatum aduersus hannibalem poenum cunctando restituit. AEmilianus vero Scipio Hannibale tandem deuicto carthaginensem triumphum egit. Vtriusque tibi nomen copulatum est. etc."

7. Fabius Maximus Cunctator, the famous Roman general (d. 203 B.C.) whose delaying tactics after Cannae (216 B.C.) gradually wore down Hannibal's forces. Aemilius Scipio, great Roman general of the second century B.C. (185-129). He destroyed Carthage in 146 B.C.

8. In Pliny (*Hist. Nat.* XX, 24, 100) theriaca is considered as an antidote against the bite of serpents. Galen wrote two works on the drug (see *Opera*, ed. Kühn, XIV, 210-94 and 295-310). Directly relevant is his sixth commentary on Hippocrates (Kühn, XVII, 336-37), where he mentions that theriaca is used against the bites of wild beasts.

9. Linacre's first translation from Galen was not published until August 1517, but it undoubtedly circulated in manuscript long before that. See below, p. 97, and notes.

PAGE 65

1. Philip Beroaldus the Elder (1453-1505), celebrated humanist of Bologna, where he held the chair of Rhetoric and Poetry. He edited many classical authors, but does not seem to have produced a Galen. In his "Declamatio Philosophi medici et oratoris" (*Varia Opuscula*, Paris, 1505, sig. A₃), he alludes in passing to Galen's book on theriaca. Pace probably means that a rhetorician like Beroaldus would be out of his field in commenting on a medical work.

2. (1428-1524), professor of medicine at Ferrara. He taught Linacre at Vicenza and Pace at Ferrara. His first publication was *De Plinii in medicina erroribus* (Ferrara, 1492). He wrote treatises on syphilis and the viper and translated parts of Aristotle, Galen, and Hippocrates. Pace's report of his death was a false rumor. The monument erected to him by Alfonso III of Este in 1524 gives his age as ninety and states that he taught at Ferrara for sixty years (Allen, 2, 489). See also p. 127 below.

3. Not an idea of Leonicenus' alone, but a general humanist position. Cf. Erasmus' letter to Henricus Afinius (Allen, 2, 493), where contemporary physicians are held up to scorn for their failure to learn Greek.

4. A term Pace introduced into the language, according to the *Oxford English Dictionary*. It means one who obstinately clings to old ways, even though they are wrong, instead of changing over to the new (*sumpsimus*). For the anecdote of the illiterate English priest that gave rise to the expression, see below, p. 103. See also Allen, 2, 323; 3, 40. Erasmus seems to have been the earliest source of the story (1516).

5. Cf. Chaucer, *General Prologue*, 425-28:
> Ful redy hadde he [the Physician] his apothecaries
> To sende hym drogges and his letuaries.
> For ech of hem made oother for to wynne—
> Hir frendshipe nas nat newe to bigynne.

6. Avicenna (980-1037), the famous Arabian physician and philosopher. Pace seems to refer to a passage in Galen's *De Differentiis Pulsuum* (ed. Kühn, VIII, 620) where *diesis* (lit. a "flowing through") is discussed with regard to the different types of pulse. Galen uses a musical analogy to illustrate his point.

7. "Proportion" is a rhythmic term in sixteenth-century music used to account for the relation of a note to its subdivisions or of the subdivisions to a note of larger value. For this and the allusion below to British musicians, see Thomas Morley, *A Plaine and Easie Introduction to Practicall Musicke* (London, 1597), sig. *4v:
> . . . proportions of *multiplicitie* might be had and vsed in any kinde without great scruple or offence: but those *superparticulars* [proportions such as 3:2, 4:3 where the larger number contains the smaller once with one part left over, i.e., 1½, 1⅓ times] and *superpartients* [proportions such as 5:3, 7:4 where the larger number contains the smaller once with any number of parts left over, i.e., 1⅔, 1¾ times] carry great difficultie, and haue crept into musick I know not how, but it shold seeme, that it was by meanes of the *Descanters,* who striuing to sing harder waies vpon a plainsong then their fellowes, brought in that which neither could please the eares of other men, nor could by themselues be defended by reason. Here was I determined to haue made an ende, but some more curious then discreet, compelled me to speake some words more, and to giue a reason why, after the proportions I haue said nothing of the *inductions*. And therfore to be briefe,

I say that all which they can say of these *inductions,* is nothing but meere foolishnesse, *& commenta otiosorum hominum qui nihil aliud agunt nisi ut iniuniant* [sic] *quomodo in otio negotiosi videantur . . . .* But to be plaine, those *inductions* be no other thinge . . . but that number which any greater notes broken in smaller do make, as for example . . . *sesquialtera* or pricke semibriefe is the induction to their *tripla,* for sing your *sesquialtera* in minimes, and you shall find three of them to a stroke [i.e., measure].

8. See above, p. 47.

PAGE 67

9. *Hist. Nat.,* VII, xlix, 162.

1. Technical terms which double the idea of possession. In astronomical language *horizon* refers to the celestial hemisphere within the horizon of a certain place. *Climate* is used in the obsolete sense of an area of the earth's surface between two given parellels of latitude.

2. Demosthenes 314.16 (ΠΕΡΙ ΤΟΥ ΣΤΕΦΑΝΟΥ).

3. Cf. St. Augustine, *De Civitate Dei,* XI, xxx (*PL 41,* 343-44); *De Genesi ad Litteram,* IV, ii (*PL 34,* 296-99).

4. For the story, see Aulus Gellius, *Noctes Atticae,* XI, ix, 1. Pace speaks of more than one orator but, according to Critolaus, from whom Gellius takes the tale, there was only one—and he was Demosthenes.

5. This is said of Demosthenes in Erasmus' *Colloquies* (transl. C. R. Thompson, Chicago, 1965), p. 611.

6. Not ordinary neuter nouns, but a form of irregular noun. Cf. Quintilian: "Nec statim diligentem putabo, qui promiscua, quae ἐπίκοινα dicuntur, ostenderit, in quibus sexus uterque per alterum apparet; aut quae feminina positione mares aut neutrali feminas significant, qualia sunt *Murena* et *Glycerium*" (*Inst.,* I, iv, 24).

PAGE 69

7. Aldus Manutius (1449-1515), founder of the famous Aldine press.

8. For the *y* spellings in *Utopia,* which occur in the two 1518 (Froben) editions, but not in the 1516 and 1517 editions, see *The Complete Works of St. Thomas More,* vol. 4 (*Utopia*), ed. E. Surtz and J. H. Hexter (New Haven, 1965), p. cxciii.

9. For Politian, see above, p. 33, n. 8. For the spelling of Vergil, see his *Miscellanea,* I.lxxvii (*Opera,* Paris, 1512, I, sig. R₄v): "Quo argumento dicendum Vergilius: non Virgilius," where he mentions several ancient in-

scriptions "quae . . . in marmore inueniuntur," with the *e* spelling. Today *Vergil* is the preferred American spelling, *Virgil* the preferred British.

1. A lexicon by John Balbi of Genoa (completed in 1286) based on Papias and Huguitio of Pisa and used as a standard book of reference in all the churches of France. Printed by Gutenberg in 1460, it was translated into French and used in the schools of Paris as late as 1759. It was despised by the humanists as an example of medieval learning. See P. S. Allen, *The Age of Erasmus* (Oxford, 1914), pp. 43 f.

PAGE 71

2. Pace's etymology is incorrect. The word *bull* is derived from the leaden seal attached to papal edicts (Latin *bulla* = any round, swelling object).

3. Pace may have a particular bull in mind. In 1516 the bull *Pastor Aeternus* reasserted papal supremacy and repealed all decrees of the Councils of Constance and Basel as well as other papal bulls. See Preserved Smith, *The Age of the Reformation* (New York, 1920), p. 15. The references to war in this paragraph are probably aimed at Julius II.

4. Pace refers, of course, to the *Adagia,* new editions of which had appeared in 1515 and 1517. The "proverb" is apparently "Qui per alium facit, per seipsum facere videtur," just cited by the grammarian. It sounds more like a legal maxim than a true adage.

5. It is unlikely that Pace refers to any actual composition of his own, but simply to some grammatical note or other. The vacancy on the papal throne was probably that of February 20-March 11, 1513, between the death of Julius II and the election of Leo X, who is referred to in the next sentence.

PAGE 73

6. Commenting on the line "corpora perque domos et relligiosa deorum" (*Aeneid,* II, 365), Servius noted "sane 'relligio' geminatur 'l' propter metri necessitatem."

7. Cf. *Epistles* 9.5.3: "Nihil est ipsa aequalitate inaequalius."

8. I Corinthians 3:16; 6:19; II Corinthians 6:16.

9. Plato nowhere makes this statement, but it was commonly attributed to him in the Renaissance. Cf. Erasmus, *Adagia*, III.III.lx, and above, p. 59, n. 1.

PAGE 75

1. Pace probably alludes to Archimedes' (c. 287-212 B.C.) work on the *Measurement of a Circle*. Aristotle refers to the problem of squaring the circle, which is impossible of geometric solution, in *Soph. Elenchus* (171b, 172a), *Physics* (185a), and *Eud. Eth.* (II, 10, 1226a).

2. The famous planetarium supposedly carried to Rome after the sack of Syracuse by Marcellus and described by Cicero, *De Re Publica*, I, xiv, 21-22.

3. Pace is apparently quoting from memory. Livy does not quite say this. He praises Archimedes as "unicus spectator caeli siderumque, mirabilior tamen inventor ac machinator bellicorum tormentorum operumque quibus quicquid hostes ingenti mole agerent ipsi perlevi momento ludificaretur" (XXIV, 34). Pace may have misread the *ingenti mole* and *ludificaretur* and arrived at Archimedes' playing with huge weights in the air. Or perhaps he was thinking of Archimedes' statement in Plutarch's *Life of Marcellus*, 7, "that with any given force it was possible to move any given weight" and "if there were another world, and he could go to it, he could move this."

4. In the obsolete sense of obelisk, a common Renaissance use of the term. In Pace's day St. Peter's Needle stood in the ruins of what had once been the *spina* of Nero's Circus and was one of the sights of Rome. Mephistophiles, for example, promises to show Faustus "the high Pyramydes / That Iulius Caesar brought from Affrica" (B, 846-47). It was not actually Caesar's, of course, but had been carried to Rome from Thebes by Constantinus (ca. 353 A.D.). In 1586 Pope Sixtus V's brilliant engineer, Domenico Fontana, finally managed to dismantle it and erect it in its present location in front of St. Peter's, winning great fame for himself.

5. Possibly by the geometric arrangement of the walls lining the harbor (Livy, XXIV, 34), but the reference is obscure. See also Quintilian, *Inst.*, I, 9.

6. For this story see Plutarch, *Marcellus*, 19; Valerius Maximus, VII, 7, Ext. 7; Cicero, *De Finibus*, V, 50; Livy, XXV, xxxi, 9-10.

PAGE 77

7. The first edition of the Greek text of Euclid was not published until 1533.

PAGE 79

8. In middle English *arithmetic* was erroneously derived from *ars metrica*, the 'art of measure' and made into *arsmetrike*. Cf. Chaucer (*Knight's Tale*, 1040), "That geometry or arsmetrike can." The modern

form, based on the Greek, gradually established itself in the sixteenth century.

9. Erasmus, *Adagia*, I.IX. xxxiv: "Leonem ex unguibus aestimare." See also Jonson's *Cynthia's Revels*, V, x, 73; "Ex unge, you know the old adage, as these, so are the remainder."

1. Macrobius, *Somnium Scipionis*, I, vi, 7; see also Martianus Capella, 7, 742.

2. Cf. the Pythagorean belief that "the principle of all things is the monad or unit; arising from this monad the undefined dyad or two serves as material substratum to the monad, which is cause; from the monad and the undefined dyad spring numbers; from numbers, points; from points, lines; . . . from solid figures, sensible bodies" (Diogenes Laertius, VII, 25).

3. Cf. *Carmen Aureum*, Pseudo-Pythagoras (ed. E. Diehl, *Anthol. Lyr. Grae.*, Teubner, 3rd ed., Leipzig), Fasc. 2, p. 87, lines 47-48.

4. Number mysteries, tending toward the cabala, were popular in the early Renaissance. Cf. the final section of Pico della Mirandola's *Heptaplus* and Agrippa's *De Occulta Philosophia*, II, i-xv. Toward the end of the Renaissance they came into fashion again, as in Sir Thomas Browne's *Garden of Cyrus*.

PAGE 81

5. The entire section is a paraphrase of St. Augustine, *De Civitate Dei*, XI, xxxi: "Hoc itaque satis sit admonere est, quod totus impar primus numeris ternarius est, totus par quarternarius: ex quibus duobus septenarius constat. Ideo pro universo saepe ponitur, sicuti est, *Septies cadet justus, et resurget* (*Prov.* XXIV, 16): id est, quotiescumque ceciderit, non peribit . . . Et, *Septies in die laudabo te* (*Psal.* CXVII, 164). Quod alibi alio modo dictum est: *Semper laus ejus in ore meo* (*Psal.* XXXIII, 2)" (*PL 41*, 344-45).

6. Cf. St. Augustine: "In decem autem Lex, in septem vero Gratia significatur; quia Legem non implet, nisi charitas diffusa in cordibus nostris per Spiritum sanctum, qui septenario numero significatur" (*PL 37*, 1961). The explanation why the Holy Spirit is represented by the number seven is somewhat more complicated and occupies most of the page and the page preceding.

7. *Adagia*, I.VII.xxvi: "Omnia octo." After mentioning a number of possible sources, Erasmus adds: "Quod si nobis quoque conceditur in aenigmate divinare, non absurde natum videri potest a fabula, quam narrat Plutarchus in commentario De Daemonio Socratis. Deliis ac caeteris Graecis oraculo responsum fuisse apud Aegyptios, ita demum malorum finem fore, si aram, quae in Delo erat, duplassent. Qui cum non intellexissent, quid sibi vellet oraculum, ridicule duplatis singulis arae lateribus, impru-

dentes solidum octuplum effecerunt, ob inscitiam proportionis, quae longitudine duplum reddit." Erasmus then goes on, in the 1515 but not in the 1508 edition of the *Adages,* to tell the story of Heliogabalus as given by Pace.

8. This work, like the one on music mentioned earlier (p. 47), was apparently never finished. Pace's friend Tunstal produced his book on arithmetic (*De Arte Supputandi*) in 1522.

9. Wisdom of Solomon 11:20.

1. Cf. Erasmus, *Adagia,* II.VI.lxxxvi: "Circulum absolvere: Est rem omnibus numeris, omnibusque partibus perfectam reddere. . . ." Erasmus goes on to cite Quintilian (*Inst.* VIII, Pr. 1).

2. A game played by guessing how many stones or nuts were in one's hand, odd or even. Horace does not say that children learn it without a teacher. He merely lists it in a series of games unsuitable for men: "Aedificare casas, plostello adiungere mures, / Ludere par impar, equitare in harundine longa" (*Sat.,* II, iii, 247-48; see also Ovid, *De Nuce,* V, 80).

PAGE 83

3. For the story, see Quintilian, *Inst.,* II, xx, 3.

4. Pace seems to be recalling, however vaguely and inexactly, Plato's famous metaphor of the charioteer (*Phaedrus,* 246 and 253 f.).

5. Lycurgus did not specifically banish arithmetic although he banished "the unnecessary and superfluous arts" (Plutarch, *Lycurgus,* IX, 3). Perhaps Arithmetic refers to the fact that Lycurgus did away with the necessity for business and the amassing of wealth and in so doing got rid of the arithmetic involved in it (Plutarch, XXIV).

6. Manius Curius Dentatus, plebian, consul 290 B.C.; noted for his frugality and incorruptibility.

PAGE 85

7. A common object of satire in the early Renaissance. According to Erasmus, Franciscans were forbidden to touch money by Pope Benedict so as to carry out St. Francis' command not to receive it: *Exsequiae Seraphicae, Colloquia Familiaria* in *Opera,* I, 871; see also 710, 739. For general background, see C. R. Thompson's introduction to his translation of the colloquy (Chicago, 1965), pp. 500-503.

8. We have not been able to discover the papal decree to which Pace refers.

9. Erasmus, *Adagia,* I.I.xcii: "Uti foro."

1. The recitation was fairly lengthy, for the whole psalm in the Vulgate [108, "Deus laudem meam ne tacueris"; 109 in the Authorized Version] runs to 31 verses. The theologian begs God not to hold *His* peace, even though he himself has been silenced.

2. A pun on two meanings of *ratio*, as the context makes clear: both *reason* (the usual meaning) and *reckoning* or *account*.

PAGE 87

3. "The ass though laden with gold still eats thistles." Cf. Massinger's *City Madam*, II, i: "wilt thou . . . being keeper of the cash, / Like an ass that carries dainties feed on thistles?" See also Massinger's *Roman Actor*, I, i and Shakespeare, *Julius Caesar*, IV, i, 21. Erasmus (*Adagia*, IV.VIII.-xxxviii) gives the proverb "Asinus stramenta mauult quam aurum."

4. For chalk in German inns, see Erasmus' colloquy *Diversoria* (trans. C. R. Thompson, Chicago, 1965).

5. The context here indicates that Pace is being deliberately humorous. "Computare digitis" is the normal Latin phrase for counting on one's fingers. Children also count on their fingers and hence know as much about it as Pace (or the Romans)!

PAGE 89

6. Thoma-Fedra Inghirami (1470-1516). Poet and orator. Certified poet laureate by Maximilian in March 1497. Librarian of the Vatican; Secretary to the Lateran Council in 1512. He died of a fall from a mule. His portrait by Raphael is in the Pitti at Florence. His funeral oration for Julius II is still extant, first printed at Rome in 1777. Erasmus noted that he was "lingua verius quam calamo celebrem" (Allen, 5, 246).

7. Quintilian's *Institutio Oratoria* and Cicero's *De Oratore, Oratoriae Partitiones, Orator*, and *Brutus, sive De Claris Oratoribus*.

8. Pace has in mind Aristotle's *Rhetoric, Poetics*, and probably the spurious *Rhetorica ad Alexandrum* attributed to him.

9. Pace applies to Hermogenes a paraphrase of Plato's epigram on Aristophanes. (*Anth. Lyrica*, I, 90, ed. Diehl, Leipzig).

1. The ten great orators of ancient Greece were Antiphon, Andocides, Lysias, Isocrates, Isaeus, Aeschines, Lycurgus, Demosthenes, Hypereides, and Deinarchus. See the Pseudo-Plutarchan "Vitae Decem Oratorum," *Moralia*, 832B-850E.

PAGE 91

2. See below, p. 99, n. 3, where this definition of the orator is cited from Cato.

3. Luke 2:46-47.

4. Erasmus' Latin translation of the New Testament, part of which was published the year before (i.e., in 1516) by Froben.

PAGE 93

5. One of Erasmus' most intimate friends. He probably arrived in England in 1504 with Silvester de Giglis, Bishop of Worcester, who was sent to carry the Papal cap and sword to Henry VII. Appointed Latin Secretary sometime before July 1511, Ammonius was the author of one small volume of poetry (Paris, 1511). He died of the sweating sickness on August 17, 1517. See the Introduction, above, p. xiv.

6. Simo's slave in *Andria*. Described as *lorarius*, or household whipper. The only time he speaks in the play is in act V, scene ii, but he says little more than *yes* and *no*. To be exact he says *quid vis?* (20) and *quem?* (21).

7. See below, p. 107, n. 6.

8. Erasmus, *Adagia*, I.II.lvii: "Mandrabuli more res succedit." The proverb means to be worse off every day: "indies in pejus labitur." Mandrabulus was said to have found a treasure and the first year offered a golden egg to Juno Samia, the second year a silver, and the third year a copper (*aeream*).

PAGE 95

9. See above, p. 51, n. 8.

1. Papias the Lombard. Compiled in 1053-63 a dictionary of Latin, "in which he marks the quantity and gives the gender and the inflections of the words, but draws no distinction between the ancient classical forms and the barbarous forms in modern use, and cares little for matters of etymology" (J. E. Sandys, *History of Classical Scholarship* [Cambridge, 1903], I, 501). The work was still in use in the sixteenth century. Papias' primary source was the anonymous *Liber glossarum*, which was in turn partly derived from Placidus. On dolls, however, Papias merely has "Pupae imagines. quas puellae faciunt" (dolls are images which girls make). See the Venice, 1496 edition, sig. s₂v.

2. Balbi of Genoa. See above, p. 69, n. 1.

3. St. Isidore of Seville (ca. 560-636). Pace refers to his famous *Etymologiarum Libri XX*, a catalogue of the entire world and a description of everything in it, which seemed childish to the humanists in its naivete and innocence. It was actually a gathering and systematization of all the learning possessed at the time. The title was taken from the contents of Book X.

4. The word means literally "a net," and hence an enigma or puzzle. See Aulus Gellius I, 4, 4. Pace may be punning on *gryps, gryphis,* the classical griffin. In any event, the "two things" that Grammar does not know in the next paragraph presumably refer to the questions about Greek and Latin nouns which Rhetoric has just put to him.

5. Pace is probably playing with the supposed derivation of the word *solecism* from the corruption of the Attic dialect among the colonists of Σόλοι in Cilicia.

6. Apollonius Dyscolus (second century A.D.). Noted for obscurity even among fellow grammarians. Of the twenty-four works of his mentioned in Suidas only four survive: his *Syntax* and works on the *Pronoun, Conjugation,* and *Adverb.* They are printed in the Teubner edition of the *Grammatici Graeci,* ed. Uhlig and Schneider.

7. Heraclitus of Ephesus (fl. c. 500 B.C.). Instead of publishing his works, which survive only in fragments, he is said to have deposited them in the temple of Artemis. Antiquity knew him as ὁ σκοτεινός, or "Mr. Obscurity." See, e.g., Cicero, *De Fin.* II.v.15.

8. Theodore Gaza of Salonidea (c. 1400-1475) was one of the first teachers of Greek to arrive in Italy from Byzantium. After learning Latin in Vittorino da Feltre's school at Mantua, he was appointed professor of Greek at Ferrara and later at Rome and Naples, taking part in the papal scheme for translating the major Greek classics. Pace refers to the first edition of his Greek grammar published by Aldus at Venice in 1495: *Theodori Introductivae grammatices libri quatuor. . . . Apolonii grammatici de constructione libri quatuor. Herodianus de numeris.*

9. A commonplace. Cf. Horace, *Ars Poetica,* 70-72:

> multa renascentur quae iam cecidere, cadentque
> quae nunc sunt in honore vocabula, si volet usus,
> quem penes arbitrium est et ius et norma loquendi.

PAGE 97

1. Physician and classical scholar (1460-1524). Linacre was in Italy from about 1487-1499; he received his M.D. degree from Padua in 1496 and later returned to England to practice. Shortly after Pace's *De Fructu* was written, he became a priest and presumably gave up the practice of medicine. Linacre was most famous for his translations from Greek into English, particularly his work on Galen.

2. Probably the lost grammar, mentioned in Erasmus' *Letters,* prepared for St. Paul's School around 1512, but rejected by Colet. An English version of it was published around 1525 under the title *Linacri Progymnasmata Grammatices Vulgaria,* with commendatory verses by More and Lily. Linacre also wrote a *Rudimenta Grammatices* for Princess Mary, which was

published by Pynson about 1523-24 and was primarily a revision of his first grammar. It was translated into Latin by Robert Buchanan and printed at Paris, where it went through at least ten editions in the next thirty years.

3. By 1517 Linacre had published a translation of Proclus' *De Sphaera* (Venice, 1499) and Galen's *De Sanitate Tuenda* (Paris, 1517), though at least parts of his major work on Galen, which was soon to appear in 1519, probably circulated in manuscript.

4. Probably in his *De Emendata Structura Latini Sermonis,* first published in 1524, but circulated in manuscript long before. It was the labor of many years. Often reprinted and long regarded as a standard work, even as late as 1669, when it was referred to by Milton in the *Preface* to his *Accedence Commenc't Grammar.* Tryphon was an important Greek grammarian in Rome under Augustus. He wrote a number of musical, botanical, zoological, and dialect glossaries, as well as treatises on disputed breathings and etymological pathology. His works are now lost.

5. Giovanni dell' Aquila (d. 1510), professor at Pisa from 1473-79 and at Padua from 1479-1506. In his day he was regarded as another Aesculapius. See A. von Haller, *Bibliotheca Chirurgica* (Basel, 1774-75), I, 170.

6. Galen is now believed to have been born in 129 A.D. He died in 199 A.D., so he actually lived seventy years.

PAGE 99

7. Baptista Pius of Bologna (c. 1460-1540). Pupil of Philip Beroaldus. Taught at Bologna, Milan, Rome, and Lucca and held the Chair of Eloquence in Paul III's College of Wisdom. Besides editing Fulgentius (1498) and Plautus (1500), he wrote two volumes of linguistic and archaeological *Annotationes* (Brescia, 1496 and Bologna, 1505). See Allen, *Eras. Ep., 1,* 507 n.

8. *Entrance* = ἔισοδος; Hesiod = Ἡσίοδος.

9. Paulus Bombasius tells the same story in a letter to Erasmus: "valde hominem risi; nec ab illo nostro qui παρὰ τὴν ἔισοδον 'id est apud Hesiodum' interpretatus fuerat, in quibusdam multum dissimilem putavi" (Allen, 3, 156, December 6, 1517). Allen is the source for the identification of the mistranslator as Pius.

1. Erasmus, *Adagia,* I.IX.xciii: "Summis labiis."

2. The proper noun Ἡσίοδος is, of course, masculine.

3. See Quintilian, *Inst.* XII, i, 1: 'vir bonus dicendi peritus.' The definition is attributed to Cato the Censor.

4. See Quintilian, *Inst.* I, 19 and 21; XI, 25.

5. In the *De Oratore,* I, vi, 20-22, Cicero said that an accomplished orator should know all the arts and sciences, but that he realized it was impossible: "Neque vero ego hoc tantum oneris imponam nostris praesertim oratoribus . . . nihil ut eis putem licere nescire." In his *De Optimo Genere Oratorum,* however, he claimed that he was looking for perfection: "Oratorem genere non divido; perfectum enim quaeso. Unum est autem genus perfecti" (I, 3).

6. The opening sentence of Demosthenes' *De Corona,* for example, calls upon all the gods and goddesses.

PAGE 101

7. These could be printer's abbreviations, which are common in the texts of the period, but since they are the only ones that occur in the *De Fructu,* it seems more likely that they are used to indicate a certain degree of cordiality and familiarity between Grammar and Rhetoric, as though they were two Rotarians slapping one another on the back and yelling, "Good-by, J. B.!" "So long, T. H.!"

8. *The Consonants at Law: Sigma vs Tau, in the Court of the Seven Vowels.* Sigma brought suit against Tau for "assault and robbery, alleging that he had stolen all the words that are pronounced with double tau."

9. Cf. Lucian, *Consonants at Law,* 9: "He [Tau; Sigma is speaking] has turned me out of all Thessaly, wanting it called Thettaly, has swept me from the *sea* (Θάλασσα—Θάλαττα). . . ." There is no mention of the Athenians, however, who are apparently Pace's own addition. He must mean that in the Athenian dialect, i.e., Attic, the form would be Θάλαττα.

PAGE 103

1. See above, p. 65. The phrase "quod ore sumpsimus" occurs in the Mass, in the "Prayer during Ablution" after the Communion.

2. Probably a fictitious person introduced to lead into the compliment to Budé below.

3. Guillaume Budé (1468-1540), great French humanist. By 1517 he had published his *Annotations on the Pandects* (1508) and his *De Asse* (1515), the latter a widely acclaimed treatise on Roman money.

4. According to Herodotus (II, ii) Psammetichos, Pharaoh of Egypt, raised two children in total silence in order to discover the original language of man. After two years they had both taught themselves to say *Bekos,* the Phrygian word for *bread,* and the Egyptians were forced to admit that the Phrygians were an older people than they. One wonders where Pace got the information that *Bekos* is Phoenician.

5. Cf. *Third Philippic,* 29, 31.

6. A vague reference to Demosthenes' constant opposition to Macedon. After the victory of Antipater at Crannon, Athens was occupied by a Macedonian garrison, and Demosthenes was ordered to be executed. He took refuge in the temple of Poseidon at Calauria in 322 B.C. and committed suicide there (appropriately) by sucking poison concealed in the end of his pen.

7. For Pace's account of More, see Edward Surtz, S.J., "Richard Pace's Sketch of Thomas More," *JEGP, 57* (1958), 36-50.

PAGE 105

8. By Lucian, included in More's and Erasmus' translation (*Luciani . . . opuscula . . . ab Erasmo Roterodamo & Thoma Moro . . . in latinorum linguam traducta* [Paris, 1506]). Bombasius' praise was probably given to Pace orally.

9. In Latin *nasus* means not only *nose,* but also *wit, derision,* or *sarcasm.* In this sense it would refer to More's famous irony. Cf. Martial, I, xlii, 18; V, xix, 17; and More's *Prefatory Letter To Giles* in the *Utopia.*

1. Pace refers to More's good nature and well-known sense of humor. Cf. Erasmus' *Preface* to the *Praise of Folly:* "suspicabor hunc ingenii nostri lusum tibi praecipue probatum iri, propterea quod soleas hujus generis jocis, hoc est, nec indoctis, ni fallor, nec usquequaque insulsis, impendio delectari, & omnino in communi mortalium vita Democritum quemdam agere" (*Opera* [Leyden, 1703], VI, 402).

2. Cf. Horace, *Epist.* II, i, 194; Juvenal, x, 33 and Democritus' own treatise *On Cheerfulness,* defining the moral ideal.

3. From *ridenda* to *deridenda,* a difference of one syllable. Pace's syllabic joke about More imitates that of Hythlodaeus to Peter Giles in the *Utopia:* "Bona uerba inquit Petrus [Giles], mihi uisum est non ut seruias regibus, sed ut inseruias. Hoc est inquit ille, una syllaba plusquam seruias." (Yale edition, *4,* 54).

4. In the spring of 1513 Colet preached against war, urging the King and those who heard him to follow the example of Christ, not Caesar and Alexander. He also quoted Cicero, whose "cum vel iniquissimam pacem iustissimo bello anteferrem" is much stronger than Pace's paraphrase of it (Allen, *4,* 525). As a result of this sermon the Bishop of London and others tried to discredit Colet to the King. See J. H. Lupton, *A Life of John Colet* (London, 1909), pp. 189-90.

PAGE 107

5. Cf. Lucian, *Demonax*, 28: "On seeing two philosophers very ignorantly debating a given subject, one asking silly questions and the other giving answers that were not at all to the point, he [Demonax] said: 'Doesn't it seem to you, friends, that one of these fellows is milking a he-goat and the other is holding a sieve for him!' "

6. *Leukomitrati*, like *albimitrati* on p. 92 above, is apparently a word coined by Pace. Both are simply transliterations of Greek and presumably refer to the Franciscans, the followers of Scotus. Erasmus uses a similar expression, μελανολεύκος, to refer to the Dominicans with their black cloaks and white robes and hoods (Allen, 2, 139). At the same time, however, Pace intends a pun since it is clear from context that the dispute here is between youth and age, the old and the new learning. Cf. Pico della Mirandola's constant address to his imaginary audience of *patres* in the *Oratio de Hominis Dignitate*.

7. Probably Pace's own conflation of Philo Judaeus and Horace's superstitious Judaeus Apella, who believed frankincense melts without fire at the threshold of the Temple (*Satires*, I, v, 100). The implication is that both are Jews, and both are crazy. Perhaps Pace is misquoting again, but in a famous passage in his *De Congressu Quaerendae Eruditionis Gratia* Philo finds the beginning of all learning in geometrical elements, though he makes it clear that the philosophical definitions of a line, surface, and point underly them and form the substratum of all things (XXVI, 146-48).

PAGE 109

8. Grammar is not quite right. Quintilian is speaking of the *grammaticus*, who was not only a grammarian, but also a teacher of literature: "recte loquendi scientiam et poetarum enarrationem" (I, iv, 2). See also I, iv, 5.

9. *Inst.*, I, i, 12-14.

1. The speaker here may be Pace, although there is no indication of a change of speaker in the Latin. This fluidity of address is characteristic of the work as a whole. Perhaps it is not so much a breakdown of the *persona* or the dramatic vehicle as an intentional and meaningful part of the overall effect, allowing Pace to address the work to Colet in his own person throughout and at the same time maintain the imaginary drama of an address to the boys of Colet's school by a series of personified abstractions. It is clear from p. 111 that it is Pace himself who is interrupted by a late-comer among the abstractions, Dialectic, whose lateness is appropriately symbolic. See the Introduction, p. xiv.

2. Ceylon was first discovered for Portugal in 1505 by Lorenzo de Almeida, son of Francisco de Almeida, Viceroy of India. The Portuguese king referred to in the next sentence was Emmanuel I.

3. Pace juxtaposes Ceylon and Utopia because Ceylon was one of the last outposts of the known world mentioned in *Utopia*. When Raphael Hythlodaeus returned from Utopia, he arrived first at Taprobane (i.e., Ceylon) and then went on to Calicut on the Malabar Coast: "Caeterum postquam digresso Vespucio multas regiones cum quinque Castellanorum comitibus emensus est, mirabili tandem fortuna Taprobanem delatus, inde peruenit in Caliquit, ubi repertis commode Lusitanorum nauibus, in patriam denique praeter spem reuehitur" (The Yale Edition of the Complete Works of St. Thomas More, *Utopia*, Vol. 4, New Haven, 1965, p. 50).

4. The only early translation of Strabo's *Geography* listed in the *British Museum Catalogue* is the one by Guarinus Veronensis and Gregorius Tifernas (Venice, 1472).

5. Cf. Erasmus, "Γεροντολογία," *Colloquia Familiaria*, in *Opera* (Leyden, 1703), I, 735: "Mihi videor tutius totum orbem obire in tabula geographica, neque paulo plus videre in historiis, quam si viginti totos annos, ad Ulyssis exemplum, per omneis terras mariaque volitarem." For the English term *mappemonde*, see Chaucer, *To Rosemounde*, "Madame, ye ben of al beaute shryne/As fer as cercled is the mappemounde."

PAGE 111

6. Pace's translation of Lucian's *Demonax* was printed at Venice in 1522, in his collection of Plutarch's *Opuscula: de garrulitate; de avaritia; quomodo poterit quis ab inimicis aliquid commodi reportare; eiusdem, de modo audiendi; ex Luciano, Demonactis Philosophi vita*. The anecdote which Pace tells here occurs in section 57 of the *Demonax*.

7. Pace takes the story from Aulus Gellius (I, 9, 1 f.) who says that Pythagoras "physiognomized" the young men who presented themselves to him for instruction in order to learn their character and disposition.

8. Again Pace's information is not quite right. The anecdote occurs in Pliny, *Hist. Nat.*, XXXV, xxxvi, 88-89, but the painter was Apelles, not Alexander, and Metoposcopus is not the name of a person, but a term for physiognomists: "Imagines adeo similitudinis indiscretae pinxit [Apelles], ut—incredibile dictu—Apio grammaticus scriptum reliquerit, quendam ex facie hominum divinantem, quos metoposcopos vocant, ex iis dixisse aut futurae mortis annos aut praeteritae vitae." Apion was a rhetorician and grammarian of Egyptian origin who taught at Rome in the time of Tiberius and Claudius. To him we owe the story of Androcles and the Lion. See Aulus Gellius, 5.14.

9. Palmistry. For the entire section, cf. Agrippa: "Habent etiam Signa, & facies signorum suas figuras, quas qui scire uelit in Astrologorum libris eas requirat. Ex istis denique figuris & gestibus, physiognomonia, & metoposcopia, diuinationum artes dependent; ipsaque etiam chiromantia, praedicentes futuros euentus, non ut causae, sed ut signa per effectus consimiles, ab eadem causa causatos" (*De Occulta Philosophia*, I, lii).

1. *Naturales Quaestiones,* IV, vi. Pace has confused the town of Cleonae with the Athenian politician Cleon. The paraphrase of Seneca continues for the rest of the paragraph.

PAGE 113

2. Terms of logic. Cf. *Utopia:* "Nam ne ullam quidem regulam inuenerunt earum, quas de restrictionibus, amplificationibus, ac suppositionibus acutissime excogitatis in paruis logicalibus passim hic ediscunt pueri. Porro secundas intentiones tam longe abest ut inuestigare suffecerint, ut nec hominem ipsum . . . nemo . . . eorum uidere potuerit (Yale Edition, vol. 4, p. 158). The problem of second intentions was a chief point in the dispute between the Thomists and Scotists. A primary perception of a person or thing as it is in itself, in its pure individuality, is known as the *intentio prima.* Secondary reflection within the mind itself, assigning the object perceived to genus or species or class, is known as the *intentio secunda.* Since it exists only in the human mind itself, it is not real in the same sense as external objects and universals, which have their existence in the Divine Mind. See also p. 127, n. 8.

3. Pace is punning on the various meanings of *intentio.*

4. This is the form given to the name Socrates in medieval handbooks of logic, e.g., in the *Summulae Logicales* of Peter of Spain. A few lines later Pace puns on the normal sense of the word (*sortes* = 'lot' or 'destiny').

5. Pace refers to Pliny's *Epistles,* VI, 11: "Quid enim aut publice laetius quam clarissimos iuuenes nomen et famam ex studiis petere aut mihi optatius quam me ad recta tendentibus quasi exemplar esse propositum."

6. Cf. pp. 23-25 above.

PAGE 115

7. For the entire section on bad companions, cf. Erasmus, *Adagia* I.X.lxxiv: "Corrumpunt mores bonos colloquia praua," in which the passage from St. Paul is cited, as well as a favorite saying of John Colet: "Joannes Coletus meus, vir pariter & eruditus & incorruptus, subinde dictitare consueuit: *Tales nos esse, qualia sunt quotidiana colloquia: tales evadere, qualia frequenter audimus.*" At the end of the discussion Erasmus makes the same application as Pace: "Jam vero quod de colloquia dictum est, idem oportet & de studiis accipere. . . ."

8. ΠΕΡΙ ΤΗΣ ΠΑΡΑΠΡΕΣΒΕΙΑΣ, 19.245. Demothenes is here requoting some iambics first cited by Aeschines in his speech defending the other side.

9. Cf. Psalm 17:27 (Vulgate): "Et cum electo electus eris et cum perverso perverteris."

1. I Cor. 15:33. The Revised Standard Version reads: "Bad company ruins good morals." A common sixteenth-century meaning of the English word *conversation* is "behavior," "mode or course of life."

2. Erasmus, *Adagia*, I.III.xxvi and xxvii: "Ilias malorum; Lerna malorum." According to Erasmus, who cites Strabo, the Lerna was a lake adjacent (*communem*) to Argos and Mycenae "in quem cum passim ab omnibus purgamenta deportarentur." The proverb therefore signifies "de malis item plurimis simul in unum congestis & accumulatis."

PAGE 117

3. E.g., Allen, 2, 443 f. In February 1517, Francis I attempted to persuade Erasmus through the agency of Guillaume Budé to join the newly organized Collège de France. Erasmus declined, not wishing to lose his independence and freedom of thought.

4. For another allusion to Erasmus' poverty, see above, p. 23, n. 6.

5. Allen (3, 218) dates this episode as occurring between September 19 and September 29, 1517, since Bombasius enters at the end of the interview (p. 121) and that was the only time he was with Pace in Constance. The episode, however, may be entirely fictitious; it would not have been unlike Pace to fabricate such a story.

PAGE 119

6. The Scotist probably refers to Rainerius de Pisis (fl. 1300-1325), a Dominican theologian whose *Pantheologia*, an alphabetical dictionary of theology, circulated widely in manuscript before being printed at Nuremberg in 1473. There were a number of later editions in the fifteenth and sixteenth centuries.

7. Mentioned in the *Iliad*, V, 784-86:
>   Hera shouted,
> Likening herself to high-hearted, bronze-voiced Stentor,
> Who could cry out in as great a voice as fifty other men.

8. Romans 1:1.

9. Erasmus, *Adagia*, I.V.vi: "Latum unguem."

1. See Acts 9:5 and 26:14. Erasmus cites the former passage in *Adagia*, I.III.xlvi: "Contra stimulum calces." Although most of the quotations in the *Adagia* are taken from classical sources, there are many places in the work where Erasmus, as Pace says, draws on biblical material. See M. M. Phillips, *The Adages of Erasmus* (Cambridge, 1964), pp. 383-90.

2. The *Adagia* had been reprinted fifteen times between the first edition in 1500 and the greatly enlarged one printed by Froben in 1515.

3. Matthew 24:7; Mark 13:8, Luke 21:10.

PAGE 121

4. Erasmus, *Adagia,* I.III.liii: "De lana caprina." See also Edward Topsell, *History of Four-Footed Beasts and Serpents* (London, 1658), p. 235: "But among the Grammarians and Poets, Lana Caprina Goates wooll grew to a prouerbe, to signifie a thing of no weight or moment."

5. Erasmus, *Adagia,* I.II.xx: "Aequalis aequalem delectat." See also I.II.xxi: "Simile gaudet simili" and Shakespeare, *All's Well,* I, i, 237.

6. It is presumably this section of the *De Fructu* that was enlarged as a result of Bombasius' criticism. See above, p. 13.

7. Plutarch has a long passage on the enervating effect of pleasure and the value of work in the "De Tuenda Sanitate," 24-26 (*Moralia,* 135C-137C). Erasmus' Latin translation of this work was first printed by Pynson (London, 1513).

8. Sophocles, *Ajax,* 866. See also Erasmus, *Adagia,* II.III.xxxiii: "Influit quod exhauritur."

9. For the story see Seneca, *Dialogues,* Book X, "Ad Paulinum de Brevitate Vitae," VI, 1 (ed. E. Hermes, Leipzig, 1905), p. 286. The Roman was Marcus Livius Drusus (b. 124 B.C., tribune in 91 B.C.), "execratus inquietatem a primordiis vitam dicitur dixisse: uni sibi ne puero quidem umquam ferias contigisse."

PAGE 123

1. Lucius Quinctius Cincinnatus, appointed dictator in 458 B.C. See Livy, 3, 26, 6; 4, 13, 14 f.

2. Cf. Cicero, *De Officiis,* III, i: "P. Scipionem . . . dicere solitum scripsit Cato . . . numquam se minus otiosum esse, quam cum otiosus, nec minus solum, quam cum solus esset." The work of Cato's is now lost.

3. Among others, probably Marcus Musurus (*ca.* 1470-1517). Allen states that Pace was helped at Padua by Latimer and Tunstal, but that "their endeavours to learn Greek met with little encouragement from Musurus" (*1,* 445). A native of Crete, Musurus was associated with Aldus, for whom he edited a great number of books in Greek. In July 1503, he was appointed professor of Greek at Padua and held the position until the University was dissolved in the wars of 1510-11. In 1504 he was a candidate for the chair of Greek at Venice against Pace's lifelong friend Leonicus. For a modern account, see D. J. Geanakoplos, *Greek Scholars in Venice* (Cambridge, Mass., 1962), pp. 111-166.

4. Cf. More, *Utopia* (Yale Edition, vol. 4, p. 60): "Itaque hac in re non uos modo, sed bona pars huius orbis imitari uidentur malos praecep-

tores, qui discipulos uerberant libentius quam docent." Ascham, of course, was a member of the same anti-flagellation league.

5. Erasmus, *Adagia*, III.III.x: "Ante barbam doces senes." After citing Apuleius' *Apologia*, "Odi puerulos praecoci sapientia," which forms the basis for *Adagia* IV.II.c, Erasmus adds: "Nec Faber placet praecox ingeniorum genus, quod negat ad frugem solere pervenire." Faber, of course, is Quintilian (*Inst.*, I.ii.3).

6. Pace's story of Cleanthes (331-232 B.C.) seems to be derived from two different sources. In his life of Zeno, Diogenes Laertius (VII, 31) records that Zeno compared his pupil and successor Cleanthes to tablets of hard wax, which are written on with difficulty, but which retain what is written upon them. Pace, however, has just quoted Quintilian on slower minds and, in describing Cleanthes, he uses a phrase (*vasi angusti oris*) which Quintilian also employed (*Inst.*, I.ii.28). Was the coalescence of the two accounts brought about by Pace's vague recollection that Cleanthes worked as a water-drawer at night and discussed philosophy by day?

7. Pace is not speaking of actual mountains, but mountains within a particular literary *topos*, in which they are always harsh in the ascent and smooth and pleasant on top. Cf. Dante's description of Paradise in the final cantos of the *Purgatorio* and Milton in Book IV of *Paradise Lost* (131-53). The *topos* goes back as far as Hesiod, *Works and Days*, 290 f.

8. Diogenes Laertius, II, 33.

PAGE 125

9. A variant of the ancient *topos generositas virtus, non sanguis*. Cf. Chaucer's *Wife of Bath's Tale*, 1109-1206; Dante, *Convivio*, IV, 3, 10, 14-15. For an excellent survey of the idea, see George M. Vogt, "Gleanings for the History of a Sentiment: *Generositas Virtus, non Sanguis*," *JEGP*, 24 (1925), 101-24.

1. Erasmus, *Adagia*, I.II.xlvi: "Currentem incitare." See also I.II.xlvii and p. 35 above.

2. Cuthbert Tunstal (1474-1559), Bishop of London and Durham. After attending Oxford and Cambridge, he received his LL.D. from Padua. William Latimer (1460?-1545). Classical scholar, tutor to Reginald Cardinal Pole. Latimer attended Oxford, traveled in Italy with Grocyn and Linacre, and completed his studies at Padua, where he acquired a knowledge of Greek. For his further relations with Pace, see p. 47 above.

PAGE 127

3. Leonicus (Nicolao Leonico Tomeo, 1456-1531) was a professor of Greek at Padua and a friend of Pace since the latter's days at Padua (1499). His translation of Aristotle's *Parua Naturalia* (Venice, 1523) was dedicated to him. See F. Gasquet, *Cardinal Pole and His Early Friends* (London, 1927). For Leonicenus, see above, p. 65, n. 2.

4. Aristophanes, *Clouds*, 1146-47. Strepsiades, who is the farmer referred to, says only: "But take this first; for it is necessary to remunerate one's teacher in some way." But the scholiast, referring back to line 669, explains, "He gives to him [the teacher, Socrates] a bag of barley-meal." See *The Clouds of Aristophanes*, ed. W. J. M. Starkie (New York, 1911).

5. See above p. 109.

6. Allen, *Eras. Ep.*, 2, 257.

7. Pace undoubtedly means *John* Stokesley (1475-1539), later Bishop of London. In 1503 he was made dean of divinity and in 1504-1505, praelector in philosophy and vice-president of Magdalen College, Oxford, where he was accused, among other things, of christening a cat. There is no record of his having been at Rome before 1514. On July 23, 1519, Erasmus described him as one of the adornments of Henry VIII's court, along with More, Linacre, Colet, and Tunstal (Allen, *4, 22*; see also *3, 357* and n.).

8. See above, p. 113, n. 2.

PAGE 129

9. A commonplace still repeated in introductions to Latin literature (e.g., Moses Hadas, *A History of Latin Literature* [New York, 1952], p. 58).

1. Not quite as Pace has it. Comparing Cicero and Demosthenes, Quintilian notes: "Cedendum vero in hoc, quod et prior fuit et ex magna parte Ciceronem, quantus est, fecit. Non mihi videtur M. Tullius, cum se totum ad imitationem Graecorum contulisset, effinxisse vim Demosthenes, copiam Platonis, iucunditatem Isocratis" (*Inst.*, X, i, 108).

2. Pace has in mind simply remarks in passing, such as "divinus aucitor Plato" (*De Optimo Genere Oratorum*, V, 17).

3. Cicero's criticism of Thucydides occurs in *De Optimo Genere Oratorum*, V, 15-16.

4. For the story, see Lucian, *The Ignorant Book-Collector*, 4.

5. Cf. Erasmus, *Adagia*, I.II.lxiii: "Bis per omnia." Erasmus gives a lengthy discussion of the way in which the proverb developed from music.

6. Erasmus, *Adagia*, I.III.lxxv: "Cornicum oculos configere . . . quasi dicas, novo quodam invento veterum eruditionem obscurare, efficereque ut superiores nihil scisse, nihil vidisse videantur." Erasmus himself was not certain how the saying originated. One of his major sources was Cicero, *Oratio pro Murena*.

PAGE 131

7. Simplicius of Cilicia, sixth century A.D. Expelled from Athens by Justinian, he taught at the court of the Persian King Chosroes and later died at Alexandria in 549. Author of a number of commentaries on *Aristotle* (*Categories, Physics, De Caelo, De Anima*). *The Categories* were most recently edited by Carolus Kalbfleisch in 1907. Pace probably used the Greek edition of 1499.

8. The Latin is simply *moderni*, the Moderns (followers of the *via moderna*) in philosophy, *i.e.*, Ockhamists, in contrast with the Ancients (followers of the *via antiqua* in the universities), *i.e.*, Thomists and Scotists.

PAGE 133

9. *Orsu* in the Latin text is an Italian exclamation meaning something like *come now, forward,* or *on.*

1. Erasmus, *Adagia*, I.IV.xli: "Alienam metis messem."

2. A bilingual pun explained in the margin.

PAGE 135

3. Erasmus wrote very little before he knew Greek. If Pace has anything specific in mind, perhaps he means the abridgment of Laurentius Valla's *Elegantiae* (not printed until 1531), the first edition of the *Adagia* (Paris, 1500), the *Enchiridion* of 1503, and various letters.

4. See Pliny, *Ep.* VII, 9, To Fuscus. The Dresden MS. of Pliny reads *provocatumque,* the Laurentian *probatumque.* Aldus' edition (Venice, 1508) has "notum, prouocatumque est." Pliny himself quotes the "ancient saying" (multum legendum esse, non multa) in this same letter.

5. *De Ratione Studii ac Legendi Interpretandique Auctores Iuuenibus Apprime Utilis,* first published in *Augustini Dathi Senensis Pancarpie Epistolae* (Paris, 1511).

PAGE 137

6. See Quintilian, *Inst.,* X, v, 1 f. and Cicero, *De Orat.,* I, 34, 155.

PAGE 139

7. A common idea in the early Renaissance. Cf. Pico della Mirandola, speaking to Lorenzo Medici of Angelus Politianus, "cuius amoenum et fertile ingenium quam antea flores litterarum varios extulerat tam nunc,

ut arbitror, solidam philosophiae maturamque adeo frugem pollicetur" (*Heptaplus,* ed. Eugenio Garin [Florence, 1942], p. 182).

8. *Ep.,* VII, 9.

9. Erasmus, *Adagia,* I.I.xli: "Sus cum Minerva certamen suscepit."

1. Quintilian says precisely the same thing about the profession of *grammaticus,* or teacher of languages and literature: "Haec . . . professio cum brevissime in duas partes dividatur, recte loquendi scientiam et poetarum enarrationem, plus habet in recessu quam fronte promittit" (*Inst.,* I, iv, 2).

PAGE 141

2. Probably the letter printed in Allen, *1,* 436-37, dated January 17, 1507. Henry was then about fifteen years old. Andreas Ammonius probably had a hand in it, but Erasmus later printed it in 1522 as proof that Henry was capable of writing his book against Luther (1521) without any help from Erasmus. For the importance Erasmus attached to the letter, see Allen, *1,* 569-70, but whether he carried it around with him in a little box wherever he went is doubtful. Pace was at Ferrara in 1508, working with Leonicenus. In December 1508, Erasmus visited him on his way to Rome and left a number of papers including the *De Copia, De Ratione Studii* and Books III and IV of the *Antibarbari,* which were later variously sold, lost, given away, and pirated.

3. Pace refers, of course, to Plato's concept of the philosopher king in the *Republic.* See above, p. 57.

4. Thessalian diplomat. Counselor and friend of King Pyrrhus; sent by him at least once to negotiate peace with Rome. See Livy, *Epitomae Periochae,* XIII; Plutarch, *Pyrrhus,* 11 f.

2. "Fidus" Achates, friend of Aeneas.

INDEX OF NAMES

INDEX OF NAMES